AF705318

'In a particularly engaging fashion, the authors explore the methodology, ethics, and importance of field research within social psychology. They point to the rich benefits of field research, two of which are especially significant. First, field research allows researchers to assess whether the effects they are investigating are powerful enough to appear in naturally occurring environments. Second, it allows the public to recognize the relevance of social psychological findings to their lives.'

Robert Cialdini, *Arizona State University, USA*

The Field Study in Social Psychology

This unique book offers a comprehensive introduction to field studies as a research method in social psychology, demonstrating that field studies are an important element of contemporary social psychology, and encourages its usage in a methodologically correct and ethical manner.

The authors demonstrate that field studies are an important and much-needed element of contemporary social psychology and that abandoning this method would be at a great loss for the field. Examining successful examples of field studies, including those by Sherif and Sherif, studies of obedience by Hofling, or the studies of stereotypes of the Chinese by LaPiere, they explore the advantages and limitations of the field study method, whilst offering practical guidance on how it can be used in experiments now and in the future. Covering the history and decline of the field study method, particularly in the wake of the replication crisis, the text argues for the revival of the field study method by demonstrating the importance of studying the behavior of subjects in real life, rather than under laboratory conditions. In fact, the results point to certain variables and research phenomena that can only be captured using field studies. In the final section, the authors also explain the methods to follow when conducting field studies, to make sure they are methodologically correct and meet the criteria of contemporary expectations regarding statistical calculations, while also ensuring that they are conducted ethically.

This is essential reading for graduate and undergraduate students and academics in social psychology taking courses on methodology, and researchers looking to use field study methods in their research.

Tomasz Grzyb is Professor at the University of Social Sciences and Humanities, Wrocław Faculty in Poland, and President of the Polish Social Psychological Society. His main area of interest is social influence and manipulation techniques. He is also a supporter of courses concerning the basics of social influence studies organized for military officers engaged in PSYOPS. He has published several articles about marketing, social psychology, advertising, and education.

Dariusz Dolinski is Professor at the University of Social Sciences and Humanities, Wrocław Faculty in Poland, and editor of the *Polish Psychological Bulletin*. He was formerly President of the Polish Association of Social Psychology and President of the Committee for Psychology of the Polish Academy of Sciences. He is the author of *Techniques of Social Influence* (Routledge, 2016) and (with T. Grzyb) *The Social Psychology of Obedience Towards Authority* (Routledge, 2020).

Research Methods in Social Psychology

1. **The Field Study in Social Psychology**
   How to Conduct Research Outside of a Laboratory Setting?
   Tomasz Grzyb and Dariusz Dolinski

For more information about this series, please visit: https://www.routledge.com/Research-Methods-in-Social-Psychology/book-series/RMSP

The Field Study in Social Psychology

How to Conduct Research Outside of a Laboratory Setting?

Tomasz Grzyb and Dariusz Dolinski

Routledge
Taylor & Francis Group
LONDON AND NEW YORK

First published 2022
by Routledge
2 Park Square, Milton Park, Abingdon, Oxon OX14 4RN

and by Routledge
605 Third Avenue, New York, NY 10158

Routledge is an imprint of the Taylor & Francis Group, an informa business

© 2022 Tomasz Grzyb and Dariusz Dolinski

The right of Tomasz Grzyb and Dariusz Dolinski to be identified as authors of this work has been asserted by them in accordance with sections 77 and 78 of the Copyright, Designs and Patents Act 1988.

All rights reserved. No part of this book may be reprinted or reproduced or utilised in any form or by any electronic, mechanical, or other means, now known or hereafter invented, including photocopying and recording, or in any information storage or retrieval system, without permission in writing from the publishers.

Trademark notice: Product or corporate names may be trademarks or registered trademarks, and are used only for identification and explanation without intent to infringe.

British Library Cataloguing-in-Publication Data
A catalogue record for this book is available from the British Library

Library of Congress Cataloging-in-Publication Data
Names: Grzyb, Tomasz, author. | Doliński, Dariusz, author.
Title: The field study in social psychology : how to conduct research outside of a laboratory setting? / Tomasz Grzyb and Dariusz Dolinski.
Description: 1 Edition. | New York : Routledge, 2021. | Series: Research methods in social psychology | Includes bibliographical references and index.
Identifiers: LCCN 2021009068 (print) | LCCN 2021009069 (ebook) | ISBN 9780367555566 (paperback) | ISBN 9780367636449 (hardback) | ISBN 9781003092995 (ebook)
Subjects: LCSH: Psychology—Research—Methodology. | Psychology—Fieldwork.
Classification: LCC BF76.5 .G79 2021 (print) | LCC BF76.5 (ebook) | DDC 150.72—dc23
LC record available at https://lccn.loc.gov/2021009068
LC ebook record available at https://lccn.loc.gov/2021009069

ISBN: 978-0-367-63644-9 (hbk)
ISBN: 978-0-367-55556-6 (pbk)
ISBN: 978-1-003-09299-5 (ebk)

DOI: 10.4324/9781003092995

Typeset in Bembo
by Apex CoVantage, LLC

Contents

Acknowledgments

Writing a book is a major undertaking. As is often the case with major undertakings, these cannot be completed solo. At this point, we would like to thank all those whose advice, support, and kindness allowed us to arrive at the very last character in this book.

Firstly, we would like to extend our gratitude to all the psychologists whose ingenious field experiments we discussed in our work. They include both pioneers of social psychology, who have made field experiments the fundamental source of scientific knowledge, as well as contemporary researchers who go against the currently prevailing scientific paradigm and still conduct such experiments. As we ourselves belong to the latter category, we would like to thank all our subjects – without your input, the very concept of this book would not have been possible. We misled you, put you in uncomfortable positions, and asked you to grant all kinds of requests. We always tried to approach our subjects with the utmost respect – even when the procedures we had devised were not particularly pleasant for them. We greatly appreciate your effort, time and involvement.

We also owe a lot to our colleagues from the broadly understood Academy. Your remarks and comments – including critical ones – allowed us to stay clear of many errors and mistakes. Our dialogue was a true source of inspiration and a brilliant intellectual experience for us. We would like to thank the following colleagues from the Faculty of Psychology at our University: Katarzyna Byrka, Katarzyna Cantarero, Malgorzata Gamian-Wilk, and Wojciech Kulesza as well as scholars from other universities: Michał Bilewicz, Robert B. Cialdini, Maria Lewicka, Romuald Polczyk, Wieslaw Łukaszewski, and Yoram Bar-Tal. Obviously, it is impossible to name everyone here. Hopefully, those who were omitted will not take offence.

We would like to express our particular gratitude to Klaus Fiedler and Christopher Carpenter, who, upon becoming familiar with the concept of this book, provided us with numerous, extremely valuable, suggestions and advice which we used throughout our work.

We are also grateful to employees of Routledge publishing house, who, through their professional approach and involvement have made publishing of this book possible. At each stage of the process, Eleanor Taylor, Alex Howard, and Akshita Pattiyani and Jane Fieldsen offered their input and help. We appreciate it a lot.

Last but not least, we would like to thank our families – we are aware that living with someone who mainly sits at their desk, muttering to themselves every now and then, is difficult and challenging. We know how much we owe to you. Thank you.

All of the above-mentioned individuals helped us make this book better. Needless to say, we are the only ones responsible for any errors and flaws.

The Authors

1 Is social psychology still a science of human behavior?

Thousands of articles appear every day in a range of psychological journals published around the world. These are most often theoretical studies, reviews of research results concerning some aspects of human behavior (and in the case of animal psychology, of animals as well), or reports from empirical research conducted by the authors. Some of these texts are fascinating, others less so. There are also weaker and boring texts. In a word: these articles are distinct in terms of both their subject matter and their quality. From time to time, however, there are articles that deal with psychology itself. If those reading such articles are practitioners of scientific psychology, the act of reading usually leads them to wonder if what they do (and often have done for years) makes any sense at all. It is this kind of text that was published in 2007 in *Perspectives on Psychological Science*. The authors of this article – Roy Baumeister, Kathleen Vohs, and David Funder – gave it the strange, not to say provocative, title "Psychology as the science of self reports and finger movements." Baumeister, Vohs, and Funder point out that while psychology is defined (by psychologists themselves as well) as a science of behavior, behavior is not the focus of its attention today. While animal psychologists and developmental psychologists actually observe and analyze behavior (as the authors jokingly suggest: perhaps because they cannot get their subjects – animals and small, illiterate children – to fill out questionnaires), in the case of social psychology, behaviors going beyond filling out questionnaires, pressing computer keyboard keys, or clicking mouse buttons are rare. The authors reviewed the then newest (January 2006) issue of the *Journal of Personality and Social Psychology*, the flagship journal of social psychology, and presented the following conclusion of their analysis: "It is undeniably a fine issue, offering important advances in the topics the articles address. The methods are rigorous, and the discussions are thoughtful. The editors, reviewers, and authors did their jobs well. But behavior is hard to find." Next, they stated that even if behavior is explored by the authors of articles, it is quite specific – "human behavior is almost always performed in a seated position, usually seated in front of a computer. Finger movements, as in keystrokes and pencil marks, constitute the vast majority of human actions" (p. 397).

Were Baumeister, Vohs, and Funder (2007) in fact correct? After all, they based their conclusions on an analysis of only one issue of the journal. Perhaps they came across some exceptional texts that were not representative of the state of the discipline. One of us (Dolinski, 2018a) therefore decided to systematically review an entire volume (six issues) of the journal. He took what was then the newest volume, 113, from the second half of 2017. It contained 49 articles, four of which were not empirical in nature. The number of articles presenting research in which real human behavior, other than completing questionnaires and answering various questions, was a dependent variable: four. This means

DOI: 10.4324/9781003092995-1

that such real behaviors were taken into account in less than 9% of the texts. The proportion of behavioral studies to all studies presented in the analyzed articles is perhaps even more telling. Out of the total number of 290 studies presented in the analyzed volume of *JPSP*, only 18 (i.e. about 6%) concerned behaviors. Let us take a look at what kind of behavior was studied, because it is quite telling. Jones and Paulhus (2017) investigated deception. The participants either took advantage of an imperfection in a computer program or overstated their own achievements. In the Chou, Haleva, Galinsky, and Murnighan (2017) study, the behavior was the number of tasks completed by the participants, and, in one experiment, behavior in the course of solving the prisoner's dilemma. Savani and Job (2017) tested the perseverance of participants in solving cognitive tasks. So, as we can see, none of these studies explored behaviors that did not involve people assuming a sitting posture and moving their fingers! There is only one (!) study in the entire volume analyzed in which psychologists explored behavior by participants other than that mentioned above. This is the study by Neal, Durbin, Gornik, and Lo (2017), in which social interactions of preschool children were observed. Baumeister, Vohs, and Funder would probably say that this exception only appeared because preschool children are not capable of filling out questionnaires to ask them what social interactions they prefer, but we prefer to keep an open mind. As the authors of the present volume, we would prefer to believe that the authors of the aforementioned articles are nothing short of exceptional, and it was their intention to examine the real behaviors of children.

Of course, the question arises as to the cause of social psychology's drastic departure from behavioral research. Baumeister, Vohs, and Funder (2007) estimate that in 1976

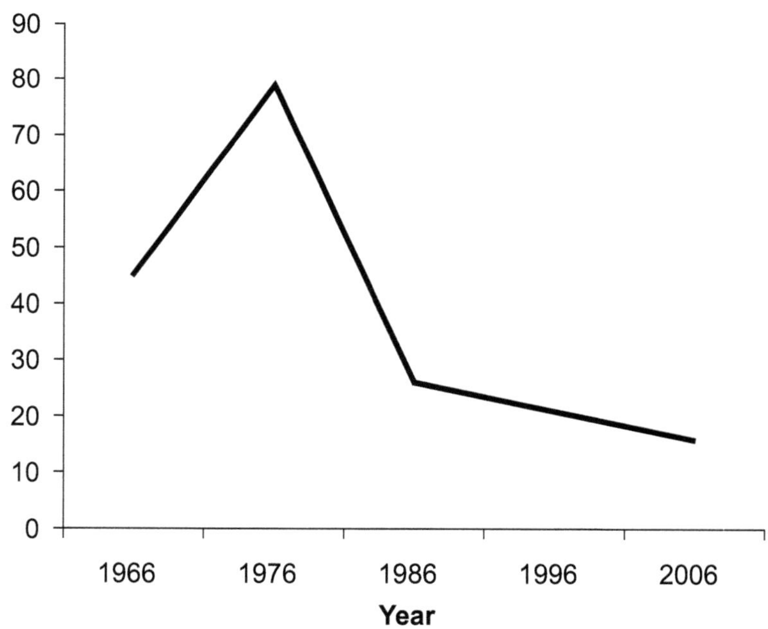

Figure 1.1 Percentage of studies from *Journal of Personality and Social Psychology* that included behavior (1966–2006).

Source: *Perspectives on Psychological Science*, *2*, p. 399. Copyright: SAGE.

about 80% of the texts in *JPSP* were devoted to behavioral research. Ten years later, this percentage was more than thrice lower! It then declined gradually and consistently to reach a level of several percent in 2006. About ten years later, it turned out (Dolinski, 2018a) that, practically speaking, there is almost no such research at all … Perhaps it is published in journals other than *Journal of Personality and Social Psychology*? Analysis of the issues of such leading social psychology journals as *Personality and Social Psychology Bulletin*, *European Journal of Social Psychology*, or *Social Psychological and Personality Science* shows that they do not differ from *JPSP* in terms of the subject of our interest here. In all of them, studies in which the causes of human behavior were examined accounted for merely a few percent (Dolinski, 2018b).

It would also seem that, regardless of the aforementioned cognitive revolution, psychology in recent decades has become more interested not in determining cause–effect relationships (i.e. when a certain behavior occurs), but rather in the psychological mechanisms that these behaviors activate. In other words, psychology has begun to consistently treat people as the subjects of their own actions and is focused on why they behave in a particular way in a specific situation. This is, of course, a very desirable direction for the development of psychology as a science about people. But the assumption that explaining why a behavior appears is more important than investigating the very causes of behavior has led to a kind of aversion on the part of psychologists to investigate behavior as such. It can be said that modern psychology explains … virtually everything except behavior. We would say that, more often than not, behavior explains not only judgments, beliefs, and biases, but even … processes of explanation.

We feel it necessary to stress at this point that, in our opinion, verbal behaviors are just as much behaviors as are those reactions that are not verbal in nature. Thus, in examining human beliefs, judgments, and opinions, social psychology examines human behavior. There is no dispute here. Nor do we believe that verbal behavior is in any way "inferior" to other human reactions. It is simply a subclass of different human behaviors. Social psychology should undoubtedly take an interest in such human reactions, and it does so in a very intensive and, we feel, effective way. But at the same time, this does not mean that we should stop studying other subclasses of human behavior, that is, those that go beyond study participants' verbal declarations. In particular, we should be aware that if someone responds to the question "Would you, in the described situation, help out a person who fell down on the sidewalk?", we are not studying altruistic behaviors, but declarations about one's own potential altruistic behaviors. We do agree that the study of such declarations can be both interesting and of import. But it should not lead social psychologists to abandon interest in the issue of whether a person actually proffers help in a particular situation. What we are opposed to is what we call "methodology instead" – instead of studying altruistic behavior, people's beliefs about their own altruism are studied; instead of examining human honesty, they are asked how they would behave in a situation where they were facing temptation.

We also seem to have a more liberal attitude than Baumeister, Vohs, and Funder (2007) to the study by psychologists of behavior that involves participants sitting in a chair running their fingers over a computer keyboard. In our opinion, the issue here is more complex. First of all, modern people spend a lot of time sitting in front of their computer. It is thus a very reasonable thing for psychologists to study such activity. What we mean is, first of all, that the very act of pressing the keys on a keyboard can be an indicator of vastly different activities. If one presses the ENTER button to confirm a transfer of money to a charity, there can be no doubt that this is a study of real behavior – altruism. If one sends an offensive e-mail to someone else – it is an act of verbal aggression, and therefore also of real behavior. However, the situation is different when participants press the keys on a keyboard to respond to a psychologist's question as to whether they would make a donation to some charity in a particular situation or, in another hypothetical situation, send an offensive e-mail. If, in such cases, researchers claim that they are conducting experiments on altruistic and moral behavior (as is usually the case in modern psychology), then this is "methodology instead." In other words, the problem is not that social psychologists conduct research in paradigms where people are supposed to press keys on a computer or smartphone. The problem is what this key pressing means, what are its subjective and objective consequences.

Of course, there would be no problem if people's declarations about how they behave comported with their actual behavior. However, there is plenty of evidence that this is quite frequently not the case. In a survey commissioned by Deutsche Bank (2014), respondents were asked what they would spend five million euros on if they won such an amount in a game of chance or inherited it. Of those surveyed, 27.5% declared that they would give a large portion of it to the poor. Reality, however, shows that winners very rarely allocate even a small part of their winnings to charity (Kaplan, 1987). Psychological research also reveals significant discrepancies between declarations about one's behavior and actual behaviors. Later in this book we give a detailed presentation of studies on the mechanism of distribution of responsibility. They examined, for example, how the number of people sitting in a train compartment affected the likelihood that a participant would react when one of the passengers robbed a woman who had left the compartment for a moment (Grzyb, 2016). It turned out, in accordance with the classic psychological rule, that participants react much more often when they are the sole witness to a theft than in conditions where there are three witnesses. However, if the situation was only described to respondents (some in conditions where they are the only witnesses and others in conditions where they are one of three) and they were asked how they would behave, information about the number of witnesses was irrelevant to their answers. Peng, Nisbett, and Wong's (1997) review of intercultural studies shows, in turn, that if you compare people living in different cultures on the basis of their verbal declarations, you get a completely different picture than when you compare their real behavior. This applies to such different areas of life as cultural behavior at the table, time spent engaged in sport activities, or maintaining cleanliness and order. Another, no less spectacular, example of the discrepancy between how people behave in real life situations and how they respond to the question of how they would behave can be found in the classic studies of obedience carried out in the Milgram paradigm (1974). In one of our studies, we showed that even people who are well acquainted with Milgram's research and its results are convinced that they would very quickly, at the very beginning of the experiment, refuse to follow the experimenter's instructions (Grzyb & Dolinski, 2017).

Why do social psychologists often declare in articles that they are investigating behavior, but in fact only ask people how they would behave in a particular situation? There seem to be at least two reasons. First, the study of real behavior is much more difficult and much more laborious than the study of verbal declarations. And the second? Observed behavior is usually of a binary nature. Someone has guided a blind person across the street or has not. Someone gave back a fountain pen found in the university corridor and someone else did not. Someone voted (or did not vote) in an election, someone marched (or did not march) in a street protest, someone signed (or did not sign) a petition. Someone made change for someone else's large bill or did not, someone stopped their car to help an unfortunate individual whose car had broken down in the middle of the road while someone else did not. The key is therefore whether or not participants behaved altruistically in a particular situation (e.g. whether or not they made a donation) and whether or not they behaved honestly in a particular situation (e.g. whether or not they stole money). Such a dichotomous character of the dependent variable, however, excludes the possibility of applying many sophisticated statistical analyses (or enables them but only with large sample sizes, which is extremely troublesome due to the aforementioned laborious nature of such studies). So if researchers want "to succeed," they prefer to avoid binary dependent variables. The problem is, however, that if we adapt our method to enable the appropriate analyses rather than seek such statistical models that would allow us to examine reality, we reduce everything to absurdity. Avoiding a dichotomous dependent variable and planning a study so that the behavior can be studied on an interval scale is, therefore, reducing the experimental study to absurdity (although, we stress, this does not have to be the case every time – in some situations it is possible, and even necessary, to operationalize the dependent variable to give it an interval character, and this need not happen at the expense of reducing the realism of the study). However, it would seem obvious that the mode of data analysis should be adapted to the analyzed problem. Meanwhile, it is often the case that the problem is defined and empirically operationalized to make the results easily counted. To put it simply: it seems obvious that the dog should wag its tail, yet it is often the case that the tail wags the dog.

Moreover, the manner in which social psychologists treat measurement scales used in psychological research supposedly for measuring behavior and, de facto, the "declared tendency toward certain behaviors" as interval scales is frequently quite problematic. A scale in which we would ask, for example, "what amount (in euros, from 0 to 100) would you allocate to charity?" is only an interval scale in name alone. In fact, the difference between no euros and one euro is only mathematically the same as the difference between, say, 33 and 34 euros. There is a tremendous qualitative difference between zero and one: nothing versus something – refusal of support versus commitment – and the difference between 33 and 34 euros is, from this perspective, trivial. The same is true for deception. Deceiving once every ten opportunities is something significantly different from not deceiving once, while the difference between deceiving six and deceiving seven times is negligible.

But maybe the tail wagging the dog looks more elegant, or at least that is what social psychologists think? Yes, how elegant, for example, the figures in articles presenting structural equation models look. When social psychologists publish their research results based on participants completing at least a few questionnaires and presenting a complex figure, they often do not even take into account that several or even several dozen alternative models could be built on the basis of their data, and in fact, there is often no reason to believe that the researcher's preferred model is better than others, as the respective fit goodness coefficients are very close to each other. The approach based on measuring almost everything that seems to make sense from a theoretical perspective with questionnaires and showing the results in the form of complex models, rich in arrows and numbers, is, of course, motivated by the desire to write an article that can be easily published. Reviewers prefer this approach, and editors approve of such texts. But this is the blind alley down which our discipline has gone. The tail is wagging the dog, which only seems to be a nice sight!

We make no bones of the fact that we are fascinated by a psychology in which behavior is measured in such a way that we can simply observe it. We do not necessarily have to be direct eyewitnesses of the behavior itself; sometimes it is just as good to note its direct and obvious consequences. If, for example, we were investigating altruism, the occurrence of a money transfer to the account of a charity from the account of a participant would be an excellent indicator of behavior, and we would not have to directly observe how the individual made the transfer. In studies of pro-ecological behavior, decreased water and electricity consumption are excellent indicators of pro-ecological behavior. The dynamics of phone bills and billing analysis, indicating who conversations were conducted with, can also be a good indicator of the dynamics of social contacts enjoyed by sick old people unable to leave their homes. The content of death certificates is also as good (and perhaps even better) as observation of the deaths of the subjects.

To properly explain the difference between a study typical of modern psychology and the approach we present, we will refer to one of the articles published in the aforementioned volume 113 of the 2017 *Journal of Personality and Social Psychology*. Schroeder, Fishbach, Schein, and Gray (2017) analyzed what happens to individuals in conditions where their need for intimacy is clearly infringed by a stranger touching their body. After a series of four experiments in which participants were to imagine themselves being touched by others, the authors announced in the article that their fifth experiment would be a field study. One could reasonably assume the reader had every right to expect that this time the real behavior of people whose intimacy has been violated would be investigated, and that it would be done so in a real social situation. It turned out that the authors did indeed use the natural context of a flu shot clinic, but … they did not study the behavior of participants during the procedure; instead, they asked them about various things (e.g. whether they would prefer to roll up their sleeve or remove their jacket, or whether they would prefer to minimize or maximize eye contact with the nurse). The field study was therefore a "field" study only in relation to the place where the investigation was conducted, but not the manner in which it was done.

In our opinion, therefore, this otherwise interesting study neither concerned real human behavior (but only subjective beliefs about the occurrence of one's behavior) nor was it a field study. If the study had been a true field study and appeared today in the flagship journal of social psychology (and *Journal of Personality and Social Psychology* is just such a journal), we would be dealing with something unique.

In 2009, *Perspectives on Psychological Science* published a text bearing the meaningful title "We have to break up." It was written by the eminent social psychologist Robert Cialdini, and it takes the form of a farewell letter from a disappointed lover who realizes that he has less and less in common with his partner. Cialdini points out that the focus of contemporary social psychology on cognitive factors explaining behavior and the associated popularization of mediation analyses actually means the death of the field studies that constitute the core of his empirical activity as a researcher. Every social psychology textbook contains descriptions of Cialdini's studies, already classic today, devoted mainly to altruism and social influence, carried out following this very methodology. The logic of field studies makes it impossible, meanwhile, to get people walking down the sidewalk, sitting in a café, or entering a library to complete a survey before measuring the dependent variable. This would be entirely incompatible with experimental realism and would strike at the very essence of the psychological field study, in which participants should not even be aware that they are engaged in the experiment (or at least they should not be aware of the actual purpose of the study). Social psychologists carry out their research with the intention of publishing it (preferably in a prestigious journal). However, they know that today the rule is "no mediation, no publication." If this is the case, then conducting research in the field study paradigm does not help advance one's scientific career.

Neither Cialdini nor we, the authors of this book, question in the slightest the need and sense of research focused on issues other than actual human behavior. It has never occurred to us to question the need for survey-based research or online studies. After all, social psychology would make no sense without examining attitudes, stereotypes, the structure of the "I," generalized beliefs about the social world or values. However, in a situation in which social psychology does not actually study behavior (and if it does, it certainly cuts itself off from the best journals), the alarm must be sounded. In social psychology there must be space for exploring not only what people think, but also what people do, and why they do it. That is why Robert Cialdini writes "We have to break up!"

However, while we completely share Cialdini's opinion on the condition of contemporary social psychology, we approach this problem with greater optimism: we believe that a rift with it (i.e. social psychology) is not a foregone conclusion. The question that psychologists conducting methodology classes often hear from their students is which method of psychological research is the best. The most sensible answer to this question is a sort of inversion: the best method is the one which is most adequate for solving a particular problem. So sometimes a competence test, other times a personality inventory, sometimes observation, and on other occasions conversation will be the best. In many situations, an experiment is the most appropriate. However, the laboratory experiment has some disadvantages which the field study does not. The field study, on the other hand, has limitations that no laboratory experiment has. Those methods can therefore be highly complementary. A great illustration of this is the research program conducted by Bibb Latané and John Darley, dedicated to the diffusion of responsibility. In many studies (Latané & Darley, 1968, 1969) they showed that as the number of witnesses to an interaction increases, their individual responsibility for helping the victim decreases and, consequently, the chance the victim will receive assistance decreases. Two of their studies are most frequently described in psychology textbooks – in one, blind but perfectly hearing participants seated in separate rooms hear an epilepsy attack suffered by one of the confederates, and in the other, smoke is let into the room where the participants are located. In both of these laboratory experiments, the results clearly showed that the chance of any reaction from participants decreases as the number of witnesses to the interaction increases. It should be recalled, however, that Latané and Darley (1970) also tested their hypotheses in natural conditions. In a very ingenious field experiment done in a liquor store, the researchers staged a theft – two men approached the counter and asked about the most expensive beer in the store. The salesman mentioned the name of the beer, then went to the backroom to check how much beer was left (in fact, he was cooperating with the researchers and this behavior facilitated the next part of the study). When the salesman disappeared behind the door, one of the men took a box of alcohol and went out in front of the store, after which he hid the box in his car. The whole scene was staged by the researchers in two versions – when there was only one person in the store, and when there were two witnesses to the situation. The obtained results fully confirmed what the researchers already knew from the laboratory studies – paradoxically, the chance of a reaction was higher when the entire situation was observed by one person rather than two. So why did Bibb Latané and John Darley decide to once again examine the same phenomenon in a much more difficult manner than through a laboratory experiment?

At least a partial answer to this question can be found in a very well known and widely commented (over a thousand citations) text by Eliott Aronson and Kevin Carlsmith (1968) on the subject of two realities in experimental research. These researchers distinguished between experimental realism and mundane realism. The former concerns the extent to which the participants of a study can be "dragged" into the situation staged by the researcher, and how important it is for them and affects their behavior. The second type of realism is related to the degree to which the scene staged in the experiment coincides with what the subjects can experience during their day-to-day activities in their "real world." Aronson and Carlsmith note that these two realisms are not part of a single continuum – an experimental scheme can be constructed in which there will be a high level of experimental realism, but a low level of "everyday" realism; Solomon Asch's (1951) study of group conformism is an example. In Asch's laboratory experiments, the study participants were strongly involved in the procedure, followed the experimenter's instructions for estimating the length of the segments shown to them, but these were activities that were very likely to differ significantly from their everyday activities. One can also imagine a study with the opposite weighting of realisms: a high level of mundane everyday realism and a low level of experimental realism. Aronson and Carlsmith cite the example of a study by Elaine Walster, Eliott Aronson, and Darcy Abrahams (1966). In one of the experiments in the series, dedicated to this issue, the researchers asked students to read a newspaper in which they included an article on problems of the legal system in Portugal; in different groups it contained different information about the system for paying prosecutors. From a certain perspective, therefore, the experiment had a high level of mundane realism (the participants did something natural for themselves, simply reading the newspaper). At the same time, however, as the results showed, it did not particularly affect their behavior, as they simply had little interest in the legal system of an unknown and quite distant country (the study was done in the USA). The level of experimental realism was therefore rather low in this case. Aronson and Carlsmith, however, claim that experiments can offer both, and therefore provide research that is as high on realism as it is on the "mundane." Almost 30 years later, Eliott Aronson, Timothy Wilson, and Robin Akert (1994) suggested the introduction of a third kind of psychological realism as an attempt to address the contradiction that sometimes exists between experimental and mundane realism. In their opinion, this is the degree to which the psychological processes that characterize the participants of a study during an experiment are the same as they could have experienced in real, everyday life. Maintaining a high level of this realism gives us – as researchers – a chance to increase the ecological accuracy of the interpretation of the results.

We also note that in modern psychology (particularly social, but not only), with increasing frequency, instead of an experiment or a single study of another kind, we are talking about an entire research program concerning a single phenomenon (Wojciszke, 2011). This offers additional possibilities to boost the level of individual realities by studying the same phenomenon using different research tools. From this perspective, the series of experiments that Latané and Darley carried out (which we write more about later in the book) seems to be perfectly balanced between the different realities, but also between the high internal validity of the experiment and its external validity. High internal validity was achieved in a series of tests carried out in the laboratory, and external validity was ensured in experiments and quasi-experiments conducted in field conditions (although this does not mean, of course, that these aspects of accuracy exclude each other). It can therefore be concluded that the series of diverse types of research (including field experiments) that led Latané and Darley to the publication of their famous book on indifferent witnesses (Latané & Darley, 1970) could serve us as a model example of the balance between different research methods used in concert to describe a psychological phenomenon.

Unfortunately, it seems that this peculiar balance from the beginning had a tendency to grow more and more unstable. Lee Cronbach – who made a great contribution to the development of research methods in psychology – wrote about two disciplines of scientific psychology back in the mid-20th century (Cronbach, 1957). He noted that young researchers concentrate on either "correlative" or "experimental" research at the very beginning of their scientific career. These concepts were deliberately given in quotation marks, as it is not a matter of using certain statistical methods, but rather a general approach to subjects and objects of research. The "experimental" psychologists, explained Cronbach, are primarily concerned with the strict control of variables, including (and perhaps even more so) those that are subject to our manipulation. "Correlative" psychologists, in turn, study those variables that people have not learned to control or manipulate (and there is little chance that they will ever learn to do so). Cronbach noted that the two groups became somewhat oppositional to each other – he saw this, for example, in the very low citation ratio of publications containing research of both types (i.e., both "experimental" and "correlative" psychologists usually ignored reports from research carried out by people outside their own group). Needless to say, he clearly criticized this situation by calling (as shown by the examples of psychological theories fashionable in the 1950s) for breaking through the barriers of own groups and joining forces to explore psychological phenomena together – using all available methods. As can be expected, Cronbach's proposals did not have the expected effect, although it should be mentioned that the text itself was a breakthrough from a certain perspective. It has been cited more than five thousand times already and remains an important reference point for researchers dealing with methods of data collection and analysis in psychology. It is also often cited when discrepancies (or, relatively less frequently, consistency) in the results achieved in field and laboratory experiments are analyzed (Colquitt, 2008; Scandura & Williams, 2000). An interesting meta-analysis of data from field and laboratory experiments was proposed by Adam Vanhove and Peter Harms (2015), who engaged in secondary analysis of the results from 203 pairs of experiments in the field–laboratory system. Their results – which should come as no surprise – showed significantly stronger effects in laboratory tests ($r = 0.25$) than in the field ($r = 0.14$). The researchers also considered a lower correlation between the effects obtained in the laboratory and the natural environment than originally assumed ($r = 0.61$). They noted that the strength of effects in the laboratory and the field was similar when the study was of a correlative nature and when used as a variable of psychological characteristics, but differed in other cases (e.g. when the actual behavior was a dependent variable). Therefore, it is not surprising that Vanhove and Harms formulated their conclusions, once again (after Cronbach and many others), encouraging triangulation and the use of different research methods to fully illustrate the analyzed phenomenon.

Robert Cialdini (2009) shows that among all the methods that can be used in such triangulation, field experiments are the least popular. The reasons for this state of affairs will be discussed later in the book; in the meantime, let us try to define this concept. What does it mean to say that a study is an experiment, and what does it mean that it is a field study? Contrary to appearances, these are not trivial questions.

The very understanding of the notion of experimentation in psychology from the beginning has been closely related to two elements: the manipulation of an independent variable and the possibilities of generating results for a population. Although, as research methods in psychology evolved, more and more complicated experimental plans appeared, the key questions asked by researchers remained these two: does the independent variable affect the dependent variable? Can the results that were obtained be applied to the population? (West, Cham, & Liu, 2014). It can therefore be concluded that the key to considering a study an experiment would be some form of manipulation of the independent variable and random allocation to experimental and control groups.

It is the violation of these assumptions that is the most common reason why it is impossible to consider an applied research method as an experiment – if we have problems with the random assignment of participants to groups (and random selection to the study itself), we must necessarily abandon calling our research an experiment. A substitute name – a quasi-experimental study (Shadish, Cook, & Campbell, 2002) – must suffice. An additional issue (which we will address in more detail later in the book) is the random selection of participants for the experiment itself, giving (depending on how this selection was made) a greater or lesser chance of generating results per population.

So we already know what constitutes an experiment. But what does it mean to say that it is fieldwork? The most important social psychology textbook, a powerful, two-volume work (1614 pages!) edited by Susan Fiske, Daniel Gilbert, and George Lindzey (2010), contains an entire chapter on "Social psychological methods outside the laboratory" written by Harry Reis and Samuel Gosling. The authors indicate that, in fact, every study conducted outside the laboratory can be described as field research, although obviously not every study will be an experiment (or even a quasi-experiment). Reis and Gosling give several reasons why researchers decide to conduct their experiments in an environment outside the laboratory. The idea is, of course, to maximize the accuracy of the external study, but also to be able to observe the natural behavior of people in their natural environment, along with (it must be noted!) the entire wealth of disruptive variables that naturally occur in the world around us. We note that, from a certain perspective, this is counterintuitive – usually, as researchers, we want to determine the "pure" influence of variable A on variable B; however, in some situations it is only by analyzing it in its natural environment that we can see the whole complexity of the social situation (and, speaking more methodologically, a complex system of interactions between the main, secondary, and confounding variables, which cannot always be reproduced in the laboratory).

Reis and Gosling (2010) point to another reason worth looking at for a moment – they write that the vast majority of field research is conducted in a way that assumes the participants are not aware of their participation in the experiment. Of course, this raises a lot of ethical questions (which we will devote a separate chapter to), but it is worth mentioning here that a field study almost always entails not informing participants of its occurrence. This, of course, has many serious consequences, both negative (the aforementioned ethical issues) and positive (no fear of evaluation by study participants, providing the opportunity to observe their natural behavior).

The book you hold in your hands is the fruit of many years of work by its authors spent on conducting such field experiments. The idea at the heart of it could be summarized as follows: we want to show that field experiments are an important and necessary element in modern social psychology, and to abandon them would be to the discipline's great detriment. We want to show both the benefits that psychology has gained (and can still gain) from research carried out in the field study paradigm, as well as some limitations that are associated with the use of this method. We also intend to discuss the technical difficulties that are associated with the implementation of such research and the ethical problems associated with this method of experimentation. In addition, we would like to point out that some of the problems that come to mind during the implementation of field experiments (both technical and ethical) can be relatively easily solved, and others can be measured in such a way that they can be overcome. Finally, we intend to show that performing field experiments can provide us with great satisfaction, and even – let us not shy away from this word – joy.

2 A strictly natural experiment

One of our daughters went through a period of her life where she felt a fear of fire. At about the age of four she decided that, because a fire can happen at home, proper preparation for it is a must. The first stage was to check what in the house was flammable (fortunately, her research method was to ask her parents about it, rather than to experimentally examine the flammability of individual objects). Then she packed her biggest treasures (her beloved drawings, books, and dolls) into a bag, which she always kept by the bed. When asked why she did it, she replied: "if you ever have to escape a fire at night, just grab the bag and all of my treasures will be saved." As her interest became slightly obsessive, the decision was taken to end the matter by installing an alarm system in the house. It was explained to her how smoke detectors work, and she went shopping with her parents to a hardware store where they bought what they needed. When the entire device was assembled and ready to be installed, the girl looked in amazement and asked: "What do you mean, you want to install it right away?" "Yes," went the response: "Have I forgotten something?" "Of course, you forgot to check if it works. Light a fire in the fireplace and put the sensor over the smoke, then we'll see if we can trust this thing."

The four-year-old being described had not (yet) been specially trained in research methodology, so it can be said with a high degree of probability that her way of getting to know the world (which can be described in the short phrase "let's check it out") is something natural, and relatively independent of upbringing. Of course, as many psychologists and education specialists (e.g. Kohn, 1998) prove, it is relatively easy to suppress this curiosity in children. Systematic use of phrases such as "when you're older, you'll understand", "don't talk so much", or "well aren't you curious" can quite effectively stop a child from asking (and checking things out), but it can be assumed that an experimental approach to the world around them is quite characteristic of children. In this chapter, we will consider what manifestations of such an experimental approach to learning about reality can be discovered in the world around us.

Let's start by looking at children. Claire Cook, Noah Goodman, and Laura Schulz, 2011) chose preschoolers as their "research subjects." In their study, they invited 60 toddlers (with an average age of 54 months, or 4.5 years) to play with specially constructed toys to see to what extent the children's behavior would resemble the model of testing hypotheses in the scientific world. The authors of the experiments put forward quite an interesting hypothesis – they wanted to check whether the experimental model is the fundamental mode for discovering reality on a daily basis for toddlers at the tender age of 4.5 years old. An experimental design consisting of three phases was developed. In the first phase, the children were divided into two groups: one, which was given the working title "all tokens," and a second, called "some tokens." The children were shown a fairly

DOI: 10.4324/9781003092995-2

standard toy from a well-known and popular children's toy manufacturer. This toy played various melodies after placing a token on it – four examples of such tokens were shown to the children. There was a difference between the groups: in the "all tokens" group, each of the tokens shown to the children would activate the toy so that it would start playing a melody. In the "some tokens" group only two of the four tokens had this function, while the other two did not activate the toy.

Now the second phase followed, the same for both groups. The children were presented with pairs of tokens connected to each other. They were shown that such pairs of chips activated the presented toy (i.e. after the two connected tokens were placed on it, the toy started to play a melody). Each time, after demonstrating how the pair of chips activated the music, the experimenter stated: "Oh, look, it plays. I wonder what makes it work?", and then said to the children: "Okay, now you can play by yourself."

This is how the third phase – the so-called free play – began. The researchers were primarily interested in whether the children would want to separate the tokens. As might have been expected, this phenomenon was practically absent among children from the "all tokens" group, who were informed that every token operates the toy. This is hardly surprising – if the children learned that every token caused a melody to be played, they would not have to check it out for themselves. Interesting things only started happening in the group that had previously been told that only some of the tokens activated the toy. It turned out that significantly more children wanted to find out which token "worked" – the toddlers disconnected the tokens and "tested" each one in turn. Let us note that, from the perspective of play, this didn't make much sense – after all, the toy was already working, and individually placing the tokens on it couldn't make it work better. Nevertheless, half of the children in the "some tokens" group separated the pairs of tokens and placed them on the toy individually in order to satisfy the researcher's curiosity in a hastily constructed experiment. It should be noted that the described study has some methodological issues (e.g. it is not known to what extent the children's actions were caused by their curiosity and to what extent they fulfilled the supposed expectations of the researcher after the question "I wonder what makes it work?") The fact that this question was also asked in the "all tokens" group does not change much here; after all, the children knew perfectly well what made it work – any token at all. It is also unclear why the children in the "all tokens" group did not try to experiment with other elements activating (or not) the toy. However, even with these issues in mind, the study highlights some interesting phenomena: curiosity about the reasons for the occurrence of a phenomenon (e.g. the playing of a melody) and a tendency to construct simple plans to verify this.

Such curiosity can be even stronger than the need to avoid aversive stimuli – Christopher Hsee and Bowen Ruan (2016) showed this in their research on the "Pandora effect." In their imaginatively planned experiments, they sought the limits to which participants in their studies were ready to go in order to satisfy their curiosity and acquire new information. This study is interesting because, as the authors note, we live in times of quite heavy information overload. As one popular comparison goes, the weekend edition of the *New York Times* contains a larger volume of information than that which the average person in the 18th century absorbed in an entire lifetime. Nevertheless, it turns out that the need to learn new things is stronger than (even!) the desire to avoid pain. Hsee and Ruan designed a study in which the invited participants came to a university building and were informed that they had to wait a while for the study to begin, and to "kill time" they could assess pens. However, these were not ordinary pens, but gag pens, known from stores offering "funny gadgets," which zapped the holder with current when pressing a button placed on them (the participants were informed of this). To be more precise, some of the pens in the box had this function (because a battery had been installed in them), while others did not. The participants' task (which they could perform or not – after all, this activity was only to "kill time") was to assess their quality and functionality, and, of course, their "fun levels."

The participants were divided into two groups, to establish the conditions of "certainty" and "uncertainty." There were ten pens in the certainty condition, with red stickers on five of them indicating that batteries were inside, and "copy" pens, and green stickers on the other five indicating that the pens are "safe." In the uncertainty condition, all the pens were marked with yellow stickers, and the respondents were informed that it was not known whether there were batteries in them, so it could not be determined whether or not they would "zap" the holder with electricity.

The study's creators assumed that the participants would be less eager to test the pens if they were not sure about their nature and the risks involved in playing with them. The risk was quite real, because the pens administered a shock of 60V. The experimenters had previously carried out a pilot study in which they checked how aversive the stimulus was. A nine-point scale from extremely negative to extremely positive was used, with an average stimulus of 3.05.

This time, research intuition led the experimenters astray – the results turned out to be exactly the opposite of what they had expected. It was the group in the uncertainty condition that was more willing to use the potentially dangerous pens (mean and standard deviations are given in Table 2.1).

Let us note that a very interesting phenomenon can be observed in the number of "safe" and "dangerous" pens (in the certainty group) – here the respondents were more likely to reach for those that could certainly shock them than those that were "safe"!

What might the reasons for this be? Hsee and Ruan point to the curiosity they think is inherent to every person. The researchers emphasized that in a series of four experiments, the participants were always more willing to perform activities whose outcome was uncertain (even if they expected negative consequences, i.e. an electric shock). The researchers called this phenomenon the "Pandora effect," because, just as in the mythological tale, doing something to open the can – in their experiment, pressing a button on a pen – had negative consequences that, nonetheless, did not prevent the curious from acting. Of course, Hsee and Ruan also did not rule out other possibilities – e.g. boredom, which the participants of the study wanted to kill with stimuli, although even this explanation seems to depict humans as beings requiring stimuli and experimenting with their dosing.

Table 2.1 Average number of pens used by participants under different experimental conditions in the Hsee and Ruan studies (Study 1)

Statistics	*Conditions*			
	"Certainty"	*"Uncertainty"*		
		General	*"Electrocuting" pens*	*"Safe" pens*
Average	5.11	3.04	1.74	1.30
Standard deviation	3.88	2.81	1.70	1.46

Source: Based on Hsee and Ruan, 2016.

But is scientific discovery done through research really exclusive to humans? In other words, are we really as unique as we think we are?

Let's start with animals, or more precisely: rats. These rodents, perhaps the most earnest contributors to psychological research, exhibit many behavioral patterns that remain a mystery to the scientists studying them (Barnett, 2007). One such behavior is their reaction to food in their environment that they have not yet encountered. If a herd comes across such food and has no previous experience with it, they do not eat it immediately (no matter how hungry its members may be). One individual from the herd is "designated" to eat the food, and the rest observe it for up to eight hours, waiting for possible symptoms of poisoning. If none emerge, the food is eaten (and is shared among all the members of the herd, including any weakened and sick individuals). Most interestingly, it is not clear how the "kamikaze" is chosen, who is supposed to check the quality of the food in its own stomach. It is known that this individual is in no particular way "different" from the others (we note that, from a scientific perspective, it would be inappropriate to choose an individual that was significantly different from the flock, as this would violate the principle of randomization). We also know that the individual agrees to its role more or less voluntarily (no resistance on its part can be observed, and the other rats do not make it eat by force). Paul Rozin (1976) writes more about the principles of food selection by rats. We refer readers interested in this problem to his work.

It is worth mentioning that the procedure applied by rats causes some trouble to exterminators, as it prevents the use of simple poisons that could quickly kill the pests. For this reason, it is quite common to use a chemical compound called brodifacoum (Empson & Miskelly, 1999) instead of poisons that cause the immediate death of an animal. Its greatest advantages from the perspective under consideration are its relatively long duration in the rodent's body, the lack of immediate symptoms, and its inducement of a blood clotting disorder (the cause of death is bleeding out from the wound, not the poison itself). The use of this chemical compound and its derivatives makes the natural link between the intake of the poison and the death of the rat virtually invisible to the rest of the herd, so the "kamikaze" method ceases to be effective from the rats' perspective.

Animals, in fact, enjoy what is, from a human perspective, an amazing capacity to achieve their goals. A small bird called the fork-tailed drongo (Dicrurus adsimilis) that inhabits the savannah uses an incredible method of obtaining food (Flower, Gribble, & Ridley, 2014). The drongo is highly reluctant to acquire food on its own (it feeds on small insects and invertebrates), so it spends a large part of its feeding time following meercats. It enters into a seeming symbiosis with them – because big birds of prey are enemies to the meercats, the drongo looks out for them and warns the little rodents of danger just in time by screaming. From time to time, however, the drongo announces danger when none is present – that is to say, it screams "attention, predator" when in fact neither it nor the meercats are in danger. However, the meercats are not aware of this, so they hide from the non-existent danger in their usual manner by ducking into tunnels they have dug. The drongo then flies off the branch it usually occupies and quietly eats all the insects and worms left behind. After a few minutes of feasting it returns to its post, the meercats exit their tunnels, and the relationship continues. Such behavior even leads some researchers (Yong, 2014) to consider whether the drongo has the ability to make inferences about the mental states of other creatures (in this case, meercats). Note that this would be a prelude to acknowledging that the drongo can have a theory of mind. Although for the time being this remains speculation, the very fact that these birds obtain their food in such a specific manner (and observations show that they can acquire as much as a quarter of their daily intake via this theft mechanism) allows us to cautiously assume that the drongo is engaged in experimentation. We point out that they do not announce false alarms all the time – they know that the meercats would then stop paying attention to them. Therefore, they must strike a balance between real and false warnings so as to fill their stomachs and not deprive themselves of the possibility of further food theft at the same time. Of course, it cannot be ruled out that the drongo can simply learn this strategy, e.g. by observing other members of the species or simply by conditioning.

Elements of experimental thinking can be observed in many animal species, even intellectually underdeveloped (but highly developed socially) ants (Beckers, Deneubourg, Goss, and Pasteels, 1990). The researchers noticed that ants of the species *Lasius niger* (the black garden ant, common in many countries, sometimes found in dwellings) have a very interesting strategy for moving around their hive. In the initial stage, they move about in a seemingly disorderly manner, in all possible directions, and their lines of movement give the impression of wandering around or spinning in circles. However, this happens only until one of the ants finds something fit to eat. Then the ant catches as much as it can carry, and makes an about-face, then retraces its exact path – it can do so because the ants continually emit a fragrant pheromone, which, like Ariadne's thread, enables them to return home (i.e. to the anthill). When the ant brings food to the anthill, it turns back again and, following the same pheromone trail, it returns to the food it found (all the while leaving behind more hints of pheromones). After some time, the path becomes so "pheromone rich" that other ants join it and also start carrying food to the anthill.

The researchers also observed that the ants are not only able to locate the right path to the food, but also to relatively quickly adjust it for shorter trips. Once again, this is related to the presence of pheromones. With a large number of ants wandering around the vicinity of the anthill, most probably others will zero in on the same food source, but it is possible that they will manage to do so by finding a shorter (faster – as we will see in a moment, it is about time, not distance) way between the food and the anthill. Once all the food has been taken to the anthill, the insects again start their seemingly disorderly circulation in the area, and when they find food, the whole story will be repeated. Observations of the actions of the common black garden ant have prompted researchers to create a species-specific pattern of behavior, as shown in Table 2.2.

Table 2.2 Behavioral pattern of black garden ants when seeking food and bringing it to the anthill

Circumstances	*Behavior*
Without food, no perceivable pheromone	Moving in random directions, leaving traces of pheromone
No food, trail with perceptible traces of pheromone	Follow pheromone trail, leave pheromone
Reaching anthill, trail with perceptible traces of pheromone	Turn around and follow pheromone trail in the opposite direction
Finding food	Take food, turn around, follow pheromone trail in the opposite direction
Carrying food	Follow pheromone trail, leave pheromone
Reaching anthill with food	Leave food, turn around, follow pheromone trail in the opposite direction

Source: Based on Beckers, Deneubourg, Goss, & Pasteels, 1990.

For the sake of clarity, it should be noted that in the case of this phenomenon, we cannot speak of a planned experiment for several reasons – mainly because the common black garden ant (a single specimen) itself cannot, of course, experiment. In the analysis of this example, however, it is rather worth noting the astonishing creativity of nature, thanks to which ants as a community (or colony) are able to optimize their activities by choosing the most advantageous from among several options (in which they apply experience).

So, even if such seemingly primitive organisms like ants are able to perform a sort of primitive "experiment" (choosing the fastest way to get to the food from among a few paths), how do humans present themselves in this area?

An example of how even in relatively primitive conditions people conduct quite advanced experiments in methodological terms is the history told by the Polish naval captain Karol Olgierd Borchardt (2003). Borchardt sailed in the 1950s on ships transporting nuts down the Amazon. Of course, in a tropical climate and due to the enormous humidity on the ships, taking proper care of the cargo was crucial. It was necessary to constantly ventilate the chambers in which the nuts were stored, to "mix" the cargo if necessary, so that the temperature and humidity in the various storage areas were more or less even, all in order to ensure that the goods reached their destination port in the best possible condition. Of course, different ships and different shipowners approached their tasks in various ways – from the perspective of freight owners, it was therefore important to find a relatively simple and at the same time effective method of verifying how carefully the sailors looked after their cargo. The difficulty was that while the state of deterioration of bananas or oranges can be easily assessed, the case of nuts is more complicated. To find out what condition a nut is in, you have to open it, and if you open it, you can no longer sell it (even if everything is fine with it). The procedure on ships sailing down the Amazon was as follows: at the port where the cargo was loaded, 100 nuts from different boxes were selected (as the methodologist would say: a random sample). The nuts were opened and a count taken of how many of them were spoiled. Then, the remaining nuts were loaded on the ship, which set off on its journey to the port of destination. At the end of the trip, the procedure was repeated – 100 nuts were again randomly selected, they were opened, and the number of spoiled nuts was counted. The difference between the number of spoiled nuts at the end of the voyage and at the beginning was a roughly objective measure of the "quality of the voyage" and the time that the sailors spent taking care of the loaded goods.

We note that the described procedure meets almost all the criteria for the experiment. Here we have a problem with the possibility of examining the whole population (in this case, it is difficult to determine the quality of all the nuts); we have a decision to base our conclusions on a sample (100 nuts drawn); and finally we have some sort of a framework for random sampling (both when taking the cargo on board and when unloading it). If we wanted to compare the procedure used to experimental plans we are familiar with (Ross, 2019), we would consider that the Amazon sailors and nut owners employed (partially) a plan with a pretest and posttest. We know nothing about systematic research on methods of nut care, but if the system of "wind catchers" described by Borchardt (special cloth chimneys that compressed air to aerate the nuts) were to be empirically verified, a complete scheme would be ready. Such a system could be installed in one of the cargo holds, in another one it would not, and by using the described procedure it would be possible to compare the results obtained via this method without particular difficulty.

The history of life at sea supplies more examples of the use of experimentation as a research tool to find ways of improving seafarer's well-being. One of the most prolific researchers in this field was James Lind, a Scottish physician and pioneer of marine medicine. Living from 1716 to 1794, he practiced as a physician during a time when seafarers dealt with the serious threat of scurvy – a terrible disease which is (as we know today) the result of a long-term deficiency of ascorbic acid (vitamin C) in the human body. The symptoms of scurvy (from general weakness, through spontaneous bleeding, difficult healing of wounds, inflammatory overgrowth of gums, to bone fractures and tooth loss) had a significant impact on the quality of life of people at sea and, consequently, on the income from sea transport (merchant navy) and the combat capabilities of a fleet (navy). Suffice it to say that during his ten-year period of command of the English fleet, Admiral Richard Hawkins recorded 10,000 deaths from this disease, then also known as rotting. No wonder, therefore, that the problem of scurvy was analyzed in a great deal of ways, and all sorts of remedies for it were proposed. For example, the London medical academy prepared a special anti-scurvy formula in the form of an elixir consisting of sulphuric acid, spirit, sugar, cinnamon and ginger. The effectiveness of this medicine was comparable to that of another agent used at the time – fumigation. In other words, zero. At the same time, however, it was still better than taking so-called Ward's peas – pills prepared by Joshua Ward, a ship's doctor, who claimed to have received a secret recipe for this substance from the Jesuits. Ships that were equipped with this medicine recorded tremendous mortality rates among the crew.

Only relatively simple experiments carried out by the aforementioned James Lind made it possible to find real remedies for scurvy. In 1747, Lind assumed a post on the ship *Salisbury*, where he found a crew fed on a diet consisting of three meals. Sailors were given oatmeal with sugar for breakfast, mutton, bread, pudding and soaked rusks for dinner, and groats, raisins, wine and sago for supper. Modern dietary science leads us to believe that this was a diet that not only did not prevent scurvy, but even increased the risk of disease. Lind selected six pairs of sailors from the crew, whom he supplied with various substances to enrich this diet and to prevent (at least in theory) the symptoms of scurvy. Sailors from the first pair received one quart (just over a liter) of apple juice a day; the next one – 25 drops of sulphuric elixir; the next two received two tablespoons of vinegar three times a day; the next a quarter of a liter of salt water; and the penultimate a special mixture consisting of garlic, mustard, horseradish and myrrh balm. The last pair received (apart from normal meals) two oranges and one lemon each, which – as we today can easily surmise – successfully inhibit the progress of scurvy. Lind published his results in 1753 in the book *Treatise of the Scurvy*, after first informing the admiralty of them. The admiralty ordered the introduction of a mandatory daily portion of lemon juice into the sailors' menus (it is unclear why lemons were chosen rather than oranges), which clearly reduced the incidence of scurvy. It also had side effects – English sailors started to be referred to as "limeys." Some of them tried to protect their good name and refused to drink the lemon juice (or poured it overboard). Loose teeth, however, quickly encouraged them to try to make nice with the lemons again while maintaining their sailorly ethos. A compromise was achieved by adding lemon juice to rum or other spirits, sometimes adding sugar or cinnamon for taste. This is how grog was created – as we may assume, experimentally as well).

The history of alcohol production is quite interesting from the perspective of thinking about experimentation. In his fascinating book *A history of the world in 6 glasses*, Tom Standage (2005) describes the role of various drinks that symbolize their respective eras (beer, wine, alcoholic distillates, tea, coffee, and Coca-Cola) in changing social reality. It shows, among other things, the incredible role that beer played in the creation of the societies of Egypt and Babylon; it also details how (experimental, of course) the decision was taken to add hops to it. The eminent beer expert Michael Jackson (1997; the similarity of his name with that of the famous pop musician entirely accidental) demonstrates, for example, that the position of Belgium as a brewing country results, among other things, from a tendency to experiment and add various additives to the drink – orange peel extract, raspberries, etc. It is worth noting for balance, however, that in many cases the Belgians do not seek to experiment. Here, travelers through the country may be wondering about the double roofs that can be found in some places – a second, new, and effective protection from sun and rain is set up over the old, already worn by the passage of time. The reason is again beer – some of the so-called top fermentation varieties lie in open vats and are not imbued with industrial brewer's yeast. Instead, the brewers wait for the wort (a malt solution, the basic raw material that becomes beer after fermentation) to be "annexed" in a natural manner by the wild yeast naturally present in the air. Since there is a high probability that the yeast's natural habitat is the old roofs, brewers do not want to risk losing them and do not allow them to be dismantled.

Here at the end we wish to return to the girl we talked about at the beginning of this chapter. Indeed, according to her wishes, a fire was lit in the fireplace, and the effectiveness of the alarm was indeed checked (the device worked quite well). A ladder and drill were used, and the sensors were installed (with the girl holding the ladder) on the ceiling. When the job was finished, she was asked if everything was now ok, and if she stopped fearing fire. "Well, yes," she replied. "We no longer need to worry about fire. But what about a flood?" Experimenting never ends.

3 The field study in social psychology

The history of research conducted using the field study method

It is unclear where social psychology would be today were it not for field experiments. In this chapter we will look at some of them – their selection is not dictated by their subjectively understood "weight," or the influence of a given study on the development of the discipline. And hats off to anyone who would try to answer the question of whether the Oak School experiment conducted by Robert Rosenthal and Lenore Jacobson, or perhaps Charles Hofling's "hospital" research was more important for psychology. The experiments described in this chapter have several aspects in common – all of them were studies conducted in natural conditions; all assumed a lack of knowledge of the participants about their participation in the experiment (or at least a lack of knowledge about its true purpose, although it should be stressed that this significantly changes the social context of such research); and all generated results that changed our thinking about the social world. We also demonstrate that many of these experiments remain salient in the world of science – despite Robert Sternberg's statement that "Nobody cites dead psychologists," it turns out that this is not entirely true – the ideas of researchers from 60 or 70 or even 90 years ago are still treated as important and interesting discoveries. What is more, in many cases they serve as the basis for further hypotheses and interesting replications of original experiments.

In this chapter we present ten different field studies that were conducted by psychologists. This is not, we hasten to repeat, our choice of the "best" or "most important" studies. We want to highlight the different experimental approaches, the originality of research ideas, and the variety of areas where field experiments have enhanced and extended psychological knowledge. In order to avoid the mistaken impression that the order in which we present these studies reflects their importance, we will present them according to the chronology of their appearance in print. We will start with experiments that were conducted before World War II, and we will end our brief review with those published at the end of the second decade of the 21st century. What is more, we want to signal here that a number of other field experiments, very important from the perspective of the development of the psychology of field experiments, are presented in later chapters of this book, illustrating the theses presented there.

1 How much you dislike the Chinese: LaPiere's experiment

One of the first researchers to demonstrate the importance of experiments carried out in a natural environment and measuring real behavior was Richard LaPiere, a scientist (B.A. in Economics, M.A. and Ph.D. in Sociology, and thus, contrary to popular belief and according to the records, not formally a psychologist) from Stanford University. His most

DOI: 10.4324/9781003092995-3

recognizable work – an article in *Social Forces* entitled "Attitudes versus actions" (LaPiere, 1934) – was revolutionary for one basic reason. The author challenged the conviction, dominant in the early years of psychology and sociology, that there is a fundamental correspondence between the declared attitudes and actual actions of individuals. Although this assumption was not, of course, accepted unquestioningly (Bain, 1928, 1930; Faris, 1928), it became a sort of foundation for social research (both in sociology and psychology) in the early 20th century. LaPiere opposed such thinking, showing that the study of attitudes by asking for declarations of behavior involves the risk of artifacts occurring. He used the example of a question that can be considered (from a certain perspective) as a sensible item on a survey analyzing attitudes towards minorities: "Would you give up your seat on a streetcar to an Armenian woman?" (Hock, 2015). According to LaPiere, the answer to a question thus posed would only be a kind of symbolic response to the description of a symbolic (and strongly hypothetical) situation, which can hardly (or not at all) be treated as a factor predicting the real behavior of the participant. LaPiere criticized the approach that assumes the potential for drawing far-reaching conclusions from declarations collected in the form of responses to such questions (and it should be kept in mind that his contemporaries not only drew conclusions about the behavior of the participant, but also, on the basis of these declarations, were capable of advancing hypotheses about the mutual relations between e.g. Americans and Armenians).

The research that enabled LaPiere to question the possibility of drawing conclusions about behavior based on declarations was conducted between 1930 and 1931. It is worth describing briefly the social setting or, more broadly, the context in which it took place. At the time, the United States of America was a country rife with very strong interethnic conflicts (Lake & Rothchild, 1998). The famous study using adjectives carried out by Daniel Katz and Kenneth Braly (1933) on students showed how strong and consistent the images of many minorities (Germans, Italians, Irish, Black – then still referred to as Negros – Jews, Chinese, Japanese) were, as well as how strongly negative some of them were. One of the most negatively stereotyped minority groups at the time was Asians, with particular emphasis on the Chinese. In Katz and Braly's research, students who were supposed to indicate the adjectives that best defined the Chinese included: superstitious, sneaky, devious, stupid (we hasten to add that there were positive words among them – loving family ties and tradition, quiet). These attitudes, presented by a part of society, were also reflected in the policies of some service providers – a number of restaurants and hotels openly declared that they did not serve representatives of specified ethnic minorities. LaPiere noted, however, that displaying a poster with the then popular slogan "We serve for white people only: no dogs, Negros, Chinese" is only a form of declaration of a certain attitude and, as he himself pointed out earlier, it is not possible to predict behavior with 100% certainty on this basis alone. Therefore, he decided to check how the employees of service providers would react when they actually had to serve (or refuse to serve) a Chinese person.

LaPiere took advantage of the fact of traveling around the United States with a young Chinese student and his wife. In the interests of fairness, it should be said that this part of the description of the research method is not entirely clear – there is a certain probability that LaPiere and his companions' original intention was not to do any research, but simply to travel around the USA, and in the course of this journey something happened that sparked the researcher's curiosity. One evening in a small provincial town known for its intolerant attitudes towards minorities, they were forced to seek accommodation. The three of them approached the reception area, asked for rooms and, to LaPiere's surprise, were served very efficiently and charmingly. Two months later, LaPiere called the same hotel and asked if he could rent a room for an "important Chinese gentleman" passing through town. This time, his request was met with a very clear and firm refusal. This inconsistency between declaration and real behavior caused the researcher to engage in a more systematic analysis of the phenomenon.

LaPiere and his companions traversed the entire United States twice – both across the continent and along the West Coast. They traveled roughly 10,000 miles during this journey. The Chinese couple traveling with LaPiere were not informed about the research being carried out because he wanted to maintain a certain "methodological purity." The scientist carefully noted all the reactions they encountered during their travels – they visited 67 places of accommodation (hotels, campsites, and private accommodation) and 184 restaurants and cafes. LaPiere – as he declared, at least – tried to make sure that his Chinese friends were the first to enter the premises and also to rent the rooms themselves (although, again, it is worth noting that he did not systematically study this influence, which is one of the weaknesses of his experiment). The results were unequivocal – out of the 251 facilities they visited, only at one were they refused service, motivated by the racial background of the Chinese couple (a campsite owner simply said "I don't take Japs"). In all the other places they were served normally, and even – as the study's author pointed out – in many of them the service was better owing to the curiosity of the owners of lodgings and of waiters and waitresses in restaurants towards guests whom they viewed as exotic. LaPiere tried to introduce a quality of service scale as a measurement tool, but since he created it and evaluated it himself, it is difficult to treat it as completely reliable – suffice it to say that in 25 out of 67 (37.3%) hotels visited (and 72 out of 184 restaurants – 39.1%), he evaluated the service as better than he could have expected if he had been traveling alone.

In the second part of the study, two months after a given stay, LaPiere sent a survey to the places visited with the question "Would you accept a person of Chinese origin at your facility?" In order to eliminate the potential effect of the in-person visits, he also sent the same questionnaire to places they had not visited, but which were located in similar regions of the country to the respondents in the first group. Here, too, the results were unequivocal – the vast majority of establishments refused (detailed results are collected in Table 3.1).

Of course, it should be noted that, as is sometimes the case with the surveys, a significant part of the surveyed institutions simply did not respond to the letters (49%), while the results obtained are so clear that they can most likely be considered more or less representative.

Table 3.1 Declarations made by hotel and restaurant owners about serving a person of Chinese origin

Response	*Places they visited*		*Places they did not visit*	
	Hotels	*Restaurants*	*Hotels*	*Restaurants*
No	43	75	30	76
Hard to say (depends on circumstances)	3	6	2	7
Yes	1	0	0	1

Source: Based on LaPiere (1934).

When LaPiere himself summed up the results he had collected in the two parts of the experiment (focused on actual behavior and declarations), he remarked on the unsuitability of surveys in research intended to analyze human attitudes. However, he did not claim that research based on the expectation of a declaration should be completely eliminated from the methods used by social sciences – he pointed out, for example, that they are useful in measuring the kinds of attitudes that, by their nature, remain exclusively symbolic. They can be used for such situations as measurements of religious attitudes or political opinion polling; however, it is not possible to predict who will vote for whom based on their results. LaPiere, summarizing his research, pointed to another element of surveys – the ease with which they are conducted. However, he treated it as one of the drawbacks of this method of data collection, as he felt that it encourages the rapid collection of large amounts of data and its mechanical analysis, which does not facilitate (or at least does not encourage) intellectual effort and "focusing on what's important."

Naturally, as could be expected, LaPiere's text describing the results of his research was a sort of stick into the beehive of social researchers of the 1930s. The obtained results (and above all the way they were collected) were criticized, although it should be noted that charges were leveled primarily against the second, survey part of the research. LaPiere was criticized for saying that the mere statement "I will not accept persons of Chinese origin" is not a *de facto* measure of attitude. It was pointed out that the phrase "persons of Chinese origin" can generate very different mental pictures, significantly different from the view of a couple – as LaPiere wrote – of young people who were "handsome, charming, quickly evoking admiration." It should be stressed that the studies discussed above have been criticized for a range of reasons (e.g. Ajzen, 1987; Blasi, 1980; Fazio, Chen, McDonel, & Sherman, 1982). For our part, we want to draw attention to their two fundamental defects. Firstly, LaPiere himself, a man with white skin, was traveling with the Chinese couple, which could have significantly affected the behavior of the participants, and above all of those who were prejudiced against Chinese people. Secondly, there are no control conditions in the studies (or more precisely, in their key aspect, i.e. the behavioral part) in which Caucasian people were the guests. It seems that LaPiere implicitly assumed that in all cases they would be politely served. Firstly, this is not certain. Secondly, LaPiere himself estimated the level of courtesy of the service, so he was able to make an objectified comparison of the behavior of the participants with the conditions we write about, and which were lacking in his experiment.

However, these critiques do not diminish the fact that LaPiere's research initiated a very important strand of experiments in social psychology concerning the relationship between attitudes and actual behavior, which has given rise to many very interesting studies and theories (e.g. Ajzen & Fishbein, 1975, 1977; Liska, 1984; Wicker, 1971); they have also shown quite conclusively that if we want to know how people will behave in a given situation, it is not enough to ask them.

2 How inter-group aggression develops: the Sherifs' experiment

The summer of 1954 saw one of the most interesting group conflict experiments in the history of social psychology ever conducted. It was the continuation of a series of studies in this area initiated by Muzafer Sherif and his colleagues in the 1940s. Sherif was of Turkish descent, born in 1906, and left for the USA after obtaining his Master's degree at the University of Istanbul in 1928. He married Carolyn Wood, who took his name, and from that time they published as the "Sherifs" – this is how they were to go down in the history of psychology. The place where it happened was Robbers Cave State Park, Oklahoma, and more precisely – the Boy Scouts of America scout camp located on its grounds.

The Sherifs wanted to understand how the attitudes and the organization of informal social groups arise. They were also interested in the processes of forming group relationships. They decided to study 11- and 12-year-old boys on a summer scout camp. It should be noted that in order to control the maximum number of disrupting variables, the roles of camp staff – educators, management, etc. – were all played by researchers. A set of various scouting exercises and tasks was prepared, which gave the boys a lot of fun, but at the same time made it possible to test the research hypotheses. It should also be mentioned that the experimental participants were carefully selected – the researchers had previously analyzed their academic results with great care, reviewed school records with reports of educational problems, and conducted interviews with their teachers and parents. The boys were also asked to complete various tests, including personality tests. The aim was to select a highly homogeneous group of healthy, socially well-adapted boys, with intelligence slightly above average and coming from well-off Protestant middle-class homes.

The research was extensive and comprised several phases. It examined how the first friendships are created, how the boys form groups, how a group hierarchy is established. An interesting example of how the latter was examined was the training session before a baseball game – targets were set up at which all of the group members were told to throw balls. The targets were constructed in such a way that the throwers and other members of the group were not able to assess the quality of the throw. Only the researchers were able to do this (a system of lights showing how close to the center the ball struck was mounted on the targets). They discovered a tendency to systematically overstate the accuracy of the throw by those passing judgment when it was performed by a person occupying a high position in the group hierarchy. When boys low in this hierarchy were throwing, their results were consistently underestimated.

During the camp in 1954 (there were others, e.g. in 1949 in Connecticut), 24 boys were divided into two groups, which generally did not come into contact with each other, although they were aware of their existence. The first phase of this study was to build a group identity in two groups of 12 – one of the manifestations of the success of this endeavor was that the groups gave themselves names. One was called "Eagles" and the other "Rattlesnakes." When it was clear that the two groups had achieved cohesiveness, the phase of confrontation began. The researchers organized a tournament of handball, baseball, and tug-of-war. The boys were sent on a treasure hunt. As was assumed, these situations provoked strong inter-group conflicts, which continued to manifest themselves after the sporting competition had ended. The Eagles, for example, who had lost the sports tournament, ceremonially burned the Rattlesnakes' flag. The Rattlesnakes, in revenge, ransacked the Eagle's cabin, overturned beds and stole private property, which initiated a series of insults and organized attacks. At the same time, the researchers began to observe an increase in intra-group cohesion, and even an increase in the willingness to cooperate and appreciate those people from their own groups who had not been treated well by them before.

After the conflict phase, the researchers attempted to reverse the situation and bring the groups together. Initially, attempts were made to test a hypothesis about the influence of pleasant social contacts on the level of conflict. However, arranged meetings (in a common dining room, during a film screening) turned into occasions to escalate the conflict rather than extinguish it. The Sherifs and their collaborators therefore decided to artificially create a situation involving a threat common to both groups. Since the two "sub-camps" were drawing water from the same spring (a large reservoir located about one mile away), the researchers faked an accident that cut off the water. All the boys were gathered together and informed of the situation, after which they were offered help in finding the sources of the leak and repairing the aqueduct. The two groups took up this task together and in harmony, which allowed them to cope with the problem. Another test of their ability to cooperate was the offer to screen an attractive film (submitted by the boys). The camp management stated that they did not have the money to rent a copy. As a result, the boys decided to finance the show themselves, after which the two groups gathered, made the appropriate calculations, voted on a specific movie, and sat down to watch it.

Probably the best known example of the cooperation between the "Rattlesnakes" and the "Eagles" was when they were informed that the truck carrying the provisions for a trip got stuck in mud and was unable to reach them. In order to free the truck, it was necessary to work together to pull a rope (as the authors say, the same one that was used early on to create conflict between the groups during the tournament). The groups started to cooperate, and shortly thereafter the truck was able to continue on.

What interested the researchers most was analyzed immediately afterwards. The Sherifs and their collaborators posed the question of how much the experience of cooperation would ameliorate the groups' shared hostility. As it turned out, this did not happen right away – at first, the groups, despite their cooperation, tended to return to their old habits (of insults and mockery), but as the experience of working together increased, these symptoms diminished. There were even friendships that developed between members of initially hostile camps. After the research was completed, their authors conducted a number of interviews with all participants of the Robbers Cave Park camp. In the summary of their research, they concluded that the meetings arranged (e.g. on social grounds) between the conflicted sides do not generally reduce the level of conflict between them – moreover, in some situations they can serve as an arena for the intensification of conflict. However, Sherif, Harvey, White, Mood, and Sherif (1961) clearly demonstrated that stimulation of cooperation for the common good creates much greater scope for conflict mitigation, especially in situations of an external threat (lack of water or food).

This study also gave rise to methodological controversies. First of all, there is no control group in which the boys would not be induced to engage in inter-group competition. Despite this drawback, the researchers' huge contribution to psychological knowledge on issues such as inter-group conflict, aggression, or the consequences of competition and cooperation cannot be denied.

3 What will people do with a found letter? The experiments of Stanley Milgram and his associates

Stanley Milgram is known in the global scientific literature as the author of one of the most important experiments in history – his studies of obedience to authority (Milgram, 1974), about which we write later in this book. However, in addition to this experiment, fundamental from so many perspectives, Milgram conducted many other, often highly ingenious studies, frequently in natural environments. Among these is the "lost letter paradigm" created by him and his colleagues in 1965 (Milgram, Mann, & Harter, 1965).

This method was first used by Milgram, and later by dozens of social psychologists as a way to check real levels of prejudice, free from the risk of self-presentation effects.

In his first study using this method, Milgram and his colleagues scattered 400 sealed envelopes with the same address printed on them around the streets of New Haven, Connecticut:

P.O. Box 7147
304 Columbus Avenue
New Haven 11, Connecticut

The envelopes, however, differed in the first line of the address – 100 envelopes each were addressed to:

- Friends of the Communist Party;
- Friends of the Nazi Party;
- Medical Research Association;
- Mr. Walter Carnap.

Milgram and his associates also examined how the place where the letter was left affected the chances of its reaching the addressee. They left the letters in four places: stores, telephone booths, at turnstiles, and under cars' windshield wipers (then the phrase "found next to a car" was written in pencil suggesting that someone had picked up the letter earlier and considered it lost by the car owner). Postage stamps were affixed to all envelopes, so the only thing potential finders would have to do to help them reach their addressee was to put them in a letterbox.

As it turned out, the overall chance of a letter reaching a letterbox was 48% – although naturally Milgram and his colleagues were most interested in the difference between the particular conditions. The percentage of letters that ultimately reached their addressees is shown in Table 3.2.

Milgram and his colleagues themselves described the results they recorded as unspectacular – after all, it can be assumed that people would prefer to help the Medical Research Association rather than the Nazi Party. However, the researchers focused on the method itself – they pointed out its limitations (e.g. that we know nothing about the person who threw the letter in the box), but also emphasized its advantages. First of all, they pointed

Table 3.2 Percentage of letters received by addressees depending on where the envelope was left and type of address

Address	*Location*				
	Shop	*Car*	*Street*	*Phone booth*	*Total*
Medical Research Association	23	19	18	12	72
Walter Carnap	21	21	16	13	71
Friends of the Communist Party	6	9	6	4	25
Friends of the Nazi Party	7	6	6	6	25
Total	57	55	46	35	48

Source: Based on Milgram, Mann, & Harter (1965).

out that the participants were not aware of the fact that a study was being carried out at all. Of course, from the perspective of contemporary discussion about ethics in social research, it is not entirely clear whether this can be considered an advantage or a disadvantage of this method, but it is worth remembering that in 1965 researchers had no qualms about it. The second benefit of using this method was the fact that it measured actual behavior, not merely declarations. The third issue seems trivial, but important from the methodological perspective – Stanley Milgram and his associates indicated a very easy way to collect data, by just looking in a mailbox once in a while and seeing what's inside. Naturally, the matter of scattering the letters seemed much more difficult from this perspective.

The method suggested by Milgram achieved considerable popularity, although of course it was also criticized (e.g. Shotland, Berger, & Forsythe, 1970; Wicker, 1969). Nevertheless, for years it has served as a popular and effective method of testing levels of prejudice towards various social groups. It has also been used to verify, among other things, the level of altruism in various city districts (Holland, Silva, & Mace, 2012). Interestingly, even the Internet revolution did not render it obsolete – a slight change in the method was made: instead of a lost letter, a "lost email" was used (Stern & Faber, 1997).

4 Get your foot in the door: the experiments of Freedman and Fraser

Social influence is an area of psychology that particularly often engages in studies carried out in a natural environment. One of the most frequently described studies in the history of psychology is the classic experiment by Jonathan Freedman and Scott Fraser (1966). The participants in the study were housewives. A phone call was made to them, during which a quite embarrassing request was made – a group of several men were supposed to visit them and take an inventory of all the household and everyday use items in the house. Only 22% of the women consented to this request. A much higher percentage was recorded when a few days earlier a short phone call was made and they were asked for a short interview on their consumer habits – then, 53% of the approached women gave their consent. Freedman and Fraser thus excluded one of the possible explanations of this effect – namely, submission to a friend. It turned out that the situation in which someone had previously made a phone call to the women and did not make any initial request of them, but only "got acquainted" with them, did not lead to significantly greater submissiveness than in the control group.

On the basis of their results, the authors of the study formulated a new technique of social influence called foot-in-the-door (FITD). To test its effectiveness, they conducted another experiment. The main request was to place in one's lawn a large and not particularly attractive billboard with the inscription "Drive carefully" on it. In the control conditions (i.e. without any initial request preceding the main request), 17% of the participants agreed to comply with the request. In the other four groups, Freedman and Fraser asked them to put a small sticker in their window or to sign a petition to the governor of the state. The message on the sticker or petition related to either road safety or environmental and waste management issues in California. Obedience in each group is shown in Table 3.3.

As we may see, the greatest obedience was recorded when the initial request was "doubly compatible" with the main request. Firstly, in terms of subject matter (it was related to road safety), and secondly, in the similarity of the activity performed (placing a sign in

Table 3.3 Percentage of subjects complying with large request in Freedman and Fraser experiment

Issue[a]	*Task*[a]			
	Similar	*N*	*Different*	*N*
Similar	76.0**	25	47.8*	23
Different	47.6*	21	47.4*	19
	One-Contact 16.7 (N = 24)			

Source: *Journal of Personality and Social Psychology*, *4*, p. 201. Copyright: American Psychological Association.

Note: Significance levels represent differences from the One-Contact condition
a Denotes relationship between first and second request
* p < .08
** p < .01

the vicinity of a house). However, it should be clearly emphasized that obedience in the remaining groups also turned out to be significantly higher than in the control group, which provides irrefutable evidence of the effectiveness of the described technique.

Even the name of the "foot-in-the-door" technique underlines the strong connection with the rule of engagement and consistency described in the literature (Cialdini, 2001). If we want someone to open a door for us, we must first put a foot in it. In this way, the name of the technique coincides with various popular sayings and folk wisdom such as "give someone an inch and he will take the whole mile." Practitioners of social influence (among the most prominent, it must be said, are all types of fraudsters) also say that the first few seconds of an interaction are the most important. If the victim "swallows the hook" and, for example, shows at least a hint of interest in a new perfume, the advantageous purchase of diamonds taken from a country overwhelmed by social unrest, or an email from an unknown bank employee in Nigeria, the damage is done. The rule of engagement and consistency is highly likely to work, and the fraudster will succeed in executing the planned manipulation.

5 The Pygmalion effect: Rosenthal and Jacobson's studies

Another study of great significance for the development of psychology (social, developmental, educational, research methodology – one could go on and on) was conducted at Oak School. This was the code name for a certain elementary school in the USA where, in the mid-1960s, Robert Rosenthal and Lenore Jacobson (1968) conducted research on the so-called Pygmalion effect. And although this study was later criticized on multiple occasions (Raudenbush, 1984; Snow, 1995), it still remains one of the most important field studies in the history of psychology.

The term "Pygmalion effect" is, of course, related to the name of the mythical king of Cyprus, who, disillusioned with living women, carved his own ideal female out of ivory. The statue was so beautiful and perfectly made that Pygmalion fell in love with it and ultimately married (according to the legend, the statue was animated by Aphrodite). The notion of the Pygmalion effect was introduced to the world of science by Robert Merton (1948), who wrote about the self-fulfilling prophecy. Since then, in research methodology we have used it to describe effects that we have in fact created by our own expectations. It should be noted that one of the stories most frequently quoted to illustrate the effect of a self-fulfilling prophecy is that of the horse Clever Hans (*Kluge Hans*). This horse, owned by the Russian–German aristocrat Wilhelm von Osten, had a quite unique skill – he was able to solve simple mathematical tasks. Von Osten rode him all over Germany to showcase these abilities at public demonstrations (while also taking the opportunity to promote his views on education). The shows went as follows: von Osten asked Hans a question (e.g., "How much is three plus four?"), and Hans stamped out the answer (always the correct one!). Of course, after a time people began to doubt in Hans' exceptional abilities and demanded that he be subjected to a series of experiments to verify them. These experiments quite quickly showed that Hans' knowledge of arithmetic mysteriously disappeared when von Osten was not nearby. As it turned out, the horse was not as smart as believed – it couldn't count, but it was great at observing its owner. The shows always followed the same pattern: after asking the question, von Osten loudly counted the pounding of Hans' hooves and, as it turned out, was unwittingly giving the horse a cue when he was supposed to stop stomping. The most important thing, from the perspective of research methodology, is that von Osten really was doing it involuntarily: he had not trained Hans, but simply believed he possessed a brilliant horse! (Dunbar, 2004). This is a good illustration of the problem faced by a researcher when conducting experiments involving people (who are far more advanced in decoding involuntary messages). At the same time, however, investigators focused on dolphins have noted that they are excellent observers of experimenters, and they are highly skilled at grasping non-verbal messages that they then use to make decisions (Bradbury & Vehrencamp, 1998; Tschudin, Call, Dunbar, Harris, & van der Elst, 2001).

The Rosenthal and Jacobson study itself began by having students in grades 1–6 take the TOGA (Test of General Abilities), a non-verbal intelligence test that diagnoses IQ relatively independent of learned skills. It can therefore be stated that this was a general indicator of the intelligence of the children tested, which omitted the skills they were learning at school (such as counting, reading, and writing). At the same time, teachers working with the students on a daily basis were informed that their pupils were being tested using the Harvard Test of Inflected Acquisition. The aim of this procedure was to make the teachers believe that it was possible to predict students' future educational achievements using this test – that is, to assume that, for example, during the following year, they would demonstrate an exceptional increase in their school skills (of course, this was not something the test could do). After completion of the test (conducted in 18 classes – three in each of the six levels), the teachers were given a list of those students whose scores were in the top 20%, and thus those who could be expected to achieve the best results in the following school year. In fact, these names were chosen at random and had no connection with any intelligence test performed earlier. At the end of the school year, Rosenthal and Jacobson visited Oak School once again and repeated the research with TOGA to see if there was a difference between the experimental group (those on the "school success forecast" lists) and the control group (the remaining students).

As it turned out, progress was indeed made, and while it was recorded in all children, it was more pronounced in the experimental group (on average, results in the whole school improved by 12.2 points) than in the control group (8.2 points). What is particularly interesting is that the improvement was not uniform in all classes – the strongest effect was observed in the first-grade groups, while the effect gradually decreased as the students got older, disappearing completely in the oldest classes (fifth and sixth grade).

Rosenthal and Jacobson showed how teachers' expectations of their students influence their achievements. They also emphasized the importance of interpersonal expectations in situations involving relationships with relatively unknown people (which could explain the strong effect in younger classes and its lack in older classes). Also noteworthy is that the researchers' results cast a long shadow over the validity of standard intelligence tests, especially in the United States, where for a time they were one of the main sources of information teachers received about pupils (Lynam, Moffitt, & Stouthamer-Loeber, 1993).

As for the issue at the heart of this book, the impact made by Rosenthal and Jacobson's research on the methodology of scientific research (especially experimental psychological research) is crucial. A number of texts (Babad, Inbar, & Rosenthal, 1982; Brannigan, 2004) pointed to the necessity of following the principles of single-blind and double-blind studies in order to avoid the Pygmalion effect in research (in clinical studies, double-blind trials or double-placebo design). The name of the effect itself has also become quite common, although – as is often the case in psychology – the same effect is described in different ways (e.g. as confirmation bias or self-fulfilling prophecy).

6 Will you fall in love when passing over a suspension bridge? Dutton and Aron's experiment

In accordance with the classical approach to the nature of emotions, each emotion consists of two components: physiological arousal and its subjective interpretation (Schachter, 1964). Many psychological concepts (e.g. Bersheid & Walster, 1974; Schachter & Singer, 1962) assume that this physiological arousal can sometimes be evoked by completely different sources than those perceived by the subject.

Donald Dutton and Arthur Aron (1974) decided to apply this idea to demonstrate that the recognition that someone awakens erotic interest in us is not necessarily related exclusively to that person's traits and behavior. The researchers used the fact that a very specific tourist attraction is located near their university (University of British Columbia, Vancouver, Canada). This attraction is the Capilano Canyon Suspension Bridge, which is about 140 meters long, less than 1.5 meters wide, and hangs 70 meters above the water. In addition, steel cables serve as handrails, and the bridge wobbles even when the wind is still. The experiment's participants were men who had crossed the bridge alone. Immediately afterwards, an attractive woman approached them and asked them to participate in a psychological study. In the other conditions, the men had passed over a short and very sturdy wooden bridge hanging 3 meters above the surface of calm water. The experimenters assumed that while crossing the latter bridge would not generate any affective consequences, crossing the Capilano Canyon Suspension Bridge would evoke strong emotional arousal among the men in the experiment. A "real man" should not be afraid, or at least should not admit it, even to himself. Men exiting such a bridge would prefer to interpret their accelerated heartbeat and other physiological symptoms as a product of something other than the feeling of fear.

Dutton and Aron provided them with just such an opportunity, by having a beautiful young woman approach them. After all, one's heart can beat harder because of her appearance, not because of the fear arising from crossing the bridge! But how to discover the truth? Dutton and Aron solved this by having the woman show the experiment participants a certain ambiguous drawing (Item 3GF from the Thematic Apperception Test), then asking them to think up a story to match it. Of course, the same request was made of the men leaving the other bridge. The stories invented by the participants were then evaluated by so-called "peer judges" to determine the amount of erotic content in them.

Table 3.4 Behavioral responses and Thematic Apperception Test imagery scores for each experimental group

Interviewer	*No. filling in questionnaire*	*No. accepting phone number*	*No. phoning*	*Usable questionnaires*	*Sexual imagery score*
Female					
Control bridge	22/33	16/22	2/16	18	1.41
Experimental bridge	23/33	18/23	9/18	20	2.47
Male					
Control bridge	22/42	6/22	1/6	20	.61
Experimental bridge	23/51	7/23	2/7	20	.80

Source: *Journal of Personality and Social Psychology*, *30*, p. 513. Copyright: American Psychological Association.

It turned out that the associations of men in the experimental conditions (i.e., those coming down from the dangerous bridge) contained more such content than those of the men in the control conditions (i.e., those who had passed over the robust bridge). The woman also offered to give them her phone number in the event they wanted to learn more about the results of the study. Of the men exiting the Capilano Canyon Suspension Bridge, almost half of those who took the girl's phone number then called her, while the percentage of those who had crossed the safer bridge was clearly lower. It should be added that there were also conditions in which a man made the request to take part in the study. Much less frequently the surveyed men agreed to take part in such research, less often they took a phone number ("to find out more about the research") and much less often they called. Most importantly, however, their reactions did not depend on whether they had just walked over a dangerous or completely safe bridge. The results of this experiment are shown in Table 3.4.

Although some researchers note that it was not necessarily the case that the men participating in the study interpreted their heart rate as a product of erotic excitement (see e.g. Kenrick & Cialdini, 1977; Aron, Dutton, Aron & Iverson, 1989), and the experiment itself provokes some methodological controversy (Szczucka, 2012), there is no doubt that the researchers demonstrated unusual ingenuity. It should also be noted that this experiment is undoubtedly a field study, even though the participants were asked to take part, which is infrequent in this particular paradigm. However, they were unaware of the substance of the study, and above all, they hadn't the foggiest idea as to what the extremely original manipulation of the independent variable (i.e. the level of physiological arousal felt) consisted of, nor were they aware that the question of whether or not they would call the person who had given them their phone number was also a (crucial!) part of the study.

7 When I'm in a good mood, sometimes I'll help you and sometimes I won't: the Isen and Simmonds experiment

Common knowledge tells us that a good mood makes us feel positive about life in general, kind, and friendly. We should also be more willing to help others. Alice Isen is an outstanding social psychologist who has spent many years exploring the issue of altruism.

Analyzing both her own research and that of others around the world, she noticed that this is not always the case. Moreover, some studies reported results indicating that a good mood in fact reduced people's inclination to help others. Isen and her colleagues (Isen, Shalker, Clark, & Karp, 1978) proposed a theoretical model that assumes that the relationship between wellbeing and behavior can be mediated by cognitive processing, involving a "loop" of positive cognitions. As regards altruistic behavior, this would mean that helping others (as any other behavior) can only result from the experience of a good mood if it is perceived by the subject as part of this positive cognitive loop, i.e. where the act of helping involves or is compatible with pleasant thoughts.

Taking up their empirical research, Isen and Stanley Simmonds assumed that if they put the participants in a good mood and then ask them for help, the good mood will only be conducive to such behavior if the act of helping itself is a pleasant activity. However, if this activity is not pleasant, being in a positive mood would not enhance one's readiness to engage in altruistic behavior. In fact, the opposite result could be expected – reduced readiness to help when experiencing a positive mood.

But how do you put people into a good mood? Isen and Simmonds (1978) took advantage of the fact that in the 1970s cell phones had yet to be invented. Since there were no cell phones, people outside the house had to use other devices. These were telephone booths, which can still be found in some parts of the world today. However, they look like an exhibit from a museum of telecommunication, because nobody in fact uses them any more (and young people probably wouldn't even know how to use them). So let us take this opportunity to explain to our younger readers that there was a telephone in such a booth, which you could use by inserting a coin in the appropriate slot. The phone also contained a special compartment, the coin return, into which the coin fell if no connection was made. Some phones also made change if the conversation was short. It was also sometimes the case (it is unclear why, probably due to a malfunction) that the phone returned the coin after the conversation. At that time, such phone booths were used by almost everyone, and almost everyone had a habit of checking the coin return of the telephone after the conversation.

The researchers assumed that if someone hung up the receiver and the telephone unexpectedly returned a dime, it would put the person making the call in a good mood (remember that a dime in the 1970s was much more valuable than it is now, and people generally like pleasant surprises). The researchers assumed that they would put just such a coin back into the return before someone looking to make a call entered the booth, thus remaining unaware she had become a participant in the study. After the conversation and the unexpected gift of ten cents was given and the caller exited the phone booth, an experimenter approached him, introducing himself and explaining that he was doing research on moods. He pointed with one hand to a booklet he was holding in his other hand and, depending on the experimental conditions, said either that the statements written in it are intended to put people in a good mood or to put them in a bad mood. However, empirical research is needed to verify whether this is the case and whether these statements were properly selected. The booklet actually contained statements – some positive, some negative – used by psychologists to induce specific affective states in people. The experimenter made the same request to the participants in control conditions. These were people who had put their fingers into the coin return of the telephone after their phone call, but found nothing there. The researchers adopted two indicators of altruism: the time the person examined spent reading the statements, and the number of statements read.

Analysis of the results showed that when the experimenter asked participants to read positive statements, those who had just found an unexpected dime in the coin return hole spent more time helping the experimenter and read more statements from the booklet than did people who simply made a phone call and left the booth. If, however, it was a matter of reading statements that were supposed to induce a bad mood, the results pattern was exactly the opposite. People who had been put into a positive mood spent less time helping the experimenter and read fewer statements than those in the control conditions.

We present this experiment here not only because it is ingenious, and not only because it demonstrates that you can influence people's mood within the field study paradigm, but it also shows that you can explore the relationship between mood and altruism. Another reason is the opportunity to show what measures can (and should) be taken to avoid the methodological pitfalls we have already talked about in this chapter when discussing the Rosenthal and Jacobson studies. Let us recall that we are referring to the Pygmalion effect (also known as self-fulfilling prophecy or confirmation bias).

What did the authors do to avoid these pitfalls? First of all, they made sure that the experimenter who asked the participants exiting the phone booth for help with their mood research did not know whether they had just taken a dime from the coin return hole or whether they had found nothing there. Indeed, prior to that, another researcher would enter the booth and either put a dime in the hole or just check if there was a coin there. The researchers also ensured that the time the participant spent helping the experimenter was measured correctly (it is easy to even unintentionally make an error with a stopwatch). The interaction time was therefore measured not by the experimenter, but by another person who observed the interaction from a distance and was unaware of whether the experimenter was asking the participant to read negative or positive statements.

8 May I use the xerox machine? Experiment by E. Langer and colleagues on mindlessness

Fewer and fewer people wear wristwatches, while more and more people use the clock in their cell phone. However, wristwatches are still popular enough that it is relatively easy to observe how people wearing watches check the time. They raise one hand while moving their other hand towards their sleeve and pull it up to reveal the dial of the watch. They now bring it a little closer to their face and read the time. If we were to approach someone just after that and ask them "Excuse me, what time is it?", we would expect a quick answer. After all, they just looked. But most likely this will not be the case. Instead, they will raise the hand on which they are wearing the watch, moving the sleeve with their other hand, bring the watch closer to their face and read the current time again. Why is this happening? Although people have given themselves the proud name of homo sapiens, there is much evidence to suggest that we do not always behave rationally. If we repeat an action many times throughout our lives in response to a stimulus, such behavior becomes a habit and can also take place when it is entirely inadequate to the situation. The watch owner previously referred to has been asked on very many occasions about the time, and to answer it, an appropriate sequence of hand movements must be performed without which it would be difficult to answer the question. However, watch wearers will probably also make these movements in a situation where doing so does not make sense.

Ellen Langer, Arthur Blank, and Benzion Chanowitz of The Graduate Center, City University of New York asked themselves "whether, in fact, behavior is actually accomplished much of the time without paying attention to the substantive details of the 'informative' environment" (Langer, Blank, & Chanowitz, 1978, p. 635). They took advantage of the fact that students from all over the world have one thing in common: when an examination session is approaching, they visit xerox machines to get copies of required course readings. (Nowadays, in the age of the Internet, this isn't nearly as common, but before you could just download the necessary files it was quite frequent). Students in possession of all of the assigned readings, that is, everything that is needed to prepare for the exam, already feel that things are under control: they can start studying whenever they like. (For some students, having "everything you need" even substitutes for actually studying for the exam, but this is a separate issue that we will set aside for now).

Langer, Blank, and Chanowitz (1978) decided to take advantage of this situation and approached the person at the front of the line to the photocopier. In one of the conditions they said: "Excuse me, I have five pages. May I use the xerox machine?" According to the researchers, this is not a typical message for someone to make a request. It lacks a reason for why the request is actually being made. If someone asks us for something, they usually explain why they're asking for it. A co-worker says: "Can you lend me $20, because I forgot my wallet?" A student says to another student, "Can you lend me your lecture notes because I've been absent recently?"

This typical form (i.e. including the reason why the request is made) was used in the message in the other conditions. This time, the person at the head of the line heard "Excuse me, I have five pages. May I use the xerox machine, because I'm in a rush?" There were still other conditions in the experimental scheme. The message was: "Excuse me, I have five pages. May I use the xerox machine, because I have to make the copies?" It was, in fact, a bit idiotic, because nobody at the copy machine would like to fry doughnuts or leave their suit to be cleaned. We note, however, that while the content of the message was silly, its structure was consistent with what we usually hear when someone asks us for something: it contained the request *per se* and its justification. The researchers call this situation "reason placebic info." It turned out that, as Langer and her colleagues expected, people relatively rarely allowed the person to jump the line and make copies when the request did not contain any justification, and more often when it did. Particularly curious is that the content of the justification was of practically no import! Indeed, 94% of participants let the person jump the line when the justification was sensible, and 93% when it made no sense at all! Apparently, the participants were functioning mindlessly: they did not analyze the content of the message, but rather reacted to its grammatical structure. If the request is accompanied by a justification, everything is "fine" and it should be carried out …

The experiment by Langer, Blank, and Chanowitz is very often presented in the psychological literature as if its design contained only the three conditions described above. However, the whole point of their concept is not that they claim people are mindless, but rather that, depending on the conditions, people act mindfully or mindlessly. In accordance with this assumption, the scheme of the experiment under consideration here was much more extensive. Langer, Blank, and Chanowitz claim that mindlessness and mindfulness are two qualitatively different states of the human mind. One of the most important factors leading us to mindfulness are the personal costs that we incur in the event of a wrong reaction. If someone asks us to jump the line because they have five pages to copy, the costs are minor. How much will we lose? Maybe 30 seconds, maybe a minute. And what if somebody says they have more than five pages to copy? By letting that person jump the line, we will lose much more time. So the personal cost of the wrong reaction

Table 3.5 Proportion of subjects who agreed to let the experimenter use the copying machine

Favor	*No info*	*Reason placebic info*	*Sufficient info*
Small	**.60**	**.93**	**.94**
N	15	15	16
Big	**.24**	**.24**	**.42**
N	25	25	24

Source: *Journal of Personality and Social Psychology, 36*, p. 637. Copyright: American Psychological Association

is high in this case. This should lead us to reflect. The researchers thus decided to see what would happen when the message of the person asking to go to the front of the line starts with "I have 20 pages to copy." Of course, this time, the participants acceded to this request less often; however, from the perspective of interest to us here, it again turned out that adding a reasonable explanation ("because I'm in a rush") increased the probability of the request being met (almost twofold!). However, this time adding an irrelevant explanation ("because I have to make the copies") was completely ineffective – the chances of fulfilling the request were the same as in the conditions without any explanation.

Clearly, when the person making the request needs to copy 20 pages, the participants function mindfully and analyze the content of the message presented to them!

From the perspective of the time that has passed since the publication of the results of this field study, the very small number of participants may come as a surprise (especially in the condition with the experimenter informing that he wanted to copy five pages). However, in the conditions in which the analyzed differences were statistically significant, this attests to the strength of the obtained results. Furthermore, the concept that mindfulness and mindlessness are two fundamental and qualitatively different states of mind has been boosted by a number of other empirical studies, some of which were carried out in the field study paradigm (see: Langer, 1989 for review).

9 Are you going to save energy? The studies of Schultz, Nolan, Cialdini, Goldstein, and Griskevicius

In many social campaigns concerning health, charity, and environmental issues, people are encouraged to start behaving in the correct or desirable way. This is often done by referring to social standards. So-called descriptive norms describe a standard – they invoke the way the majority of people behave. The idea seems intuitively obvious: if we declare, correctly, that the vast majority of public transport users pay for their ride, we will encourage (and perhaps embarrass) freeloaders to pay as well. People do not like being deviants. The problem, however, is that in many cases you can become a deviant by departing from a social norm constituting an average, typical behavior in two directions. If, for example, we tell students that the residents of their dormitory drink an average of 20 cans of beer per month, both one who drinks four cans per month and one who drinks 40 are deviants. Of course, the intention of such a message would be that those who drink 40 beers should reduce their alcohol consumption. However, those who drink just four beers (i.e. "too few") will also feel like deviants. The problem is that referring to descriptive norms in persuasive appeals may reduce the scale or intensity of undesirable behaviors, but at the same time it may increase the manifestation of undesirable behaviors in those people for whom such behaviors are rare or not very intense. How to deal with this problem? According to the focus theory of normative conduct (Cialdini, Kallgren, & Reno, 1991), in addition to descriptive norms, we can employ other types of norms – injunctive norms – in persuasive messages. While descriptive norms refer to what is typical and common, injunctive norms refer to what is culturally desirable and approved. Thus, in conditions where referencing in a descriptive message could exert an undesirable effect on some addressees (following our example: students who were previously drinking very little alcohol would increase their alcohol consumption), adding an injunctive message indicating that it is precisely their current behavior (occasional consumption of alcohol) that is appropriate and desirable should prevent the emergence of inappropriate behavior. Those who have been drinking little should not start drinking more.

There is no debate that humans have contributed the most to pollution and environmental degradation (Anderegg, Prall, Harold, & Schneider, 2010; Cook et al., 2016). One of the actions we can take to reduce the scale of this human destruction is to conserve electricity. Wesley Schultz, Jessica Nolan, Robert Cialdini, Noah Goldstein, and Vladas Griskevicius (2007) decided to examine how invoking descriptive and injunctive norms would affect levels of electricity consumption. The study was conducted on a sample of nearly 300 households in San Macros, California. Electricity meters were on the outside of those homes, and the researchers had access to them. This allowed them to determine the average level of electricity consumption in the surveyed neighborhoods, and then inform some of the participants that they consume less energy than average users, while informing others that they consume more energy. One more measure was applied to some of the participants. Apart from using a message referring to a descriptive norm (i.e. informing about average energy consumption), in half of the cases, a drawing was made on a sheet of paper given by the researcher to participants with information about energy consumption: the researcher drew a smiling face when consumption was lower than the average in the neighborhood, and a sad face when it was higher.

When, a week later, the researchers read the electricity meters, it turned out – as they had predicted – that the use of a descriptive message itself is a dual-edged sword: while those who used to consume a lot of energy began to consume less energy (by as much as 1.22 kWh per day), those who previously consumed little energy recorded an increase in consumption (by 0.89 kWh per day on average). But what if the descriptive message was accompanied by a face drawn by the researcher? Let us recall that in the case of people who were previously informed that they consume significantly more energy than the average user, a decrease in energy consumption was noted. However, it turns out that this effect was even stronger when the researcher drew a sad face on a piece of paper with information about the meter readings. In this case, energy consumption decreased by up to 1.72 kWh! And what if the respondents learned at the beginning that they consume less energy than the average resident of their neighborhood, but this message was accompanied by a smiling face drawn by the researcher? It turned out that this face has an almost magical power: the rise in energy consumption was minimal (and statistically insignificant) in such conditions. The results discussed here are presented in the upper part of Table 3.6.

And what's in the bottom part of the table? The researchers decided to check if the changes in energy consumption would retain their shape after a somewhat longer period of time. So they thus took a reading of the meters three weeks later. As we can see, the pattern of the results is almost identical to that in the upper part of the table.

Table 3.6 Changes in the daily energy consumption of households previously consuming more than average and less than average in particular experimental conditions

SHORT TERM			
Below Average		*Above Average*	
Descriptive Alone	Descriptive & Injunctive	Descriptive Alone	Descriptive & Injunctive
+ .89 kWh daily	+.24 kWh daily	−1.22 kWh daily	−1.72 kWh daily
LONG TERM			
Below Average		*Above Average*	
Descriptive Alone	Descriptive & Injunctive	Descriptive Alone	Descriptive & Injunctive
+.98 kWh daily	+.10 kWh daily	−1.04 kWh daily	−1.23 kWh daily

Source: Based on Schultz, Nolan, Cialdini, Goldstein, & Griskevicius (2007).

There is probably nothing better than research carried out in a natural environment and concerning a specific social problem to demonstrate the great strength that lies in a small smile sketched on a piece of paper delivering a message about electricity consumption.

10 Will you turn off the light when leaving the restroom? The research of Leoniak and Cwalina

Our short review of experiments conducted in the field study paradigm ends with a presentation of a study that was published at the end of the second decade of the 21st century. And, as befits modern times, technology, or to be more precise, a tiny device hidden between ceiling panels, played a large role in this experiment.

Krzysztof Leoniak and Wojciech Cwalina are Polish researchers who, like the American experimenters described earlier, were interested in how appeals referring to descriptive norms can influence pro-ecological behavior. Leoniak and Cwalina (2019) decided to take a closer look at behaviors conducive to saving electricity that are, on the one hand, trivially easy for people, but on the other hand, unfortunately, not at all common. Namely: switching off the light when leaving a room. The researchers were primarily interested in the issue of how people can handle a discrepancy between the content of a message addressed to them and the reality before their very eyes. For example, we could hear the message that most people don't smoke, yet while out taking a walk we would pass by people with cigarettes dangling from their mouths.

Leoniak and Cwalina state that when entering an empty public restroom, sometimes we don't have to turn on the light because the last person to leave didn't turn it off. If we see a sign hanging in the restroom asking us to turn off the light, suggesting that most people do, the content of this appeal will be entirely divergent from what we have just experienced. On the other hand, if we had to turn the light on when entering the restroom because it was dark, then such a message would be consistent with what we had just experienced.

The researchers decided to compare the frequency with which people leaving a public restroom turn off the light, creating several different conditions in their experiment. In some situations, they hung a sheet of paper with a drawing of a light bulb on the door of the restroom, with a beautiful green leaf in the middle and an inscription above it: "Turn off the light when leaving the restroom." In other conditions, this inscription was accompanied by an additional one: "The vast majority of people turn off the lights when leaving a restroom." (As we can see, the researchers used here a reference to a descriptive standard.) Other conditions assumed that the participants would read an inscription located alongside the request to turn off the lights: "It is commonly approved that the light should be turned off when leaving a restroom." (This time, we are faced with an injunctive norm.) The experimental design also includes control conditions. In this situation, there was no sign in the restroom encouraging people to turn off the light after leaving it. As we have mentioned, a device that allows for registering whether the light is on or off when someone enters the restroom and whether it is off when someone leaves it played a huge role in this experiment. A tiny device with a rather mysterious name, the HOBO Occupancy/Light Data Logger, model UX90-005, was hidden between ceiling panels in a place completely invisible to the participants. This allowed Leoniak and Cwalina to record not only how the participants behaved in four different experimental conditions, but also to observe the effect in individual situations of whether they were entering the restroom when the light was already on or had to turn it on themselves. The results of this study are presented in Figure 3.1.

As we can see, the results ultimately turned out to be quite complex and, in addition, distinct for both genders. Also, whether one entered a dark or already lit room generally had more influence on the behavior of men than on women's reactions. On the other

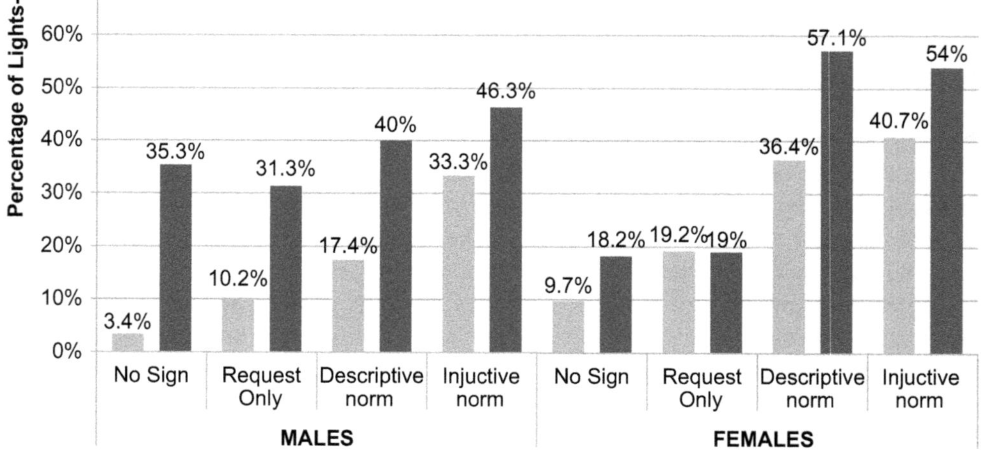

Figure 3.1 Percentage of males and females who turned off the lights after leaving restroom in each experimental condition, including the division into the light status upon entrance.

Source: *Journal of Environmental Psychology*, 64, p. 6

Copyright: Elsevier.

hand, in conditions where the participants entered a room with the lights on, women turned it off more often than men, ending their visit to the restroom.

According to the authors, these gender differences are explained by the greater sensitivity of women to ecological issues. In their opinion, this is why women are more likely than men to turn off the light in the conditions in which it is shining when they enter the restroom (i.e. when there is a contradiction between the situation they face and the content of the message encouraging them to turn off the light). However, the authors' interpretation struggles to explain why women are not more willing than men to behave pro-ecologically even in conditions where they have to turn on the light themselves when entering the restroom.

In our opinion, the results obtained by Leoniak and Cwalina lend themselves to an entirely different explanation. If we take a closer look at Figure 3.1, we will notice that women's decisions about turning off the light when leaving the restroom depend to a lesser degree than men's decisions on whether the participant was entering a lit or dark restroom. In other words, the information "the light was on/off when I entered the restroom" has less effect on women's decisions to turn off the light than on men's decisions. Why is this the case? Have you ever seen a long line of women waiting for the toilet (e.g. in a mall or gas station)? We have seen it many times! And a line of men? Much less often, and if so, it was shorter. Why? This is simply due to anatomical differences. Women need more time to relieve themselves! (Setting aside that they can also fix their makeup in the restroom, which they often do). What is the significance of this? The fact that the time that elapses from entering the restroom and the fact that the light is on/off until a decision is made to turn off the light (or not) is usually longer for a woman than for a man. According to the authors' assumptions – and it is difficult to disagree with them – information about whether or not they had to turn on the light when entering the restroom should at least potentially be taken into account by the participant when deciding whether to turn off the light when leaving it. If we assume that the availability of information that may affect the decision to take an action (in this case, the decision to turn off the light when leaving the restroom) decreases over time, the availability of information "how things were when I entered the restroom" is simply less for women than for men. To put it even more simply, a man leaving the restroom remembers better than a woman whether the light was on or off when he entered.

How to check if our interpretation is correct? There is no better option but to conduct another field study in which we measure the time spent by each of the participants in the restroom! And this is, in our opinion, the best example of how the field study paradigm is an irreplaceable method for solving some social psychology issues!

*

In this chapter we have presented ten different studies on different problems, testing different theories, using different ideas of independent variable operationalization and dependent variable measurements. These studies were conducted and published at different times. All of them, however, have one thing in common – the quality of "real-life credibility." When reading about the results obtained in these studies, one gets the feeling that they "hit the nail on the head." No wonder that students attending social psychology lectures are most eager to hear about such studies, and textbook authors are eager to write about them. They do so despite the fact that sometimes these experiments seem archaic, and from the perspective of today's methodological standards, sometimes flawed as well.

Summarizing this chapter on the history of field experiments in social psychology, it is worth noting one more aspect, relatively rarely raised as an argument in disputes about the importance of such research. It is worth remembering that such experiments have incredible potential for popularizing the discipline – they demonstrate to people from outside the academic world the importance of social psychology discoveries far better than even the best moderational analyses conducted on data collected from representative samples drawn from the population. As it often seems when doing science, we forget that in addition to communicating the results of our research to colleagues "in the business" we should from time to time present them to "ordinary people" who (this is also worth remembering) often finance our experiments by paying their taxes. Research conducted in a natural environment and recording the natural behavior of participants in experiments is irreplaceable in such situations.

4 Field study vs. other research methods

A comparison

In the book *Not by Chance Alone: My Life as a Social Psychologist* (2010), Elliott Aronson describes a conversation with Gordon Allport that took place in 1960 at Harvard. Allport, listening to Aronson's descriptions of experiments, asked him – with slight indulgence, as one may suppose – why he doesn't simply ask people how they would behave instead of conducting those "deceptive experiments." Aronson discovered, with some astonishment, that the eminent psychologist and specialist in the psychology of personality and social psychology was absolutely clueless about conducting research in the social world – and particularly about the limitations of research done through interviews or questionnaires. It would seem that 55 years after that conversation, many psychologists might repeat exactly those postulates Allport himself put forward.

But what does this state of affairs cost us? Can results obtained in, say, survey studies be of similar value to those obtained in a field experiment, or in an experiment (laboratory, natural, participatory observation) in general? Are there any situations in which the mere selection from a wide range of methods of data collection in social psychology determines (to a greater or lesser extent) the results we will obtain? We wrote a little about this issue in Chapter 1. Let's take a closer look at it now.

Research methods in social psychology usually comprise the content of one chapter, or at least a subchapter, in most social psychology textbooks. Kenrick, Neuberg, and Cialdini (2020) ask "How psychologists study social behavior?" They are echoed by Heinzen and Goodfriend (2017) with "How social psychologists answer the questions they ask." Most often, however, these titles are more literal and directly state that there will be a presentation of psychological research methods. Daniel Barret (2016) titles a chapter of his textbook "Doing research: An introduction to research methods," and Heinzen and Goodfriend (2017) use the simplest and shortest title of "Research methods." Of course, all these chapters of social psychology textbooks describe different ways of acquiring scientific knowledge in the field of social psychology. For the sake of clarity, let us try to summarize the pros and cons of each of them. Naturally, we make no claims of this study offering a full description – we will focus only on the most characteristic elements of each of the social psychology research methods (Table 4.1).

It should be recalled that the methods listed in the table in no way exhaust the possibilities and modes of collecting data in social psychology. This discipline is sometimes an extremely creative one – for example, studies at the intersection of social psychology, anthropology, and evolutionary psychology conducted by Boguslaw Pawlowski and Slawomir Koziel (Pawlowski & Koziel, 2002). They dealt with factors increasing the attractiveness of women in the eyes of men and men in the eyes of women, using an extremely interesting methodology – they analyzed the effectiveness of dating ads published in the

DOI: 10.4324/9781003092995-4

Table 4.1 Selected advantages and disadvantages of various research methods used in social psychology

Method	*Advantages*	*Disadvantages*
Surveys	• Fast, cheap and relatively easy to carry out • Broad possibilities for statistical analysis (especially seeking effect mediators) • High intersubjectivity (application of similar surveys around the world)	• Susceptible to self-presentation by participants, does not analyze behavior, at best imagined or remembered • Susceptible to artifacts in case of improperly selected sample (or interaction of features of the method itself and sample characteristics)
Individual interviews	• Potential for in-depth analysis of responses • A good source of data to make hypotheses for further studies	• Complicated, requiring qualitative (more complex and susceptible to the influence of the researcher) analysis of data • Practical impossibility to generalize obtained results • Susceptible to self-presentation by participants
Focus group interviews	• Possibility to pursue interesting threads during the course of the study, allowing for deviations from the scenario, if necessary	• Susceptible to group dynamics (people dominating the narrative and imposing their opinions on others) • High risk of self-presentation by participants
Observations	• Slight (or no) interference with the actual environment • Potential to observe real behavior (sometimes in natural environment)	• No possibility of introducing manipulated explanatory variables • Difficult (or impossible) to infer about causes and effects
Laboratory experiments	• Tight control of independent variables (primary, secondary, and disruptive)	• Only partial possibility to reproduce real situations
Field experiments	• High environmental relevance • Ability to analyze the causes and effects of the real behavior of research participants in the real environment • High mundane realism	• Incomplete (or significantly impeded) ability to control variables • Labor-intensive and cumbersome to carry out • Significant ethical issues

Source: Own elaboration.

press. They used 551 advertisements posted by men and 617 by women. Pawlowski and Koziel were primarily interested in the "success rate" of an ad defined by the number of responses (and thus the number of potential partners interested in contact) that the advert generated. The researchers examined which factors conditioned this success – they demonstrated, for example, that from women's perspective, key features of men were ones such as education, age, growth, and material resources offered (each of these factors was positively correlated with the number of responses to an advertisement – therefore, a well-educated, older, tall, and affluent man had the best chances). Interestingly, in the case of ads placed by women, the results were quite different – here factors such as weight, height, education, and age were negatively correlated with the chance of an answer being received. The study by Pawlowski and Koziel is additionally of interest to us because it shows the possibilities for undertaking analysis not only of living people, but also of their creations – in this case, personal ads. Of course, this is not a flawless method – in the case described, we cannot rule out (and perhaps we should even cautiously assume) that we are dealing with a pre-selected sample: after all, physically attractive, well-educated women can find partners very quickly and without posting personal ads. Women less attractive from the perspective of this "market," on the other hand, can still place ads which no one responds to (the same, of course, also applies to men).

However, it is worth considering to what extent the research method itself influences the results obtained – the question arises of whether the same (essentially) phenomenon examined via different methods will produce similar results. To obtain the answer to this question, a study was conducted to explore the recognized and widely described *bystander effect*. A series of experiments investigating actual behavior under laboratory conditions conducted by Darley and Latané (1968) revealed a significant relationship between the number of witnesses to an interaction and the chance of receiving help. They demonstrated that the greater the number of people see or hear that a person needs help, the less chance that the person in need actually gets it. Darley and Latané, as well as those following in their footsteps (Fischer et al. meta-analysis, 2011) have shown the durability and stability of this effect in many ingenious natural and field experiments. As the legend often repeated at social psychology lectures goes, their inspiration for carrying out this series of experiments was the tragic death of Kitty Genovese, a young girl murdered in Queens (a borough of New York City) on March 13, 1964, at 2:30 in the morning. This tragic event occupies a permanent place in the canon of psychological knowledge as an example of a total lack of reaction from outsiders to harm being done to another person. According to the official version, Genovese's murderer (Winston Moseley) beat her several times, tortured her, and finally killed her in front of more than 30 people who failed to react at all, in a way permitting the young girl to die. The case was widely reported in the national and international media, demonstrating, as the narrative adopted by journalists and supported by the police would have it, the enormous indifference that afflicted American society in the mid-1960s. The problem is that the facts, to put it mildly, are out of sync with such conclusions. Steven Levitt and Stephen Dubner (2009) carefully analyze the police records of the incident and show there is no justification for the claim of no reaction by witnesses to the murder – what is more, it was thanks to reactions by those witnesses that the perpetrator was caught a few days later. These authors prove that the Kitty Genovese case is a classic example of media manipulation by the New York police to divert public attention from scandals in their own ranks. However, regardless of the truth of the crime, in social psychology it has become the symbolic beginning of a whole series of studies first carried out by Latané and Darley, followed later by other scientists. These studies highlight an entirely counter-intuitive phenomenon – the more witnesses there are of a person in need, the less chance that someone will actually react. This phenomenon, called "diffusion of responsibility," has long been an important concept in social psychology, used to explain phenomena such as those related to altruism.

The question arises, however, of whether Latané and Darley would have recorded similar results if they had followed Gordon Allport's advice mentioned at the beginning of this chapter to simply ask people about their likely reaction to a situation indicating that someone is in need of help. We have examined this in two studies of our own.

The first one was conducted in an express train running between Wrocław and Poznan, two of the biggest cities in Poland. We should note here that this journey takes about three hours. Two students entered the train car at the railroad station and took their seats in the compartment in a manner that indicated they did not know each other (at roughly the same time, from two different sides of the car). The research assistant had previously selected a car that satisfied the experiment criteria. In the first version, there was one person in the compartment; in the second one (with the expected bystander effect) there were three. However, their behavior in the compartment (e.g. related to maintaining physical distance between the seated persons) must clearly suggest that they are strangers to each other.

After entering the compartment, the students took off their coats and sat down on seats opposite each other. After about five minutes, one of them turned to the other and said: "Excuse me, miss, I'm going to the bathroom for a moment, would you be so kind as to keep an eye on my coat?" The other responded: "Yes, of course." One minute after the first woman left for the bathroom, the second went up to her coat, took out her wallet and removed a PLN 50 bill (roughly $15) from her wallet. She hid the bank bill in her pocket and put the wallet back into the coat, and then returned to her seat. About two minutes later, the girl returning from the bathroom entered the compartment and resumed her place. If the other passengers failed to react, the women would leave the compartment as the train approached the next station.

The dependent variable in the study was defined as any reaction that led to a situation where the "robbed" woman learned of the theft. This could be prevention of the theft, loudly drawing attention after the victim returned, a threat to call the police, or (which also happened) a small note stating "this lady robbed you." In other words, any situation leading to the theft being revealed. The study was carried out over one day on the railway between the two cities. Twenty attempts were made, ten in each situation (one vs. three witnesses of the theft).

Out of ten situations in the first variant (one witness), nine responded and informed the robbery victim; out of ten situations in the second variant (three witnesses), the theft was reported in four situations (Figure 4.1). The obtained relationship was statistically significant, despite the small number of research situations created.

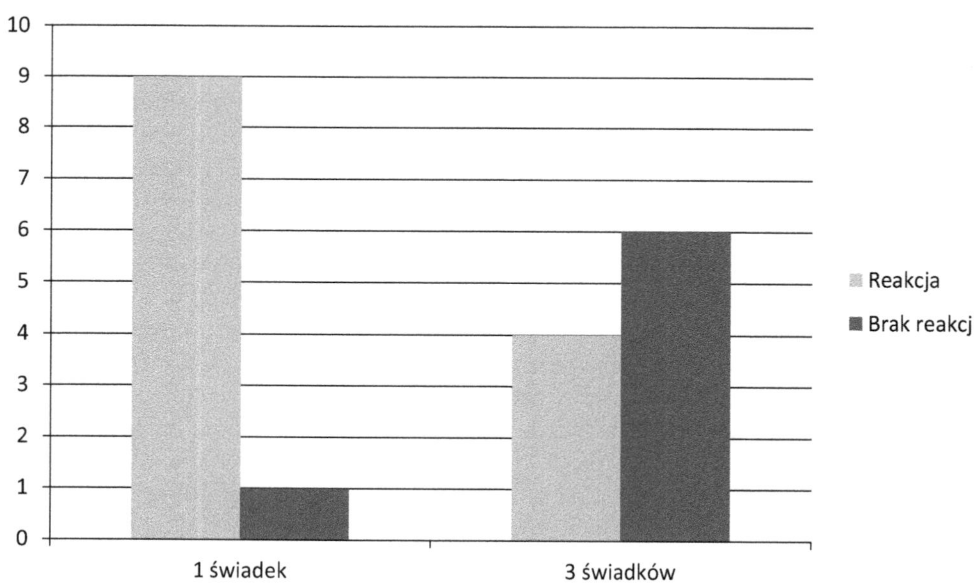

Figure 4.1 Number of people reacting to visible theft depending on number of witnesses to the interaction.

Source: authors' elaboration.

The obtained results confirmed the assumed hypotheses. Exactly as in the experiments by Darley and Latané, there was a correlation between the number of witnesses of the interaction and the desire to help a person in need. However, it should be recalled that the aim of this study was only to empirically confirm that a situation arranged in nature would generate results similar to those obtained by previous experimenters. In the next study, we decided to check what would happen if a survey study were done instead of the actual arrangement of the experimental situation.

A survey was prepared with the following description of a situation:

> Imagine the following situation – you're on a train, traveling in an eight-person compartment alone/together with two other people. At the next station a young woman joins you, and a moment later another one. After a few minutes, one of the women says to the other: "Excuse me, miss, I'm going to the bathroom for a moment, could you keep an eye on my things?" "Yes, of course," says the other woman. When the first one leaves, the second one waits for about a minute, walks up to the second woman's coat on the hanger, takes out her wallet from the pocket, removes a PLN 50 bill from it and hides it in her pocket. She puts the wallet back in the coat, smoothes it out so that it appears undisturbed, and then sits down. What do you do in this situation?

Each group received only one version of the questionnaire to be filled in (indicating how many people were in the compartment) – comparisons were made between the groups.

In order to increase the ecological accuracy of the experiment, the study was carried out on platforms at railroad stations, approaching people who were present there. The participants were randomly selected for the study and randomly assigned to a particular group (you are traveling alone or with two other people). Under the description of the situation there was a blank field in which they were to write down their most probable reaction. These descriptions were then transcribed into a spreadsheet and competent judges were asked to evaluate them in respect of helpfulness. Four competent judges (two women and two men) were asked to read the description of the situation (without information about the number of people in the compartment) and to assess the response on a scale from 1 to 5 (1 – complete lack of response, 5 – very helpful response to the problem).

The study involved 80 participants (40 in each group, half of which in each group were women). The average ratings for the helpfulness of the reaction in conditions of traveling alone and in conditions of traveling with two other witnesses of the interaction were very similar (3.78 and 4.01 respectively), and the difference between them was statistically insignificant. The number of responses rated "1" in particular groups was also checked (i.e., situations that the judges described as completely without response). There were six such people traveling alone, and five in the second group.

The results obtained in the second study show a completely different picture than the one shown in the previous field experiment. There were no differences between the groups, either in the witnesses' helpfulness assessed by the judges, or in the number of people completely unresponsive to the situation. We may also observe that the participants predicted that their own reactions would be quite clearly aimed at helping the robbery victim (average just below 4). Thus, the participants described their probable behavior as significantly more beneficial (e.g. from the perspective of their self-assessment) than that observed in the actual experimental study.

Another example of discrepancy between the regularities found in field experiments where real behavior is observed and in studies where people are only supposed to imagine that they are in such a situation may be the results of experiments on social influence techniques. One such technique assumes that in order to increase the chances of fulfilling a request, a person's arm or forearm should be gently touched while making the request. Chris Kleinke (1977) was the first to demonstrate this in his field experiments. Research in various countries around the world has shown that this rule operates regardless of the gender of the person making the request and the gender of the person to whom the request is addressed (e.g. Goldman, Kiyohara, & Pfannesteil, 2001; Gueguen & Jacob, 2006; Hornik, 1987; Hornik & Ellis, 1988). In an experiment carried out in Poland (Dolinski, 2010), this relationship turned out to be slightly more complex. In this study, a young person (depending on the experimental conditions: a woman or a man) approached a lonely passer-by (a woman or a man) near the railroad station and asked him to send a letter. The justification given was that the young person wanted the letter to have the stamp of the local post office on the envelope, and it was impossible to send it in person as they were in a rush to make the train. In half of the cases, the experimenter touched the arm or forearm of the person being addressed, while in the other cases he did not do so. The envelope contained a sheet of paper describing the experimental conditions (e.g., "the experimenter Eve asked a man to touch him"), and letters were sent to the same address in another city. This allowed us to see not only how many people took the letter from the experimenter, but also how many people sent the letter. It turned out that touch increases the chances of fulfilling the request (both when considering taking the letter from the experimenter and sending it) in only three out of the four situations. This was the case in both conditions in which the request was made by a woman, and also in the situation where a man made the request of a woman. However, if a man asked another man, touching the arm or forearm of the addressee reduced the chances of the request being fulfilled – see Figure 4.2a and 4.2b. (Additional research has shown that this is associated with strong male homophobia in Polish society.)

We described the idea behind this experiment to postgraduate students (but without presenting its results) and asked them to imagine that someone of the same sex as them (and in alternative conditions: of a different sex than them) asked them to send a letter. The participants were supposed to answer whether the fact that the person addressing them would touch them on the shoulder or the forearm while formulating this request would change the likelihood that they would take the letter from them. The participants were asked to choose one of three options: this fact will reduce the chances of it, increase the chances of it, or will not have any significance. It turned out that the vast majority of the women surveyed were convinced that regardless of the gender of the person formulating the request, they would react less favorably in conditions in which they were touched by a stranger. In the case of men, the situation was more complex. Most of them thought that a woman's touch would have no impact on their reaction, while the convictions of the others were evenly distributed – almost exactly the same number of participants believed that touch would help a woman to achieve the goal as thought that it would reduce the chances that they would decide to help her. In conditions in which men considered a situation in which another man approached them, the most common belief was that his touch would not make a difference, but a slightly smaller number of people said that the touch of another man would discourage them from fulfilling the request. Only two men (out of 84 participants) assumed that another man's touch would increase their chances of acting charitably.

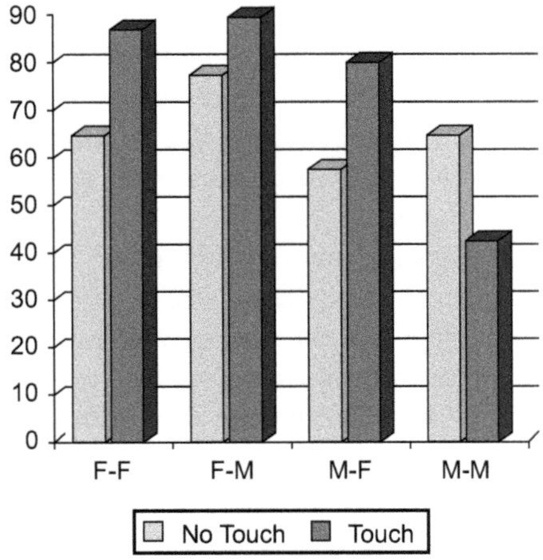

Figure 4.2a Percentages of compliance with the request to mail a letter in each of the experimental conditions. N = 40 in each condition; F–F: Female asking female; F–M: Female asking male; M–F Male asking female; M–M: Male asking male.

Source: *Journal of Nonverbal Behavior, 34*, p. 183. Copyright: Springer Science + Business Media.

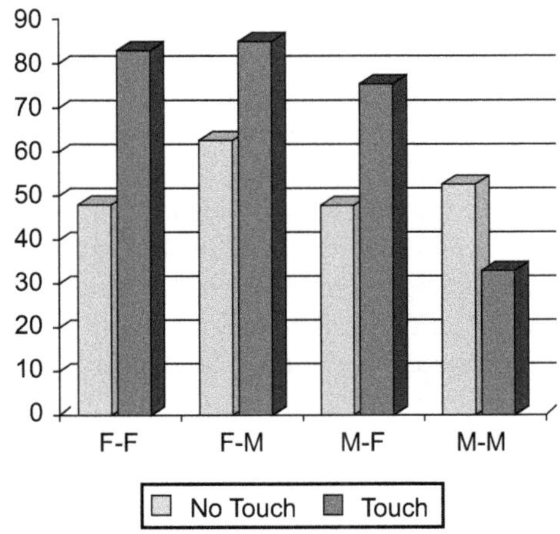

Figure 4.2b Percentages of participants who actually mailed the letter in each of the experimental conditions. N = 40 in each condition; F–F: Female asking female; F–M: Female asking male; M–F Male asking female; M–M: Male asking male.

Source: *Journal of Nonverbal Behavior, 34*, p. 184. Copyright: Springer Science + Business Media.

So we see that the relationship between a real situation and the accuracy of imagining one's own reaction turned out to be very complex. For women, touch, a factor which clearly increased the chances of meeting the request in the experiment in which we examined real behaviors, is an element that they believe would reduce the chances of doing so. Men, in turn, are more consistent in this matter. Although they underestimate the role that can be played by a woman's touch, in the conditions in which they are supposed to imagine that they are being touched by another man, their predictions are essentially accurate. There are clearly more participants who believe that touch would reduce the chances of a request being fulfilled in this case than those who believe that it would play a facilitating role.

Our research on the diffusion of responsibility and the role of touch is not, of course, the first ever to reveal the differences in results obtained through the analysis of actual behavior and from a questionnaire. Another experiment conducted under natural conditions, which, from a certain perspective, is a milestone in the understanding of obedience to authority while at the same time demonstrating the difference between survey and field research, was the so-called Hofling hospital experiment (Hofling, Brotzman, Dalrymple, Graves & Pierce, 1966). This study, for reasons not fully understood, is much less known and popular than, for example, the classic Philip Zimbardo experiment or Stanley Milgram's study, although it shows a high level of obedience in an area of particular social importance (health care) and in natural conditions (and with all due respect, it is impossible to say this about the experiments that Milgram conducted). What is more, Hofling and colleagues' hospital experiment has another extremely important advantage – it confronts the knowledge from a field experiment with data from survey research. As can be expected, these results are in fundamental contradiction with each other.

In the field portion of the experiment, a man introducing himself as a doctor called a nurse's office at night and told the person answering the phone to find a medicine called Astroten in the medicine cabinet. When the nurse found the drug (which had been placed there earlier by the researchers), Dr. Smith (as he introduced himself) asked her to give patient Jones 20 mg of the drug, adding that he was in a terrible hurry and would sign all the necessary papers later when he returned to the ward.

The nurse had several reasons not to follow the doctor's instructions. Firstly, Astroten (a completely fictitious drug, invented for the study and consisting of glucose) was not on the list of drugs approved for use in this hospital (and drugs not on the list were forbidden). Secondly, the drug label clearly indicated that the maximum daily dose of Astroten was 10 mg, while Dr. Smith expected a single dose of 20 mg. Thirdly, the administration of each drug in this hospital could only come after the doctor had signed an order – it was forbidden to administer a drug without an order, and it was completely unimaginable to give such an order over the phone. In addition, the person giving the order was completely unknown to the nurse.

Hofling and colleagues made 22 attempts (each, of course, with a different nurse). Out of the 22 people, 21 decided (let us emphasize, contrary to all the rules, not only regulations, but also common sense) to administer a completely unknown medicine in a dose double that of the daily dose after an order given by a complete stranger claiming to be a doctor.

For comparison, Hofling and colleagues created a detailed description of this experiment and handed it over to final-year nursing students for them to read. At the end of the reading, they were asked the question: "What would you do in such a situation?" All the future nurses who were asked about it replied that they would not give the medicine under the described conditions.

Hofling's research has been repeatedly discussed (and, of course, criticized) primarily from an ethical perspective (Krackow & Blass, 1995). Attempts have also been made to replicate it – one of the most interesting (albeit unsuccessful) attempts was made in the mid-1970s (Rank & Jacobson, 1977). The researchers asked nurses to administer a drug to patients in a manner similar to the original experiment, but introduced two important changes in relation to the paradigm applied by Hofling. First of all, the nurses could freely communicate with the doctor giving the order (no phone call was used, and the doctor was always available for a face-to-face conversation); secondly, the medicine they were supposed to give was a familiar one – it was the quite common and still popular Valium. As it turned out, the introduction of these two changes led to far-reaching differences in the results – in the experiment by Rank and Jacobson, only two of the 18 nurses agreed to carry out the order, while 16 refused. These results once again show how important it is to precisely control variables in field experiments, both independent and side variables, which can often have a decisive influence on the results (we will return to this issue later in the book).

The Hofling experiment had another very serious consequence worth mentioning. The results prompted the people and agencies responsible for the system of training and supervision of health care workers to introduce changes into the regulations and decision-making processes of nurses (Bucknall, 2000; Ley, 1981) in order to reduce, at least in principle, the chance of such improprieties occurring in the future. This is essentially another argument demonstrating the importance of field experiments and their results for social life.

A good example of research affirming the necessity of precise analysis of variables in the natural environment (although in a slightly different research context) is an experiment by Steven Levitt and John List, who applied a field variant of the economic games "Dictator" and "Ultimatum."

Perhaps none of the decision games in the history of psychology have been as successful as these two (save for perhaps the "prisoner dilemma" and tasks based on it). Since the publication of the first scientific article (concerning the game "Ultimatum") in 1982 (Güth, Schmittberger, & Schwarze), they have formed the basis of a dynamic branch of science called behavioral economics (Levitt & List, 2007). On the basis of the games and their results (we emphasize that each time they are obtained in laboratory conditions, and after participants are informed that they are participating in an experiment), a simple theory was formulated: people are generous and altruistic, and willing to share their resources with others (Henrich et al., 2004). How did this astonishing thesis come about? First we have to explain the mechanism of these games.

"Dictator" is a game created in 1986 by Daniel Kahneman, Jacek Knetsh, and Richard Thaler. The mathematical basis of this game can be formally described as follows: Player 1 receives an amount of X, which he divides between himself and player 2; that is, he gives player 2 the amount of y, where $0 \leq y \leq X$. Player 2 cannot reject this offer. Player 1's payout is $(X - y)$, and Player 2's payout is y." To make things a little simpler: The game is played in pairs, where one player has a certain amount of money (e.g. $20) to spend between himself and the other player. He can divide it as he sees fit, and the other player cannot influence this decision in any way – figuratively speaking, he takes what they give him. Kahneman and colleagues used this game to show how an approach accounting for purely economic benefits (in which case the participants should take all the money for themselves) is different from an approach accounting for social norms (participants should give some of the money to their partner in the game). In the classic study by the creators of the game "Dictator," it turned out that in 75% of cases the participants shared their money "equally," giving the partner exactly half of the sum. This prompted the researchers to claim that human nature is altruistic. Colin Camerer (2003) performed a meta-analysis of the results obtained by the researchers in different variants of "Dictator" and was able to identify several regularities – on average, player A gave 25% of the amount he possessed to player B; the range of the amount offered to player B varied between 10% and 52%; moreover, it was significantly influenced by the context of the study (and thus the "altruistic" nature of the subjects was susceptible to manipulation in the laboratory – e.g., leading phrases related to religion increased the participants' propensity to give money to the other person; Shariff & Norenzayan, 2007).

To sum up, it can be concluded that in the "Dictator" money distribution scheme, on average, the participants left $4–5 out of the $20 to be distributed to their "fellow players," although they were under no obligation to do so. It was sufficient, however, to slightly reconstruct the game and apply it in its natural environment, without informing the participants of the study that they were engaged in it, to make the results completely different (Levitt & List, 2007). Levitt and List described their doubts regarding the results from various economic games in a piece given the significant title of "What do laboratory experiments measuring social preferences reveal about the real world?" (2007). In one of the studies, they arranged, for example, a situation in which a player was informed that, apart from the option to take the entire $20 for himself, he could go even further and, if he wanted to, take a dollar from the other player.

People in this study proved to be not only reluctant to give money to their partner in the interaction, but when it was acceptable in the situation, they even took his money (i.e., instead of a 20 – 0 division, they opted for the distribution of 21 – (–1), taking the dollar belonging to the "co-player"). Only 35% gave anything to the other player (nearly half as much as in the original "Dictator"), 45% gave nothing to him, and 20% decided to take one dollar out of his pot. In other words, all that altruism we wrote about earlier disappeared as soon as the "scale" of the behavior was "shifted" – so it was acceptable to behave even worse (less socially acceptable) than to take the whole pot for yourself.

In other words, when the situation changed from an "economic experiment" to "normal life," the behavior of the participants was significantly modified. List obtained similar results when he constructed a field experiment based on the design of "Dictator." For this purpose, List used the hobby of collecting baseball cards. The researcher arranged the purchase of collector's cards with baseball stars at a market devoted to fans. In the first condition, he randomly selected card sellers and buyers and asked them to take part in an "economic experiment." He took customers to the back of the booth and asked them to declare how much they wanted to pay for one baseball card, choosing from five possible prices (from low $4 to high $50). After giving the price, the seller gave the customer a card which, in his opinion, corresponded to this value. Each of them (both buyer and seller) participated in five such trials, although every time they involved a different interaction partner. Let us note that this situation resembles a game of "Dictator" – there is a certain pool of money that can be divided among the players more or less equally (when the value of the card proposed by the seller corresponds to the sum declared by the customer) or unevenly (when the card is clearly undervalued, the seller benefits; when the card is more valuable than what the customer has offered, the customer benefits. Analysis of the decisions made by the sellers showed that in the condition of an "economic experiment," of which both the seller and the buyer were aware, the distribution of money was more or less fair – the buyers made relatively high offers (which showed some form of trust in the seller), while the sellers themselves provided the buyers with cards corresponding to the value of their declarations. Their behavior could again be explained by an inborn tendency towards altruism. List, however, did not limit himself to this version of the study, conducting a subsequent one in which the sellers were no longer informed that they were participating in a study, but were only provoked to play "Dictator" completely unaware that they were participating in such a game.

The experimenter approached a randomly selected booth and said: "Give me the best card you can with Frank Thomas for $20" (in the second version, he changed the value of the card to $65). Note that this is almost a perfect recreation of the "Dictator" scheme – we inform the other party that there is 20 (or even 65) dollars to be divided, while the other party makes the *de facto* division (i.e. decides whether or not to cheat us by giving a better or worse card). In a situation such arranged, it turned out that practically all the participants consistently abandoned the altruism demonstrated in laboratory studies and systematically cheated their customers by giving them cards of much lower value. This was the case both for 20 dollars and for 65 dollars. List noted an interesting regularity – the frauds were more frequent and for larger amounts when the sellers were passing through (i.e. they did not live in the city where the market was taking place). This seems quite understandable – both the risk of revenge from the customer and the risk of damage to the seller's reputation was greater when the seller was a frequent visitor to a particular market. The experiments by List and the analyses he undertook together with Levitt and Dubner show quite clearly that when it comes to examining people's inclination to engage in altruistic behaviors, relying only on laboratory experiments or (particularly!) declarations of behavior can generate knowledge quite divergent from factual behavior.

Another interesting example showing that merely asking people for their opinion or potential imagined behavior is not always the best solution for a researcher comes from studies involving the so-called "honesty box." This is a popular form of distribution of various goods in many countries (most often products from farms) consisting in selling them without the presence of the seller. The owner simply puts up a box with apples (carrots, beets, potatoes, etc.) at the side of the road and hangs up a price list detailing how much to pay for what goods. Passing drivers stop, take what they need, and leave the amount due in a can or basket. This model is beneficial for everyone – the farmer has time to take care of other things and does not have to wait for customers all day, and customers can buy products a bit cheaper. However, one particular thing is crucial – the farmer must trust the buyers to such a degree that he will risk leaving his produce (and the money left by previous customers) unattended. The ease of this procedure has made it a tool for diagnosing social honesty. Such diagnoses are sometimes made by scientists, and sometimes, due to the ease and suggestiveness of the procedure, by journalists. In Poland, for example, journalists from *Gazeta Wyborcza* conducted an honesty test among inhabitants of various Polish cities. They placed eggs on a table along with a piece of paper detailing how much they cost, and a can for collecting money. Although this was more of a happening than a real study, the journalists concluded that people are, in principle, honest.

We decided to verify the veracity of this statement in a more controlled manner. Additionally, we also wanted to see how the results would be influenced by the awareness of participants that they were engaged in an experiment. The study was held in two small towns, Lubliniec and Kluczbork. In both towns it was conducted twice – each time at the same time (between 9:00 am and noon). Lubliniec was the city where the participants were informed of their involvement in the experiment. A week before the initiation of the study procedure, a local weekly magazine published information about the planned field experiment entitled: "Studying the honesty of Lubliniec residents." The residents were informed that the experiment would take place in a central location downtown, and that it would be conducted by SWPS University researchers. In addition, in this version of the experiment, a piece of paper was placed on the sales stand to remind people that they were participating in an experiment to examine honesty. In the alternative version of the experiment, which was conducted in Kluczbork, the sales stand looked exactly the same, but passers-by were not informed that they were participating in an experiment nor what its purpose was. A self-service sales stand consisting of a table on which 90 eggs were laid out on paper trays was constructed for the study. On the table there were bags and egg containers, a money can and the information "Self-service, 30 cents per egg." In addition, the stand was marked with information about the origin of the eggs and their expiration date.

After three hours (during which the stalls were observed by the experimenter's assistants nearby), the number of eggs sold and the contents of the can were checked. The results are presented in Table 4.2.

The first conclusion that emerges during analysis of the results relates to the difference in the number of eggs sold under the conditions of information about the experiment and the absence of this information. Of course, the reason for this may be certain doubts that people encountering a new and atypical form of selling food can feel. Informing them that they

Table 4.2 Results of "trust box egg sales"

	Informed participants (Lubliniec)	*Unaware participants (Kluczbork)*
Number of eggs sold	142 (78.8%)	69 (38.3%)
Money collected	43.20 zł	19.71 zł
Average per egg	30.4 gr	28.5 gr

Source: Own elaboration.

are involved in an experiment is an indirect way of attesting to the quality of the eggs themselves (I am not dealing with an anonymous seller, whom I do not see and do not know, but with some research institution that at least indirectly guarantees the quality of the product).

The second interesting result is the average amount that was obtained for one egg in both variants of the study. Let us recall that the price per egg was specified as 30 cents, and this should be labeled as the reference value. Note that in the conditions in which the participants were informed of their involvement in the experiment, the sum collected in the can exceeded the amounts due – the average exceeded 30 cents. In the absence of this information, the average fell to 28.5 cents, which was still 95% of the amount due. Therefore, it can be concluded that in both conditions people proved themselves to be quite honest, and the fact that they were informed about being involved in research did not significantly affect the tendency to underpay.

But what would happen if we asked people to predict the results of such an experiment? We conducted such a study using the Ariadna web research panel. This panel is essentially the Polish equivalent of mTurk – it allows for creating practically any random sample from over 100,000 registered and verified users. It is also certified by recognized Polish and international organizations comprised of companies performing social research (including ESOMAR). The survey was conducted on a sample of 1453 people, representative for Poland. The participants read a description of the experiment and were asked the question: "What do you think, how would an experiment like this conclude if it were carried out where you live? Try to quantify it – the seller put out eggs worth PLN 100 (approx. $25). How much do you think was in the can at the end of the day (all the eggs were sold)?"

The obtained results are presented in Table 4.3.

Table 4.3 Average (from PLN 100 due) predicted by participants as result of the experiment involving "trust-box egg sales"

Average money collected (from PLN 100 due)		
Total		77.35
Sex	Women	72.92
	Men	82.22
Age	18–24	94.24
	25–34	82.57
	35–44	84.08
	45–54	70.50
	55 or older	67.45
Locality	Village	74.15
	Small city (up to 20,000 residents)	74.70
	Medium-size city (20,000 to 99,000 residents)	86.98
	Large city (100,000 to 500,000 residents)	74.73
	Very large city (over 500,000 residents)	78.30
Education	Primary	67.83
	Vocational	69.41
	Secondary	81.31
	Tertiary	74.69

Source: Own elaboration.

We can observe that the predictions of the participants did not match the actual results obtained. Moreover, research on what is referred to as "collective narcissism" would indicate that people tend to overestimate the morality of an own group (e.g., their own nation), believing that it is morally superior to other groups (Golec de Zavala et al., 2020). In the meantime, we are dealing with the opposite phenomenon, which is difficult to explain – underestimation of the integrity of one's own group. Also interesting is that the youngest group of participants does not follow this pattern. They have the best opinion of their compatriots and, significantly, it is the closest to the truth.

The examples of the studies described here (particularly those comprising part of a longer or shorter series involving various methods) are also an interesting exemplification of a certain model of conducting research proposed by Robert Cialdini (1980), who termed it "full cycle social psychology." He assumed that a study's starting point may be when we notice an interesting phenomenon in the real world – for example, the seemingly strange behavior of a street vendor asking us how we're doing. Natural observation of this phenomenon leads to the formation of a hypothesis concerning its character, which is then verified by means of research (usually a series of experiments, including field experiments). The results of these studies are presented in scientific and (later) popular science publications in the form of a more or less methodologically advanced theory. Then, as is most often the case with news from the psychology of social influence front, it features in workshops for salespeople. They, in turn, apply these methods in their day-to-day activities, often adding their own flourishes, like minor changes to phrasing. This change is again observed by researchers, and the cycle begins itself again (Mortensen & Cialdini, 2010). We can present this in the form of a diagram (Figure 4.3).

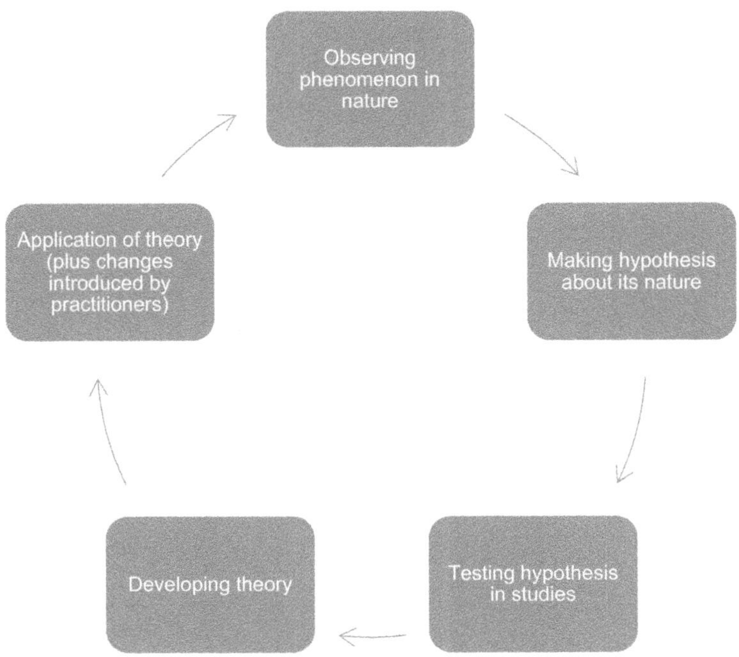

Figure 4.3 Full cycle social psychology.

Source: elaboration based on Cialdini (1980).

While this model, considering the present author's interests, best describes research in the field of social influence psychology, it is not restricted to this field alone – after all, many phenomena in social psychology have been studied in this way. In addition, the field experiment is perfectly suited to it as one of the methods for verification of hypotheses. Importantly, the "full cycle" proposed by Cialdini emphasizes the role of practical application of the results obtained in studies. They can at times be of great social significance (for example, studies on the influence of disinformation on the testimony of witnesses in court – Szpitalak & Polczyk, 2010).

The results of studies carried out using the range of methods described in this chapter also highlight the unique features of each of them – both the positive ones, which increase the accuracy of conclusions and the degree of certainty of the results achieved by the researchers, and the negative ones, which make it difficult to properly identify the causes and effects of various psychological phenomena. However, it should be very clearly emphasized that they must not be treated as a method without flaws – on the contrary, as we could see (and will be able to see as we continue our deliberations), there are many flaws present in the field experiment. By no means should it be considered superior to other methods applied in psychology. Therefore, it should not be – for sure – put in opposition to other methods used in psychology. The statement "only natural experiments with unaware participants make sense" is an unjustified oversimplification. The field experiment is rather an important part of a greater puzzle, which allows us only when complete to obtain a complete view of the situation and to draw the most accurate conclusions about the nature of social phenomena. Both the field experiment itself (without other research) and analyses performed using other methods (without field experiment) are simply incomplete, and in the vast majority of cases prevent us from obtaining clear answers to the questions posed in psychology.

5 Internal and external validity

Enemies or friends?

The essence of science is to find out the truth and explain why it is what it is. Social psychologists try, for example, to determine in what conditions people behave altruistically, and in which they behave aggressively, then explain why those conditions evoke such reactions. The means of achieving these goals is empiricism, while only research of an experimental nature is able to clearly show the cause and effect of certain human actions. If we observe, for example, that children who view a lot of aggression on TV are aggressive in real life (e.g. when playing with their peers), it does not mean that viewing aggression on TV is the cause of their real-life aggression. In fact, it may be the case that exactly the opposite is true – real-life aggression makes them more inclined to watch aggression on TV. It may also be the case that some third factor (e.g. their temperament, or the way they were raised, favors both watching the aggression and their aggressive behavior). Psychologists understood this long ago, and treating correlative relations as grounds for declarations of cause and effect relationships is regarded as one of the most serious methodological mistakes that a researcher can make.

As social psychologists, we are clearly in favor of experimentation as the primary and most important research method. As we already know, in psychology there are essentially two types of experiments – laboratory (we include online experiments in this category, or at least a significant number of them) and field experiments. Whatever form of experiment we are dealing with, it must satisfy certain criteria for us to be able to claim that its results advance scientific knowledge.

In an experiment, the researcher creates at least two different conditions and randomly assigns participants to each of them. If it occurs that the behavior of the participants in the groups is different, key questions about the reasons for this will arise. If we rule out the possibility that these are merely accidental differences (or at least we consider that the probability of this is very low), we will face the question of what factor led to these differences. To put it more precisely, the question is whether this is for sure the factor of interest to the researcher – the one that, according to the hypothesis or the research question posed, supposedly influences the distinct behaviors of the participants in particular experimental conditions. It is possible that a completely different factor, of which the researcher may not even have been aware, caused the aforementioned differentiation. The process associated with the preparation and implementation of an experiment aimed at eliminating alternative explanations for the results obtained (i.e. eliminating alternative factors that could have caused those differences) is linked with the researcher's attention to internal validity. With regard to the experimental research of interest to us here, internal validity can therefore be defined as the degree to which the experiment demonstrates the actual cause–effect relationship between the independent variable (manipulated by

DOI: 10.4324/9781003092995-5

the experimenter during the experiment) and the results, or the behaviors displayed by the participants (i.e. the dependent variable the researcher has measured). In other words, internal validity can be understood as the degree to which the results are attributable to the independent variable and not some other rival explanation.

Another important feature of an experiment is external validity. This concerns the extent to which conclusions from research results obtained in a particular experiment can be generalized to other populations and other situations. In social psychology, researchers usually ask the question "can the research be applied to the real world?" (This makes external validity conceptually close to what is known as ecological validity, although it should be noted that close does not mean completely the same.) It is worth noting that this understanding of different types of validity is logical in nature rather than statistical or mathematical (Campbell & Stanley, 1963; Cook & Campbell, 1979).

Since it is commonly assumed that it is easier to control various factors that can interfere with the course of research and avoid confounding variables in laboratory experiments than in field experiments, while in the latter it is much easier to obtain results that directly relate to the "real world" than in the former, readers of our book could arrive at the conclusion that, as a staunch supporter of the field study paradigm, we consider external validity more important than internal validity. Let us disabuse you of that notion by stating that not only is this not the case, but we consider internal validity to be of greater importance! Why?

Internal validity is absolutely crucial when assessing the value of any empirical study. If an experiment cannot claim high internal validity, then the empirical relationships noted by the researcher are caused (or at least are very likely caused) by something other than what the researcher had assumed. So if the experiment does not meet the internal validity assumptions, determining its external validity is a pointless exercise that would simply contradict the logic of science! We can say that if an experiment does not have high internal validity, it also does not, by definition, have what we might call the essence of external validity. (So, although it may be possible to replicate it accurately and get the same results, when the ratios of independent and dependent variables change, the results will be different.) Besides that, we don't always need our experiment to fulfil criteria for external validity. As Douglas Mook (1983) rightly pointed several decades ago, the famous wire mother and terry-cloth mother Harlow experiment involving rhesus monkeys, which all students of psychology learn about during their developmental psychology course, demonstrated something fundamental: the hunger reduction interpretation of mother love does not work. And it doesn't matter that the wild monkeys don't live in labs, but in the jungle instead, or whether the monkeys living in the jungle would also choose a terry-cloth mother. Mook also convincingly proves that many fundamental studies in psychology do not have any external validity, but they are fundamental to understanding human functioning.

If we consider that the task of social psychology is to explain real human behavior, we have to give consideration to the issue of external validity. Therefore, from this perspective, field experiments are more than justified. However, these experiments will only generate knowledge about "real life" if they have high internal validity.

Internal validity is linked to the rigorism of research planning (first and foremost, the development of a proper research design) and the rigorism of the research itself. Careful randomization and a research design that controls for various potential confounding variables is absolutely fundamental to the experimenter's technique. Let's examine the key factors that can affect internal validity at the stages of both planning and conducting research.

1 Effects related to the person conducting the study

In Chapter 3, we discussed the effect of the self-fulfilling prophecy. The experimenter's expectations about the pattern of the results can be translated into the way the experimenter functions in particular experimental conditions, and thus influences the results achieved in the study. This can be a process that the experimenter is entirely unaware of. Obviously, this lowers the internal validity of the study itself, and therefore it is assumed that the people conducting the study should not know the hypotheses being tested. However, at this point we would like to draw attention to another element related to experimenters themselves. They may exhibit a specific appearance, smile, clothing, or gesture. All these factors may cause participants to behave differently towards them than if someone else were conducting the study. To make matters worse, these are factors whose effects usually cannot be predicted a priori. This is why we recommend employing more than one experimenter to conduct studies, with the obvious assumption that each of them does the research in all experimental conditions. Then, in the first step of statistical analysis, we examine the main effect of the experimenter, and the interactive effects, in which one of the variables is the experimenter. Thus, we check whether, regardless of other experimental factors, the individual experimenters achieve the same results (e.g., whether they induce people to perform an act of charity or to cheat), and whether any potential differences between individual experimenters are the same in particular research conditions. While the occurrence of a main effect should not trouble us (after all, it's no wonder that there are people who, irrespective of the situation, e.g. arouse more trust or pity, and there are those who have more difficulty doing so), the occurrence of an interactive effect is a problem. The researcher should at least clearly describe the essence of this effect. In the event the experiment was carried out by two experimenters, it is advisable to replicate this study with new experimenters; in the event there were several or a greater number of experimenters, we would recommend removing the results obtained by a "particular" experimenter. (However, the article must describe the pattern of the results that this experimenter obtained and to justify the reasons for eliminating those results. It is also appropriate to describe what the results would be if this operation had not been carried out).

2 Historical events

It is obvious that certain historical events can influence participants' behavior. We are writing this book in 2020 – at a time when the coronavirus pandemic has taken over the world. It can be assumed that most people are more anxious, more self-centered, and probably more irritated and tired because of various restrictions and limitations than they were, for example, a year ago. So, would research conducted today be worthless because of the specific nature of the situation? Of course not – in fact, just the opposite! But the researcher should clearly describe the historical conditions in which the study was conducted, consider (and describe in the article) how this specificity might have affected the results, and it would be optimal if the study were replicated under "normal" conditions. We note that, from the scientific perspective, it would be both interesting and significant to obtain the same pattern of results, as it would to show the differences in the results of both studies.

We would like to emphasize here that the results obtained in a specific historical time (e.g. during a war, immediately after a war, or during a pandemic) are in no way "worse" than the results obtained at a time when nothing in particular is happening. They can be even more interesting and valuable! The researcher must be aware, however, that they can be "different." If she knows this, and includes the reservations described above in her article, nobody will be able to accuse the research of having low internal validity. However, if she either does not know this or does not inform the reader about it, the historical event has a negative impact on internal validity.

Another element related to the impact of this source of disruption to internal validity is interaction with experimental conditions – in other words, a situation where an event affects only one of the groups (for example, the control group), and in consequence affects the emergence of intergroup differences. Imagine, for example, a longitudinal study in which we want to examine how contact with the culture of a hitherto unknown ethnic group influences the level of stereotyping applied to it. In a study planned to run for six weeks, one of the groups participates weekly in workshops that give participants a chance to become familiar with the culture of an unknown ethnic group, to learn about its cuisine, rituals, traditions. During this time, the control group meets up at other workshops, completely unrelated to this ethnic group. Let us now assume that people assigned to the control group, while waiting for the bus after class, witness blatantly stereotypical behavior by a random passer-by towards a representative of the group whose culture the experimental group is learning about. Will this event affect the attitudes of the people in the control group? We may assume that it will – however, the crucial thing is that that this change will occur only in people from the control group, and what is more, the researcher conducting the experiment can be completely unaware. In this way, the interaction of historical events and membership in experimental groups can be a source of disruption to internal validity.

3 Contacts between participants of an experiment

An important factor that can be destructive for the internal validity of an experiment is contact between the participants (both those who are assigned to a defined experimental condition and those who have been and will be involved in different conditions). The fact that the participants are (or are not) familiar in advance with some elements of the experimental procedure, or whether they think about how they will react in a given situation, has a very negative impact on internal validity. It should be noted that the risk of this issue occurring is clearly higher in the case of laboratory experiments (where, e.g., participant students describe to each other their impressions from their visit to the psychological laboratory) than in field experiments, where the participants are usually not even aware that they have just participated in some experiment.

4 Maturation and testing

In certain types of experiments, especially those in which the same people are involved several times, we may be faced with other types of factors that impact internal validity. We are referring to factors known as "maturation" and "testing." In the first case, the point is that the researcher may not take into account that the participants have simply become less fit physically or intellectually because of age or fatigue (when some phase of the test takes place in the evening). In the second case, if people, for example, complete some test a second time, they can either do it more efficiently because they are learning (when it is, for example, a test of some skill), or they are motivated to give the same answer every time (perhaps because they think that someone is checking whether they are telling the truth). However, we will not devote extensive space to the issue in this book, because these are problems that arise relatively infrequently during field experiments.

5 Attrition

Relatively rarely is attention turned to the attrition factor within the context of the internal validity. Haotiaz Zhou and Ayelet Fishbach (2016) note that if the level of attrition is minimal (e.g. 1%), it will not significantly affect the pattern of results. However, the situation will change if there is a high rate of withdrawal of participants during the experiment Let's start with a situation in which this withdrawal is at different levels within the various experimental conditions. Imagine a field experiment in which we want to examine whether adding the phrase "but you are free to accept or refuse" to the request increases the willingness of those being asked to fulfill the request. Additionally, we are interested in the time of day when the request is formulated. Let's assume that in the afternoon almost all the people (say 98%) we approached listened to us until the end. In the control conditions, the request was fulfilled by 30% of the participants, while in the experimental conditions (with the message "but you are free to accept or refuse") by 55%. In the evening, however, people were usually reluctant to talk to the experimenter, and after hearing the words "I have a request to you …" they usually interrupted him, saying "I'm sorry, but I'm in a hurry" and left. Here, the attrition rate was as high as 75%, with those who did not interrupt their participation in the experiment equally often (at 70%) fulfilling the request regardless of whether it ended with the phrase "but you are free to accept or refuse" or not. Does this pattern of results indicate that the social influence technique consisting in increasing the chance of a request being fulfilled by emphasizing the freedom of choice that the respondent has (Gueguen & Pascual, 2000) does not work in the evening? The results seem to indicate this. However, it is very possible that the high attrition rate in the study conducted in the evening led to a group consisting almost exclusively of very kind people being examined. Such people fulfilled the request regardless of whether they were subjected to some kind of social influence technique or simply asked politely. By the same token, it would be incorrect to conclude people are generally more likely to fulfill requests in the evening than in the afternoon.

Serious issues with attrition may also arise in conditions where the level of discontinuation by participants of their involvement in the experiment is the same in all conditions. Imagine that we are studying the level of altruism in a large city, comparing the behavior of participants in the morning and late evening. The experimenter stands on the sidewalk holding a can for collecting donations and approaches every tenth person who looks like an adult. In both cases, about 30% of those approached did not allow the experimenter to complete the request for a donation and walked away. So it would seem that there is no cause for concern, because the attrition rate is the same in both conditions. However, it could be that in the morning those who refused were people in a hurry to work, while in the late evening they were afraid of encountering a bandit pretending to be a volunteer. As a result, in the first case we were dealing with people who were in no hurry, and in the second case with those who were not afraid. Let us now assume that we have noted differences between the behavior of respondents in both conditions. They were more likely to toss money in the can in the morning (or, if you prefer, in the evening). However, unfortunately, we have a confounding variable: whether we have studied differences in altruism resulting from different times of day (morning vs. evening), or whether we have studied differences resulting from specific emotional and motivational states (no hurry vs. no fear). The abandoning of studies is particularly frequent in the case of on-line studies (Zhou & Fishbach, 2016). We will return to this issue later on.

Although we have focused so far on methodological difficulties arising from attrition, it is also worth mentioning that the withdrawal of participants during an experiment can sometimes allow the researcher to draw important conclusions for the relationships being tested. We will tell a story about a situation where we had the opportunity to do this, but failed to take advantage of it. Many years ago (so long ago that the participants completed surveys using pen and paper rather than on a computer), we initiated a research program with the late Professor Andrzej Szmajke, dedicated to the role of confidence of self-esteem. The participants in one of our experiments were high school students, who, in the first phase, held at school, completed a questionnaire measuring the level and confidence of their self-esteem. The next stage was to be conducted a week later at a university building. We wanted to compare efficiency in the performance of various tasks by people characterized by the aforementioned parameters of self-esteem. We invited all the students who were engaged in the first phase, telling them that they would learn several interesting and important things about themselves. However, those who came to the university building were almost exclusively those who had reported high confidence in their self-esteem! We figured that, unfortunately, our experiment had failed, and we threw all the documentation into the trash. It only hit us a few weeks later: the fact that almost no one characterized by uncertain self-esteem came to learn something about themselves is itself an extremely interesting result! After all, this may indicate that such people avoid diagnostic information about themselves! Alas, it was too late …

This case, while involving a laboratory experiment, may be a good example of how people's withdrawal from the experiment while it was underway, not showing up, or not following the study procedure are not only factors that impact internal validity, but also a phenomenon that may supply the researcher with very useful information about the phenomenon they are investigating.

6 Researcher dishonesty

Another highly specific destructive factor for internal validity is scientific misconduct (i.e. the fabrication of data or the omission of those cases that "do not fit" into the researcher's hypothesis). Here, by definition, the independent variable does not in fact cause the changes to the dependent variable our dishonest researcher claims that it does. The only place where such an empirical dependency appears is in an empirical article published by the researcher. (We will return to the issue of scientific misconduct as an extremely important issue in this book in a slightly different context.)

7 Confounding variables

Our brief review of factors that can negatively affect internal validity concludes with a crucial issue that plagues experimenters. Manipulation of some factor in experimental research, unfortunately, usually involves the unintended manipulation of another factor. For example, we want to check whether lowering the participant's self-esteem will impact aggressiveness, and the result we obtain in the experiment confirms this dependence. However, before we can announce our success, we need to ask ourselves a few questions. Can a worsening of one's self-esteem lead to their mood deteriorating? Surely it can. Can it evoke anger? Most likely, yes. Frustration? Clearly, and especially if the participant expected to hear from the experimenter how wonderful she is. And if this is the case, then what evoked aggression in our experiment? Bad mood, anger, frustration, or lowered self-esteem? Experimental psychologists are well aware of the complexity of what they are investigating, and they very carefully try to control the influence of the various factors on the dependent variable. In particular experiments they measure various mental states or prevent their appearance in certain experimental conditions (or, on the contrary, create conditions conducive to their appearance). Of course, in creating such a list of potential confounding variables, psychological knowledge about both the co-occurrence of different variables and the cause–effect relationships between those variables helps them enormously.

However, it is sometimes the case that the researcher takes the utmost care in planning the experiment so as to eliminate all confounding variables, while chance leads someone else to discover such a variable much later. We have long been involved in studying social influence techniques. Many years ago, Daniel Howard (1990) wrote an article in which he described a study on foot-in-the-mouth techniques. We freely admit that we found the technique described by Howard fascinating, as well as research testing its effectiveness. The researcher assumed that if we want to persuade people to join a charity campaign to benefit others, we should first ask them how they are feeling. If they declare a very good (or at least positive) mood, which is the norm in the USA, and then hear a request to join a campaign for the homeless or people in need of food, they will easily grasp the huge contrast between their own, rather comfortable situation, and the awful position those unfortunates are in. Consequently, they will be more motivated to help them. Howard carried out an ingenious field study aimed at testing these assumptions. In the control conditions, he simply introduced himself and said he was organizing an action to help the hungry. If his interlocutor agrees to be involved, a charity worker with a pack of cookies will approach him in a few minutes. The income from their sale will be used to organize a dinner for hungry residents of Dallas on Thanksgiving Day. In the experimental conditions, the investigator also introduced himself at the beginning, but before offering to sell cookies, he asked the participant:

"How are you feeling this evening?"

If the response was positive, the experimenter's response was "I'm happy to hear that," while if the participant complained (which happened quite infrequently), the response was "I'm sorry to hear that." Immediately afterwards, of course, there was a request to buy some cookies, and thus to contribute to a fund to help provide a meal to people in need.

The results were entirely consistent with Howard's assumptions. The participants asked about their well-being agreed to buy the cookies more often than those in the control group. Moreover, this rule did not apply to those (very few) respondents from the experimental group who declared a negative mood (after all, they could not perceive the strong contrast between their own situation and that of the people who were starving).

Dear reader, do you see any confounding variable in the scheme of this experiment? … We didn't either. However, we were interested in whether the question of well-being would be as important in Poland. Poland, unlike the USA, is a country where the cultural standard is one of complaining (about the government, president, traffic jams, prices, salary, boss, subordinates, etc., etc.) This includes complaining about one's mood. Many years ago, W. B. Johnson (1937) did a study in the US in which his students filled out a very simple 11-point scale every day for 65 consecutive days to determine their mood compared to their typical, normal mood. If their mood on a given day was "like usual," they were asked to mark [0], which was in the middle of the scale; if their mood was slightly worse than usual, they were to mark [–1]; if it was slightly better than usual they marked [+1]. The number [–5], which was on the left-hand side, meant a mood so bad that the participant had never experienced anything like it before, while the number [+5] was the best it ever was. Of course, we usually feel about the same. Sometimes a little bit worse, but just as often a little bit better … So, after 65 days the typical participant should have an average close to 0. Of course, there will be those who enjoyed a particularly great time in life (those with an average above 0), and there will be those going through a worse time (those with an average below 0). However, the average of the averages for all participants should be very close to 0. But in fact the average was over 1! This means that Americans (or, in any case, the Americans asked in the period before World War II by Johnson) are usually in a better mood than usual. When we replicated the Johnson study in Poland, immersed in a culture of complaining, and extending it to 100 days, we achieved exactly the opposite effect. It turned out that Poles (or, in any case, the Poles we studied in the last decade of the 20th century) usually feel worse than usual (Dolinski, 1996).

So, if, following Howard's procedure, we ask people in Poland "how do you feel?," the typical answer will not be "good!" or "I'm OK," but rather: "could be better," "I'll manage," "don't bother asking." In such a situation, it is difficult to expect such people to easily perceive the contrast between their own feeling and the situation of those who are supposed to be recipients of charity. However, it turned out that asking people in Poland about their well-being also encourages them to engage in offering such help, despite complaining about their own feelings (Dolinski, Nawrat, & Rudak, 2001). Thus, it turned out that although the social influence recommended by Howard is an effective one, his proposed interpretation of that effectiveness does not comport with the results we obtained. This, of course, prompted us to take a careful look at the study procedure itself. Our attention was drawn to the fact that, in the control conditions, the researcher initiates a monologue (he first introduces himself, then talks about the purpose of the collection drive, and finally asks them to buy the cookies) and under experimental conditions the researcher, after introducing himself, asks the participant a question, listens to the answer, then comments on it and only then discusses the purpose of the campaign and asks the participant to take part in it. In other words, in those conditions, there is no monologue on the part of the experimenter, but rather a dialogue between the experimenter and the participant. What difference might this make? We assumed that while monologue is typical for contacts between people who do not know each other, dialogue is a normal form of communication between people who do. If we then add the quite obvious assumption that we are much more likely to fulfil minor requests from friends than from strangers, it can be assumed that in conditions where someone has entangled us in a dialogue, we initiate established schemes for responding to people familiar to us and, as a consequence, we fulfil the request made of us. Looking at it from this perspective, we decided that in Howard's experiment, the crucial element might not be that the participants were asked about their mood, but rather that they were involved in a dialogue about a light topic. In other words, the mode of communication (monologue in control conditions vs. dialogue in experimental conditions) was the confounding variable here. In a series of field experiments, we demonstrated that actually engaging another person in a dialogue (not necessarily about how they feel, but e.g. where they study, or which gender has greater sensitivity to smell) makes them more susceptible to social influence (e.g., Dolinski, Nawrat, & Rudak, 2001; Dolinski, Grzyb, Olejnik, Prusakowski, &

Urban, 2005; Grzyb, Dolinski, & Kulesza, 2021). Engagement in dialogue may also be a factor improving the effectiveness of various social influence techniques. In one study, we collected donations for Afghan refugees (Dolinski, Grzyb, Olejnik, Prusakowski, & Urban, 2005). When presenting a donation box to participants, in half of the cases we said "Even a penny will help," invoking a technique first described and studied by Cialdini and Schroeder (1976). The researchers assumed that people who refuse to donate to a charity justify this to themselves by saying that they are not rich enough to help all those in need. However, such a message makes it difficult for them to explain their refusal in this way (after all, giving anything is enough, and one needn't be rich to do that), so people are more inclined to pull out their wallets in such a situation. Irrespective of that, in our experiment we tested the technique of entanglement in dialogue. Before asking people for a donation, we had a short conversation about refugees (dialogue related to the fundraising topic) or about impact of weather on human mood (dialogue not related to the fundraising topic) with some of them. The results of this experiment (percentage of people who made a donation and average value of donations) are shown in Table 5.1.

Let's move on to the problem of external validity, which we consider to be particularly important when studying people's social behavior. It is commonly believed that high external validity is in a way inscribed in the very essence of field experiments. Mook (1983) rightly emphasizes, however, that an experiment conducted in "real life" is being carried out in concrete conditions. It cannot be assumed a priori that it will generate the same results in other real-life conditions. There will always be potential cultural, historical, or age-related limitations exhibited by participants. It is important to remember that external validity is not a term implying that the results of an experiment should be generalized to other situations and other populations. "External validity is not an automatic desideratum: it asks a question. It invites us to think about the prior questions: To what populations, settings, and so on, do we want the effect to be generalized?" (Mook, 1983, p. 379). Therefore, we cannot make a priori judgments about the possibility of generalizing results, we can only put forward hypotheses and empirically test to what extent they can be generalized.

However, it is undoubtedly the case that if field studies are carried out in accordance with all the requirements of the methodology, their external validity is related to "real life" – the results can be considered accurate for the place and population in question, and then possibly test whether an analogous pattern can be obtained in other places, with the

Table 5.1 Percentage of persons complying with experimenter's request and mean donations in each experimental condition

	Mood				*Issue*			
	Monologue Mode		*Dialogue Mode*		*Monologue Mode*		*Dialogue Mode*	
	% compliance	*M donation*	*% compliance*	*M donation*	*% compliance*	*M donation*	*% compliance*	*M donation*
Even a penny will help	16.7	.54	53.3	1.03	33.3	41.1	63.3	.83
Standard request	16.7	.38	36.7	.50	23.3	.21	50.0	.64

In all experimental conditions $N = 30$. 1 Polish zloty = approximately US $ .25

Source: *Journal of Applied Social Psychology*, *35*, p. 1156. Copyright: V.H. Winston & Son, Inc.

participation of other populations and, very importantly, other ways of manipulating independent variables and other indicators of the dependent variable. The role of the location where we carry out field research is described in this book in more detail in Chapter 10.

Here, however, we would like to look more closely at the issue of indicators of the dependent variable. Imagine that we are interested in the subject of altruism. We want to establish if the tendency to help strangers varies from country to country. Of course, we do not believe in verbal declarations and decide to do a field experiment. This is the situation Levine, Norenzayan, and Philbick (2001) found themselves in. They conducted an intercultural study in 23 cities, the largest metropolitan areas of each respective country. In each of these cities they studied how often people at a crosswalk would lead a blind man standing at the edge of the road to the other side; how often they would help a man who passes them in a hurry, puts his hand in his coat pocket and drops a pen that he accidentally pulls out; and how often they would help a person who has his leg in a cast but has inadvertently dropped a pile of papers on the sidewalk that he is trying to collect. In all these cases, we are undoubtedly dealing with altruism – providing help to another person. However, as we see in Table 5.2, in Prague, for example, all the participants led

Table 5.2 Cross-cultural differences in help-giving

City, Country	*Overall Helping Index*			*Blind Person*		*Dropped Pen*		*Hurt Leg*	
	Rank	*Z Scores*	*%*	*Rank*	*%*	*Rank*	*%*	*Rank*	*%*
Rio de Janeiro, Brazil	1	1.66174	93.33	1	100	1	100	4	80
San Jose, Costa Rica	2	1.52191	91.33	1	100	7	79	1	95
Lilongwe, Malawi	3	1.14903	86	1	100	2	93	13	65
Calcutta, India	4	.91598	82.67	6	92	16	63	2	93
Vienna, Austria	5	.79946	81	12	75	6	88	4	80
Madrid, Spain	6	.68293	79.33	1	100	9	75	14	63
Copenhagen, Denmark	7	.56641	77.67	15	67	4	89	8	77
Shanghai, China	8	.49650	76.67	17	63	9	75	3	92
Mexico City, Mexico	9	.42658	75.67	6	92	17	55	4	80
San Salvador, El Salvador	10	.35667	74.67	6	92	4	89	20	43
Prague, Czech Republic	11	.37997	75	1	100	17	55	9	70
Stockholm, Sweden	12	.17023	72	18	58	3	92	11	66
Budapest, Hungary	13	.10031	71	15	67	8	76	9	70
Bucharest, Romania	14	−.06282	68.67	6	92	14	66	19	48
Tel Aviv, Israel	15	−.10943	68	10	83	13	67	16	54
Rome, Italy	16	−.43570	63.33	12	75	21	35	4	80
Bangkok, Thailand	17	−.59883	61	23	42	9	75	11	66
Taipei, Taiwan	18	−.73866	59	21	50	15	65	15	62
Sofia, Bulgaria	19	−.87849	57	11	80	12	69	23	22
Amsterdam, Netherlands	20	−1.11154	53.67	18	58	19	54	17	49
Singapore, Singapore	21	−1.50772	48	21	50	20	45	17	49
New York, United States	22	−1.74077	44.67	12	75	22	31	22	28
Kuala Lumpur, Malaysia	23	−2.04374	40.33	20	54	23	26	21	41

Source: *Journal of Cross-Cultural Psychology*, 32, p. 551. Copyright: SAGE.

Note: Overall Helping Index is the average of the *z* scores for each of the three situations. For the other measures, scores represent the percentage of help received in each country (1 = *most helpful*).

the blind person across the street, while only 55% of people seeing the man drop his pen bothered to point out to him that he had just lost it. In Stockholm, on the other hand, only 58% of people helped the blind man, but as much as 92% informed the person who had dropped his pen. We note that if we were to take helping the blind as an indicator of altruism, we would consider the inhabitants of Prague to be clearly more altruistic than the inhabitants of Stockholm, but if the indicator were helping an unlucky person who had lost his pen, the results would be exactly the opposite!

The researchers avoided such problems by using an aggregated indicator of altruism, which took into account the reactions of people in each of the three situations described above. We note, however, in the context of external validity, that if these were three completely different situations (e.g. helping a stranger who had fainted in the subway, helping a driver who had punctured a tire in his car and was changing the wheel herself, and helping a person who had no change pay for a parking meter), the results could be radically different. Thus, it is not only important which variable we study (in this case altruism), but which indicators of this variable we account for in the experiment.

At the end, let us return to the title of this subsection. We believe that a researcher should never face the false dichotomy of focusing on either internal or external validity. Of course, achieving high internal validity is crucial, but the pursuit of high external validity of the experiment does not have to be an obstacle to achieving it. A good field study is one in which internal and external validity are friends rather than enemies.

6 Ethical aspects of field studies

What the code says and what common sense dictates

The word "ethics" comes from Greek and means simply "custom" (ἦθος – ethos). Therefore, as we seek appropriate descriptions of the ethical principles that we should follow during experimental research, we can refer to certain customs, norms that have been adopted in psychology for conducting such research. The problem, however, is that these norms have evolved together with the development of psychology as a scientific discipline and changes in the way we think about research participants as objects (historically earlier) and subjects (historically later) of experimental research. Research was conducted differently in the 1930s, differently in the 1950s, and differently now, in the second decade of the 21st century. We should naturally assume that changing environmental conditions (e.g. the ubiquitous monitoring of people's behavior, the migration of a significant portion of life to the Internet) will also change the customs and norms applicable to conducting experimental research. One thing, however, should remain the same – the focus of the researcher's interest should be to maximize the benefits for science and minimize the potential damage to the research participant. Ron Iphofen points out in *Ethical Decision Making in Social Research* (2011) that, in fact, the consequences of our actions as researchers are very often difficult to predict – because we are unable to predict whether, for example, a manipulation that seems perfectly innocent, or even a question will not evoke a violent emotional reaction on the part of the participant. A good illustration of this phenomenon is the Philip Zimbardo prison experiment, which, despite careful selection of the participants (rejecting those who exhibited any tendency toward behavioral disorders), did not predict how far the participants would actually be able to go in making life miserable for others (Haney, Banks, & Zimbardo, 1973). Should abandoning experimental research (or perhaps research with people in general) be a natural consequence of such a case? Certainly not. However, from the moment we begin thinking about a study, we should put ethics (understood as respect and concern for the welfare of the participants) first.

Sometimes, however, this may mean that we do not prioritize the issue of the potential harm that conducting a study may bring to its participants above all else. We rather ask: "Does the study make sense? Has it been sensibly designed? Will its execution generate answers to important questions? Are there any methodological errors in it that make it impossible to clearly verify the assumed research hypotheses?" and so on. In other words, we first ensure the methodological correctness of the study design itself. Does this mean that the welfare of the participants is of less importance to us? Absolutely not – quite the contrary. This can be put differently: the most unethical study is the one that is poor from a methodological perspective – because it is a waste of the participants' time and energy.

DOI: 10.4324/9781003092995-6

First and foremost, their engagement should be respected, and their energy should not go to waste. And this is what happens when we conduct a study full of mistakes – we waste the time and the effort of the participants of the study without any sense, for nothing. Nevertheless, this naturally does not mean that by virtue of being methodologically correct, a study is automatically ethically correct as well. In a very similar spirit, Robert Rosenthal, one of the most eminent methodologists in psychology, wrote the text "Science and ethics in conducting, analyzing, and reporting psychological research" (1994). One section of this article was entitled "Bad science makes for bad ethics." Not because some specific harm is done to participants, but because their time, energy, and commitment are simply being wasted. Jerzy Brzezinski (2016, 2017) also writes quite interestingly about such fundamental issues in experimental research ethics.

We note that framing the matter in this way assumes giving consideration to ethics at a very early stage of research design. This means that the starting point in the planning of an experiment is a certain assumption about the people who will participate in it. This assumption says that they are partners in the acquisition of scientific knowledge, and as partners they should be treated with due respect. We cannot "use" them – we should cooperate with them. It should be recalled that this has not always been the case in psychology. This can be seen by following the evolution of the term used in scientific texts. At the beginning, they were simply "objects," while later evolving into "subjects." In contemporary literature, the dominant term is "participants" (to further emphasize their subjectivity, the term used is "human participants"). This, contrary to appearances, is not just a lexical game of little meaning. Giving a proper and dignified name to those people on whom the potential success of our research directly depends is an important starting point. In a way, it defines our further thinking about the people who will take part in the experiment we are preparing.

If we are seeking milestones on the way to achieving an understanding of ethical principles in research involving human participation, one of the most important (if not the most important) would certainly be the *Belmont Report* – a report issued by the US National Commission for the Protection of Human Subjects of Biomedical and Behavioral Research. But before we examine this report, we should consider its origins. It was inspired by the Tuskegee experiment (Lederer & Davis, 1995; Sims, 2010).

Tuskegee is a small town in Alabama, known to lovers of 1980s music mainly for the fact that Lionel Richie was born there. However, for scientists dealing with ethics in human research, it has far more negative connotations – it is a place where one of the most shameful clinical experiments in history (or, to be more precise, a series of such experiments) was conducted between 1932 and 1972, significantly referred to as the *Tuskegee Study of Untreated Syphilis in the Negro Male*. The studies' authors posed questions about the nature of what was in the 1930s one of the most dangerous venereal diseases – syphilis. There would be nothing unusual in any of this if it was not for the fact that, despite the existence of more or less effective cures for this disease (e.g. salvarsanum), doctors (in cooperation with the Public Health Service, PHS) did not actually treat patients, but only observed the course of syphilis to its very end, i.e. the death of those infected with *Treponema pallidum*. Around 600 poor Black farmers from the Tuskegee area participated, and subsequent experiments were done mainly to convince them that they were receiving specialist treatment (an additional motivator for these extremely poor people was the fact that they received free meals and the promise of a payment of $50 to their families in the event of their death during the study). The doctors were mainly interested in observing the course of untreated syphilis, thus, despite the availability of effective medications (such as penicillin, available since 1947), they spent 40 years analyzing how the disease developed and spread throughout a population of poor Black farmers in the Tuskegee area. Let us emphasize that the researchers did not inform participants about the dangers of having sex with infected people; in fact, they did not even inform them about the nature of their illness (they were told that the doctors were treating their "bad blood"), did not provide them with any treatment, but only observed the course of the disease and its spread. As a later investigation showed, the deaths of more than a hundred people resulted from a disease that could have been cured, and of whose true nature the patients were ignorant. Things came to a head when the Associated Press published the details of the experiment in July 1972. The program was immediately halted, and an investigation was followed by a subsequent trial; $10 million in damages were awarded, and a special Tuskegee Health Benefit Program (THBP) was created to benefit the living participants of the study as well as the wives and children of farmers who died during the experiments. A side effect of this study was to task the aforementioned National Commission for the Protection of Human Subjects of Biomedical and Behavioral Research with the development of a canon of ethical principles to be followed by researchers conducting experiments involving human participants.

The *Belmont Report*, whose title is taken from the Belmont Conference Center located in Elkridge, Maryland, was published on April 18, 1979. The report and its annexes, including letters to the President of the United States, the Presidents of the Senate and the House of Representatives, constitute a 40-page document describing the three fundamental principles that should be followed when conducting research involving human participants. It also contains a number of practical proposals on how to implement them. The most important are summarized in Table 6.1.

Table 6.1 Suggestions for principles of studies involving human participants as formulated in the *Belmont Report*

No.	*Principle*	*Application*
1	Respect for research participants • Participants should be treated as individuals making decisions independently • Individuals who are not fully independent should be given special care	Informed consent: participants should be able to decide what they will and will not participate in during the research. Informed consent must be based on three elements: • information • understanding • voluntary participation
2	Welfare of the participants • No harm should be done to study participants • Research should maximize scientific benefits and minimize risk to participants	The nature and degree of risk (and potential benefits of the study) should be systematically monitored and controlled
3	Justice • Both the benefits from the research and the risks involved should be distributed fairly	Selection of participants • Fair procedures should be adopted for the selection of research participants *

Source: based on the final *Belmont Report* (1979).

* As you might suppose, the report's authors were referring directly to the skin color of the Tuskegee experiment participants – the concept of fair procedures should be understood here as non-discrimination based on gender, age, social group, skin color etc.

It is worth noting, however, that even a quick glance at the basic procedures for research conduct described in the Belmont Report gives the impression of their being very general and at a very high level of abstraction. A more detailed reading of the document only reinforces this impression. However, a significant detail is the role of the so-called IRB (Institutional Review Board) in the research design process. In the United States, the Belmont Report (an indirect consequence of Solomon Asch's experiments in the 1950s, Stanley Milgram's experiments in the late 1960s and early 1970s, and the Tuskegee and Philip Zimbardo experiments in the early 1970s) initiated an increase in the importance and necessity of obtaining acceptance for research projects from the IRB (also sometimes called IEC – Institutional Ethics Committee, ERB – Ethical Review Board, REB – Research Ethics Board: all these acronyms are variants of the words "ethics," "research," and "council"). Today, in the United States (and in many countries around the world that have adopted this system), psychological research involving human participants requires the approval of such an institution (in some cases, approval is also required for sociological research – especially if it is publicly funded). This, of course, gives rise to considerable problems – particularly among researchers in the social sciences. We note that the findings in the Belmont Report were primarily a product of improper practices in biological and medical sciences, and the simple "copy+paste" of preventive solutions to the social sciences did not necessarily lead to the best results. One interesting example is that of ethnographers who determined that the data they had collected (e.g. in the form of unstructured interviews, recorded stories, anecdotal stories and the like) did not meet the criteria for human research and should therefore be excluded from the IRB's "jurisdiction" (Ritchie & Shopes, 2003).

An important issue that ethics committees take into account is observance of the principle of informed consent from the participant. The expectation here is usually a clear one: if the psychologist–researcher is to observe the principle of voluntary participation in research, it is vital to obtain consent from the participant to be engaged in the experiment. This means that it is absolutely necessary for a potential research participant to be informed that such an experiment will take place, most likely to clarify doubts regarding the procedure itself, and to receive consent to the study (in written or oral form). Naturally, there are various alternatives for experiments without the informed consent of the participants – however, awareness of certain difficulties related to their implementation is necessary. One proposed method is the active role-play method – a kind of psychodrama in which participants are informed that they are supposed to assume the role of participants in an experiment and behave as real participants would behave. Among reports describing such procedures, worthy of mention is the work of Don Mixon, who used the active role-playing technique in his research to replicate Stanley Milgram's experiments with electric shocks (Mixon, 1972). He invited 40 students from the University of Nevada to participate in one of his studies, asking them to play the role of a participant in the Milgram experiment. The students were supposed to imagine that they were in a psychological laboratory (in fact, they were sitting at a table in one of the university's offices) and operating a device that administered electric shocks (in fact, writing down their decisions on a diagram drawn on a sheet of paper). Mixon's results were partly in line with those recorded by Milgram in his experiments, and they allowed for the further development of his research program. For example, he examined how different degrees of precision in the instructions on how a role should be played affect the results as declared by participants. Mixon's research and reflections on active role-playing techniques were also described by John D. Greenwood (1983).

It is also worth noting one more element related to ethical assessment of the experimental research program on obedience carried out by Stanley Milgram. As Eliott Aronson (Aronson & Aronson, 2018) writes, Milgram himself sadly told him that a significant part of the criticism leveled at him following publication of the results of his obedience research concerned not so much the procedure itself as the results obtained by it. In other words, if the participants in Milgram's studies had behaved less obediently during the procedure, the public's reception of the research itself would have been entirely different. This is a very important observation, because it shows that the ethical evaluation of the experimental design (which the researcher can influence) is related to the results it produces (which the researcher cannot, or in any case should not influence). This theoretical question was to some extent answered in the study by Leonard Bickman and Matthew Zarantonello (1978), which asked participants about the degree of harmfulness of the procedure presented to them, modeled on that used by Milgram. However, the participants were divided into groups – some of them were told of the actual results obtained by this procedure, while the others were informed that almost none of the participants reached the end of the scale of the machine generating the electric shocks. As it turned out, this clearly influenced assessments of the ethics of the procedure itself – when the participants surveyed by Bickman and Zarantonello knew that almost nobody wanted to electrocute another person, they viewed it as far less harmful than those who knew the real results. This conclusion is consistent with the position of some contemporary philosophers dealing with ethics and moral judgments, writes Thomas Nagel (1979). In his opinion, the moral and ethical evaluation of conduct depends to a significant extent on its consequences, on which the subject of the event may have little or no influence at all. However, this does not change the fact that observers hold this person responsible for the consequences of actions taken. This was empirically demonstrated by Elaine Walster (1966). In her experiments, she told the participants the story of a young man named Lennie, who parked his car on a hill. Because of a defect in the handbrake, the car started to roll away from the parking space. At this point, the stories began to diverge. One group learned that the car stopped on a stump in the ground, and there were no major consequences. The next group was informed that the car sped out of control and completely destroyed a tree growing at the bottom of the hill. The third presented a version of the ending in which, although nobody was hurt because the car stopped, the risk of something bad happening was high because there was a salesman and a child in a small store at the bottom of the hill. In the fourth and final version, it was reported that the car sped up, rolled down the hill, smashed the store window, stunned the child and seriously injured the salesman. Assessments of Lennie's responsibility varied greatly, ranging from low when no one was hurt to high when the consequences were more serious. The same seems to be true for moral and ethical judgments of Milgram's research – if it had turned out that the participants were disobedient and did not want to electrocute the "student," accusations of the experiment's unethicality would probably have been much weaker, or perhaps nonexistant.

Let us return to the "active role-playing" technique. It could be supposed that the methodology proposed by the researchers gives rise to considerable doubts about the reliability of the results – they are derived from what is perhaps nothing more than a very specific sample. While in Milgram's research we were dealing with a sample that was quite diverse in terms of age, social background, and occupation, in the situation described, the generalization of results may concern at most a population of young people, students. However, the true value of the active role-playing technique may lie elsewhere – namely, in showing how determined we are to adhere to the principle of informed consent of research participants. The importance of this can be seen, for example, in the 2009 special issue *64*(1) of *American Psychologist* entitled "Obedience – then and now," containing an entire series of articles analyzing the possibilities of conducting research on obedience to authority in a way that is as ethically uncontentious as possible.

So let us assume for a moment that ethical rigor here is nonnegotiable and in every case we must obtain the informed consent of potential participants to take part in the study. Let us also assume that there is no deviation from this rule. How do we benefit, what methodological consequences do we have to face? From the perspective of a researcher who conducts field experiments, it is worth declaring clearly that such field research in many fields of psychology is utterly useless. This has been known for a very long time – for example, from Martin Orne's (1962) experiments described elsewhere in this book. Similar conclusions can also be drawn from another study, carried out in 2014 in Wrocław.

In this study we wanted to examine how awareness of taking part in a field experiment influences the behavior and decisions of the participants in a quasi-experiment. The participants were passers-by in the vicinity of the main railroad station in Wrocław. The day of the week and time of the study (from 9.00 am to 5.00 pm) were randomly chosen. The participants were selected for the experiment by identifying every fifth person who did not have a chance to observe the interaction with the previous participant. Based on tables of random numbers, a randomization list was also created assigning the participants to an experimental or control group.

The main request in the study was a question of agreement to reducing the number of parking spaces for people with disabilities in Wrocław and opening them to drivers without disabilities. The request was deliberately formulated in an unobvious manner, requiring some thought from the survey participants. This is because there is no particular reason not to agree to increase the number of parking spaces for drivers (the vast majority of residents are familiar with the problem of finding a free parking space in the downtown area), but the information that this would take place at the expense of disabled drivers makes the endeavor somewhat questionable. The experimenter in the control group asked exactly this question:

> Good morning, Sir/Madam. As a resident of Wrocław, I am collecting signatures for a petition to the mayor about reducing the number of parking spaces for the disabled. The point is simply to make these places in the city more accessible for other drivers, because sometimes there are too few. Would you sign this petition?

Then, after hearing the answer (yes or no), he added:

> I have some samples of letters to the mayor on this matter. You can take them and give them to your friends. How many letters will you take?

Let us take this opportunity to point out that we have collected both dichotomous data (consent vs. disagreement) and data measured on an interval scale (how many letters the participant took). Later in the book we will present the consequences of such an approach for the possibility of performing various statistical calculations.

Returning to the description of the procedure, let us clarify that participants in the control group were presented with the request immediately, while in the experimental group it was preceded by a short interaction with an assistant to the experimenter. A few dozen seconds before the actual interaction, he approached the participant and said:

> Excuse me, I have a huge request – I am a student of psychology and I am conducting research for my Master's thesis. In a minute or so, a person will approach you and ask you for a small favor. It will be a small psychological experiment, you will be able to withdraw at any time. There will be no money, you will just fulfil the request or not. Everything will take no more than a minute and a half. Do you consent?

If the person gave consent (which they did in almost 70% of cases), the experimenter's assistant walked away, and after about half a minute the experimenter appeared, starting the procedure described above. The study involved two male experimenters and two female experimenters, randomly altering roles. We examined whether the sex of the experimenter influenced results – the analyses showed that there was no such effect.

The study involved 60 participants (30 in each of the experimental conditions). We checked how the information about participating in the experiment influenced the decision to sign the petition – the percentage of consents and refusals given in each group is collected in Table 6.2.

The difference was statistically significant: $\chi^2(1) = 4.887$; $p < 0.05$; $\varphi = 0.202$; Cohen's $d = 0.534$. We also checked whether the two groups differed in the number of letters taken for friends. Averages and deviations for both groups are summarized in Table 6.3.

The results clearly show an increased willingness to help in the group informed about participation in the study. How can we explain these results? There are at least a few possible answers. The first indicates the possibility of a "foot-in-the-door" effect (described in Chapter 3 on the history of field experiments in social psychology). This effect could

Table 6.2 Percentage of participants agreeing to and refusing the request depending on prior notice of participation in an experiment

		Group	
		Informed	*Unaware*
Decision	Agreement	66.7	46.7
	Refusal	33.3	53.3

Source: own data.

Table 6.3 Average number of letters taken for friends depending on prior notification of participation in the experiment

Group	*Average*	*SD*
Conscious participation in the study	4.45	5.24
Unaware of participation in the study	1.32	2.71

Source: own data.

occur because the request to sign the petition was the second one (the participant had already agreed to participate in the experiment). This highlights the first problem related to the necessity of obtaining permission to take part in a study – we obtain a group biased by prior consent to take part in the experiment. Another reason is the fact of performing the selection – after all, some of the potential participants who were asked to take part in the experiment refused. This means that a distinct group has already been included in the study itself, and the selection criterion (willingness to help) was strongly linked to the later analyzed dependent variable, thus impacting the results obtained.

It should also be kept in mind that the participants in both groups performed completely different roles. In the control group they were ordinary passers-by asked by someone on the street to sign a petition – in big cities this is a relatively common occurrence that does not evoke any particular emotional reaction; passers-by are accustomed to it, and they treat it more or less naturally. In the experimental group, however, after giving their consent, they became PARTICIPANTS, with all the attendant consequences. What are these consequences? At a minimum, those previously reported by Milton Rosenberg (1965) and Stephen Weber and Thomas Cook (1972). Namely, the fear of potential judgment (which is often expected) by the researcher, and the specific ability of the participant to guess research hypotheses and act accordingly. In other words, research participants often feel the need to be a "good participant" – that is, one whose participation in the experiment helps the researcher to confirm (and not just falsify) the research hypotheses. Many years of experience in conducting laboratory research allows us to state that the questions "how did I do?," "did I do everything right?," "are my results good?" are, firstly, extremely common among participants, and secondly, they clearly show that participants are usually just good, helpful people who want to "do well" in the experiment (which is something significantly different from the natural behavior they are usually asked to demonstrate).

One element of the experimental procedure that is also applied in field research is what we call debriefing. This procedure, as Dana Dunn (2012) writes, performs several functions. The first is to explain to participants the experiment's purpose, the significance of the various procedures applied and, if possible, to present the results so far. While the true purpose of the study was masked during the experiment, this is a good time to tell the truth. Debriefing is also supposed to perform an educational function – to show to the participants why the experiment was performed, to inform them about the meaning of the results for science and society, to broaden their knowledge, and to construct an image of the psychologist–researcher as a transparent and responsible participant in scientific and social life.

Debriefing is also – and this is frequently viewed as its most important role – considered to be the point at which the researcher is supposed to ascertain the well-being of the research participant. Obviously, researchers should strive to ensure that participants do not feel worse after participating in the experiment than before. The problem, however, is that sometimes the desire to safeguard participants' well-being clearly interferes with their right to full information and with the course of the study (e.g., when a participant has behaved in a socially inappropriate manner during the study, and we further inform the participant that this behavior has been observed and recorded).

Moreover, in some cases, simply informing participants that they have participated in an experiment seems to have a greater negative influence on their well-being than keeping them in the dark. Imagine conducting a study on charitable giving and we are exploring how information about the purpose of a fundraiser affects the generosity of potential donors. Such a study took place in the fall of 2012, checking whether information about the purpose of donations for animal welfare would increase the chance of their being made. Randomization of experimental conditions was performed using random number tables, study sites were drawn, and data collection began. In the control group, the request was worded as follows:

> Good morning, I am a volunteer for a foundation raising money for a homeless shelter, would you be willing to help us with a donation?

In the experimental group, the request was almost the same, but one word was added:

> Good morning, I am a volunteer for a foundation raising money for a homeless ANIMALS shelter, would you be willing to help us with a donation?

The experimenter had two cans in his backpack, and depending on the conditions he would take out one or the other; each can was labeled with the logo of an authentic foundation authorized to conduct public collections (for the purposes of the study, the experimenters cooperated with two foundations in Wrocław and, of course, transferred all the money collected to their accounts). The results, while they may not be highly relevant to the topic at hand, were extremely interesting. A total of 120 participants were involved, 60 in each experimental condition (gender was controlled for, and the number of men and women was equalized). More than twice as many people who were presented with the request to donate to an animal rescue organization chose to do so compared to those asked to donate to support homeless people. Moreover, the average donation (measured with a special "counting can") was significantly higher in the former group than in the latter.

Now imagine that we want to be entirely methodologically and ethically correct, and we thus decide to conduct a debriefing. It seems that there is no other way to do it than what follows:

> I owe you an explanation – in fact, the real purpose of this fundraiser is to see if people are more likely to give money to homeless people or homeless animals. There are some psychological theories about helping, or altruism, that we want to verify in this study. Well, it just so happened that you decided not to donate. Do you have any questions for me?

Of course, this is slightly exaggerated, but as you might imagine, it illustrates the problem at hand quite well – to what extent can we risk aggravating people who have just unwittingly helped us by participating in an experiment? Especially since this field study was not at all dissimilar to everyday events we might experience out on the street. Obviously, in situations involving a procedure that manipulates the participants' mood, enmeshing them in various processes related to the social psychology of cognition, testing their willingness to help in some dramatic enactment (as in the case of the "Good Samaritan" study done by John M. Darley and C. Daniel Batson in 1973), we owe them a full explanation and, moreover, support to people we have made feel uncomfortable. However, for many studies in the field of social influence, it will be more uncomfortable for participants to know that "they did a study with me and I didn't behave like I was supposed to" than "they asked me for a donation today, but I was in a hurry

(I didn't have change, the person didn't inspire my confidence, etc.) and I didn't give anything."

Another important issue, especially from the perspective of field experiments, is the practice of recording (audio and video) the behavior of study participants. When we are discussing how we register the course of the study, it is worth taking a moment to review the increasingly frequent expectations of major scientific journals to provide documentation of the course of the study to publicly accessible repositories. These may include pictures of the experiment, films showing the participants' behavior, etc. Of course, there is a scientific justification for this – namely, it is significant assistance for experimenters who would like to replicate our study. However, this poses another ethical problem for researchers, this time concerning protection of study participants' image. It seems that this issue can be resolved quite sensibly with a compromise – if we wish to use audio and video recordings of the study in any way, we must have the written consent of those whose voice and/or image have been recorded. Obviously, the use of such materials in activities intended to popularize science is excluded – if we want to prepare short film materials to present the course of the study at popular science conferences or on websites, we should recreate the behavior of the subjects in the experimental situation by using actors (they do not necessarily have to be professional actors; it is enough to involve e.g. students, with their clear and informed consent). It is perhaps obvious that using the images of participants to popularize science (or, even worse, to popularize the scientist) is unacceptable, and this probably does not need to be spelled out in codes of ethics.

If we are discussing codes, we should refer to the set of ethical guidelines found in the *Ethical Principles of Psychologists and Code of Conduct of the American Psychological Association* (APA, 2017). This set of standards devotes a significant amount of space to describing the conduct of the psychologist as a researcher. It talks about responsibility for research participants and the principle of voluntary consent. Section 8.06, however, is described as "Dispensing with informed consent for research." It states that a study can be performed without obtaining consent from the participant in certain cases. Psychologists may dispense with informed consent only

1 where research would not reasonably be assumed to create distress or harm and involves (a) the study of normal educational practices, curricula, or classroom management methods conducted in educational settings; (b) only anonymous questionnaires, naturalistic observations, or archival research for which disclosure of responses would not place participants at risk of criminal or civil liability or damage their financial standing, employability, or reputation, and confidentiality is protected; or (c) the study of factors related to job or organization effectiveness conducted in organizational settings for which there is no risk to participants' employability, and confidentiality is protected, or
2 where otherwise permitted by law or federal or institutional regulations.

As you can see, the standards proposed by the APA are quite liberal. It is worth noting that, when combined with the necessity of obtaining the consent of local university ethics committees for practically every study, this results in fairly strict control over the course of the study and a guarantee that high ethical standards will be maintained – this is a course of action worth considering. Perhaps the starting point here should be the question of why we need an ethics committee at all?

Ethics committees contained within the structures of a university generally act as bodies either granting or refusing permission to conduct research. The procedures of such committees are not uniform – in some cases applications are considered periodically (e.g. several times a year) and debated by the whole committee. Other committees operate continually; applications submitted electronically are sent to reviewers (as well as from outside the committee if, for example, the subject matter requires it), and the committee itself takes a decision on-line based on the information provided by reviewers and its own opinions regarding the application. This system offers many advantages – it makes it possible to respond quickly to the research needs of faculty members, allows the committee to seek the opinions of specialists, and at the same time to ask the researcher making the submission for additions or clarifications, if necessary. It also has one disadvantage, which is a kind of "original sin" of many (if not all) ethics committees. It does not allow for a normal, scientific discussion between the submitter(s) and the committee members.

Note that in the vast majority of cases the ethics committee is presented with a proposal, with language and justification of varying quality, to which it may or may not consent. There is no room for the question: "Are you really convinced that this is the only (or best) way to get an answer to the question posed?" There is no room for discussing the sensibility, including the scientific merit, of the proposed study or series of studies (although some committees do invite the applicant to a session). As a rule, the committee is supposed to evaluate only ethical aspects. But is it not a breach of research ethics to submit an application that, in principle, should not cause harm to participants' well-being, but raises legitimate concerns about its wisdom from a scientific perspective? Trivializing the issue a bit (but only a bit) – if someone wants to check for the two-hundredth time whether extraversion correlates with actively seeking social contacts, should the committee give its permission without a second thought because, after all, filling out two questionnaires does not raise ethical concerns? As it seems, given the way things are structured today, it could hardly do otherwise.

An additional issue, which is not often thought of in terms of the ethical dimension, is determining a sample size for a study that will allow us to confidently accept or reject the hypotheses being offered. Most people believe that the more information we have, the better decisions we make. In respect of data from studies, this means believing that the more cases that are examined, the more reliable the relationship obtained.

It seems obvious that the sample should be large enough for the results obtained to provide unambiguous justification for making a decision as regards the hypotheses (we are talking, of course, about the power of the statistical test in the experiment, today usually determined by computer programs such as GPower). It should also be remembered, however, that for ethical reasons the sample should be exactly the same size and not one person larger. Each additional participant means potential (and unnecessary) fear of evaluation, stress resulting from involvement in the study, or even just a simple waste of time for someone who could spend it doing more pleasant things. Add to this the often unnecessary use of taxpayers' money for research. An additional consequence of such an increase in the number of people tested is the risk of artificially increasing the chance of obtaining statistically significant results.

As the empirical science methodology guru Jonathan Cohen writes (1990, p. 1308):

> The null hypothesis, taken literally (and that's the only way you can take it in formal hypothesis testing, is always false in the real world …). If it is false, even a tiny degree, it must be the case that a large enough sample will produce a significant result and lead to its rejection.

He then concludes with the ironic statement: " So, if the null hypothesis is always false, what's the big deal about rejecting it?"

The fundamental problem is that the larger the sample size, the greater the risk of the error of statistical testing showing a difference that, realistically, does not exist. If, for example, we precisely examined the lengths of the feet of 100,000 residents of the left bank of the Mississippi and 100,000 residents of the right bank of that river, we would find that the difference between the averages is statistically significant (although we need not guess at which of these populations has longer feet). The trap that a researcher's desire to study as many people as possible can become is convincingly demonstrated in articles by such authors as Fiedler and Kareev (2006, 2011).

As Jorge Faber and Lilian Fonseca (2014) write, "Statistical tests were developed to handle samples, not populations"; with very large samples there is therefore a risk of rejecting the null hypothesis in a study where the effect being tested is in fact of marginal importance and negligible size.

Fortunately, modern psychology has moved on from basing conclusions about relationships between variables solely on significance levels, which are very sensitive to sample size. The larger the sample, the more likely the researcher is to obtain the magic value of $p< .05$. The magic of this .05 is puzzling to say the least. Rosnow and Rosenthal (1989, p. 1277) quipped that "God loves the .06 nearly as much as the .05," and Jonathan Cohen (1990) responded pithily to that remark by simply saying: "Amen." Indeed, psychologists' assumption that achieving a significance level of .05 is something marginally and qualitatively better than, say, .0499 has little to do with rationality (Wasserstein, Schrim and Lazar, 2019). Moreover, we should put more faith in the difference found in two experiments in which significance levels were close to .05 but did not reach that magic figure than we do in the one study in which the .05 level was successfully reached.

It seems that psychology is slowly abandoning its fascination with the category of statistical significance. Statistical inference is increasingly taking into account effect-size based decisions that disregard sample size. The rule that an author must provide an indicator of the strength of an effect (Cohen's d, phi, r, $\eta 2$) is required by a growing number of journals, and one of them, *Basic and Applied Social Psychology*, does not even allow its authors to state the size of p.

In concluding this chapter, we are tempted to outline the procedure for implementing a field experiment. It would be a set of steps, conceived as a kind of road map. The idea is to have a procedure that, taking into account the knowledge and research findings presented in this chapter, would at the same time be a series of questions that researchers should answer before going into the field. The important thing about it is that all of them must be posed at an early stage of the study – before any additional steps are taken.

So how does one behave ethically when planning and executing a field experiment? Below are what we consider some key considerations and pieces of advice.

First, think about what you want to examine and whether a field experiment is really a sensible way to obtain the knowledge you seek. If you can find answers to your questions in a way that causes less discomfort to your participants than the field experiment you are planning – do it. There are many such suggestions – consider a design where deception is not necessary; consider whether you can use the active role-playing technique; perhaps you can perform *ex post facto* research. If you decide that these options are not reasonable, and that a field experiment would be the best solution, then continue down that road.

Consider whether the volume of knowledge that this experiment may yield is worth infringing on the participants' right to freely decide to participate. This is not a trivial matter; you are responsible for the people who will become participants in your study without their informed consent. Consider trying to obtain consent after the study, when the participants have a grasp of the entire procedure they took part in and the knowledge that was obtained from the study. Consider consulting with other researchers – even those you know are generally against research that does not satisfy the informed consent principle – their opinions may be valuable to you if you keep an open mind.

Create a thorough and precise experimental design. When operationalizing the variables, remember that it is best to set up the situation so that it resembles as closely as possible what the research participants might encounter in real life. Talk to colleagues who work in similar areas and ask for their opinions. Try asking people who are not involved in psychology or research – how would they react if they were in this situation? Would they be surprised? Would they consider their personal freedom and dignity violated if someone treated them this way? The answers to these questions will be crucial for you to determine the risks of the procedure you are developing.

Correctly and precisely define the sample you need to test – both in terms of its size and selection criterion. You don't want to have too small a sample (because the results will turn out to be inconclusive) or too large (so that you don't involve more participants than is really necessary).

Plan your debriefing – explaining to participants that they were involved in a study – very carefully. What do you want to tell them? Can you explain your hypotheses? How will it affect their well-being? Remember that these people deserve an apology; after all, you deceived them by concealing your true identity. Allocate sufficient time in the experimental design for this procedure. Consider whether you should appoint a special person (perhaps a clinical psychologist) to carry it out.

There are situations in which a debriefing might seem unnecessary – if you are investigating, for example, how putting up different versions of a poster saying "don't vandalize the bus stop" affects the frequency of acts of vandalism, chasing down every person who looks at the poster seems pointless. Nevertheless, don't take this as permission to abandon the procedure – you need to decide for yourself whether and how to conduct a debriefing.

Once again, discuss the study design with people who have a different view of field experiments than you do. You don't have to agree with their comments – but listen to them carefully and consider what they say. They may (or even certainly will) point out consequences you haven't thought of and ask questions you wouldn't have asked. You need to think them through carefully.

Change the design of the experiment to accommodate the criticism as much as possible, but do not lose the sense of the study.

Present a description of the study to the appropriate ethics committee. If the committee's view is that the study does not satisfy the ethical criteria, ask for a joint meeting. We are all interested in the ethical aspect of research, so we should resolve such matters via discussion. Maybe you will be able to suggest modifications to the experimental design, maybe the committee will accept your arguments, or maybe they will propose a solution that satisfies you. If, after the discussion and implementation of changes, the committee comes to the conclusion that you proceed with the experiment, consider it a success. If not – think about what you can change to investigate the same phenomenon in a slightly different way. It is best to start by going back to the beginning of these deliberations.

7 Who should be the participants?

The problem of randomization in field studies

In one of the most fundamental, for the field of psychology, textbooks on the methodology of studies, Susan Fiske, Daniel Gilbert, and Gardner Lindzey (2010) present very interesting views on who are the most frequently chosen subjects participating in psychological studies. According to the authors, the majority of psychological studies are carried out with psychology students or basic psychology course participants as the subjects. Needless to say, this problem has been known for some time now; it was already in 1952 when *American Psychologist* featured a brief, one-page article by Maurice Farber symptomatically entitled, "The college student as laboratory animal" (Farber, 1952). It was as early as 60 years ago, when Farber highlighted the fact that university students represent a prevailing group of subjects for many of the phenomena described in the literature, while also emphasizing how questionable it is to use them as the only source of data. The author claimed that a heavily homogeneous group composed of individuals who are similar to one another in many respects (social background, level of affluence, life goals, social and political views) must not be treated as a reasonable sample in social studies (and in any case as the only basis for drawing conclusions applicable to a broader population). At the same time, Farber was able to pinpoint the reasons for which researchers often chose to analyze the reactions (answers provided in a survey, declared behavior, etc.) of members of this particular demographic. He highlighted at least three groups of such reasons:

1 Researchers acknowledge that after all (apart from all other qualities) students are human beings, i.e., they belong to the species of *Homo sapiens*. Therefore, there is no reason to believe that psychological rules of human behavior do not apply to them. (Farber notices, rather wittily, that this deduction mechanism is typical of those researchers who have switched to analyses conducted on humans rather recently and whose previous focus was on white laboratory rats. In order to be able to fully understand this tease, one should bear in mind that he wrote those words in 1952, which makes it a rather overt allusion to behaviorists.)
2 Students make easily accessible subjects. You simply enter a lecture hall, distribute one hundred (or even more) surveys and collect them by the exit. Farber does not consider this data collection method to be equivalent to laziness, he believes it to be an intelligent and effective approach. After all, as he puts it, students are the embodiment of a researcher's (as well as a traveling salesman's) perfect candidates: "prisoners with nowhere to run." A researcher can count on getting all of his surveys back completed or can be certain that there will be "volunteers" willing to participate in his studies: this would not happen in real life, i.e., outside of a lecture hall (or, let us highlight, outside of a prison, even though, paradoxically,

DOI: 10.4324/9781003092995-7

prisoners enjoy a greater degree of freedom in terms of being able to refuse to take part in a study than an average student involved in various interrelations with their professors).

3 Students have reading comprehension skills and can answer questions. They know what a "stereotype," "discrimination," or "potential" means, and they are also capable of introspection; one can assume that the same cannot be said of all individuals that make up society. This makes life easier for the researchers, e.g., when it comes to drawing up their surveys and questionnaires. It will suffice to use the language they understand and it will be very probable that their students will also be capable of understanding the text.

The malicious comments made by Maurice Farber were all too clear, which does not mean they were unfounded. We ourselves can particularly relate to the last argument: the one related predominantly to researchers and students sharing a similar language and a similar system of values. As students, we were sometimes hired as interviewers for the purpose of studies (both scientific and marketing ones) and it was quite often the case that our respondents were completely unable to understand the questions prepared by the researchers. As the studies were based on a randomly selected sample, this included representatives from all spheres of society, including groups with poor reading comprehension skills or who were unable to comprehend multiple sentences. Nevertheless, and this would be confirmed by anyone who has had anything to do with survey-based studies or who has any psychological intuition at all, when people are faced with an open-ended question like, "Taking into account market rate fluctuations on the Tokyo Stock Exchange, how accurate do you think estimates for the growth of the European GDP are?", they rarely reply with, "I don't understand the question." They are more likely to reply with, "Yes," "Within the norm," or "Just write something down so that it sounds right." It was only once that one of our associates almost got beaten up by a farmer, who was asked the following question included in the survey: "When looking at the Alpha Proxima Centauri star, are we seeing the light it is emitting at the moment of looking at it or over four years earlier?"

Despite the fact that Farber warned researchers not to base their studies on students as early as in 1952, in the following decades the problem not only did not disappear but it even escalated. In 1986, the *Journal of Personality and Social Psychology* published an article by David Sears of UCLA (Sears, 1986), which analyzed the percentage of texts published in the leading social psychology journals (*Journal of Personality and Social Psychology, Personality and Social Psychology Bulletin,* as well as *Journal of Experimental Social Psychology*) based on studies conducted on students (with a particular emphasis on psychology students). The results are significant enough (also because Sears analyzed the portion of the investigated studies that was conducted in laboratories and the portion conducted in the natural environment) to have a closer look at them. Table 7.1 presents exact numbers for the year 1980.

When Sears repeated his analyses in 1985, the results demonstrated an even greater dominance of studies conducted on psychology students: 83% of all articles described studies where the subjects were psychology students, whereas studies conducted on a non-student sample and in natural conditions (outside of a laboratory) represented only 13% (the analyses encompassed 178 articles published in *JPSP*, *PSPB*, and *JESP*).

Unfortunately, this trend has not slowed in any manner, and furthermore, in the case of some journals, the tendency has intensified. Other researchers (Endler & Speer, 1998)

Table 7.1 Studies published in *JPSP, PSPB* and *JESP* in 1980 by location and subject type

	Category	JPSP	PSPB	JESP	*Total*
Subjects	American university students	70%	81%	81%	75%
	American psychology students	52%	23%	57%	53%
	American university students with other majors	18%	28%	24%	21%
	Other (non-American) university students	12%	0%	8%	7%
	Adults (non-students)	18%	19%	11%	18%
Study location	Laboratory	64%	75%	95%	71%
	Natural conditions	36%	25%	5%	29%
Total	University students in a laboratory	58%	73%	78%	64%
	Non-students in natural conditions	17%	16%	3%	15%
The number of articles the analyses was based on		191	73	37	301

Source: prepared by the authors based on Sears, 1986.

analyzed the percentage of studies conducted on students during the period between 1993 and 1995 based on articles published in five major psychological journals (devoted predominantly to personality psychology). The percentage of articles that used data obtained through studies conducted on students varied among the journals, but the figures were high across the board: *European Journal of Personality* – 42%, *Personality and Individual Differences* – 52%, *Journal of Personality* – 60%, *Journal of Personality and Social Psychology* – 65%, *Journal of Research in Personality* – 87%. Meanwhile, other researchers (Wintre, North, & Sugar, 2001) analyzed articles published in six prestigious journals: *Journal of Abnormal Psychology, Journal of Experimental Psychology: Learning, Memory, and Cognition, Journal of Experimental Psychology: Human Perception and Performance, Journal of Personality and Social Psychology, Journal of Personality*, and *Journal of Experimental Social Psychology*. For the purpose of the analysis, 1,719 articles from 1975, 1985, and 1995 were selected (to capture the possible differences). Of these articles, 1,559 featured studies with human subjects. The percentages of studies involving students in certain years were as follows: 1975 – 69.8; 1985 – 66.7; 1995 – 68.2. The researchers concluded that despite the fact that the problem with studies involving samples made of students has been widely addressed in the academic discourse, the percentage of articles describing the results of such studies has not changed.

Perhaps the problem is being blown out of proportion. Perhaps using undergraduates as subjects is not such a bad idea. Perhaps their reactions, opinions, and answers given in surveys are not that different from those of the rest of the population. Robert Peterson and Dwight Merunka (2014) investigated the method for collecting the so-called convenience samples, that is, samples with the main advantage of being readily accessible and easy to analyze. These two authors used the following quotation by William Wells (1993) as the motto of their article: "This is not to say that findings based on students are always wrong. It is only to say that findings based on students are always suspect. Our findings would be substantially more credible if students were not so often the first and only choice" (p. 491). Their findings seem to clearly correspond with the quotation by Wells: in most cases students are, indeed, the first choice.

Peterson and Merunka chose the area of business ethics as the subject of their research. They came to the conclusion that the area is sufficiently well explored to use the interrelations identified therein as "reference values" to be compared with those obtained from convenience samples. They prepared a survey, including 27 items across two scales, to measure the attitude of the subjects toward ethics and capitalism. In the survey, they included eight demographic variables (sex, age, occupation, year of studies, religiousness, major, citizenship, as well as academic degrees earned). According to earlier studies, the following three hypotheses are valid:

1. Female students show a higher level of acceptance for ethical principles in business than male students.
2. Business-oriented majors show a positive connection between the level of acceptance of ethical principles in business and the level of religiousness.
3. Business-oriented majors show a positive connection between the level of acceptance of ethical principles and attitude toward capitalism.

The researchers sent their request for assistance in the study to 64 business schools in the USA. In each school, an assistant was appointed (remunerated with a small amount) who was told to conduct the study in such a manner as to make sure it resembles, as much as possible, the traditional method for collecting convenience samples (i.e., the assistant was expected to go to a lecture hall and ask the students to fill out the survey). Ultimately, data from 49 colleges was accepted for the purpose of the analyses (in the remaining cases, the number of completed surveys for a single convenience sample was below 30, which was the minimum threshold set by the authors of the study). The results came from 30 American states, and in all cases the sex ratio corresponded to the average for business schools (50/50). In general, 2,761 students participated in the study (on average 56 individuals per one convenience sample).

Despite the fact that the study was essentially conducted on a very homogeneous group (similar age and major, all subjects were students in the USA), it was already at the level of simple comparisons among the groups that differences emerged. For example, the samples differed from one another in terms of the level of religiousness, which also affected other variables (the attitude toward ethical principles in business and toward capitalism). The differences among the groups were also evident at the stage of verifying the proposed hypotheses. The first one (the relation between one's sex and the level of acceptance of ethical principles in business) turned out to be true when all students were analyzed as a single group. Nevertheless, when the students were divided into convenience samples, a significant relation was evident only in 16% of the samples, with the remaining 84% of the relations being statistically insignificant (it needs emphasizing that in ten cases, the relation – even though still insignificant – was opposite to the assumed hypothesis). As far as the relation between the level of one's religiousness and the level of acceptance of ethical principles in business is concerned, the hypothesis was confirmed in the case of two samples. In 44 samples, the relation was statistically insignificant (and the correlation coefficient ranged from –0.37 to +0.24; it was positive in half of the cases and negative in the other half). In the case of the third hypothesis, there was also a relation (between the level of acceptance of ethical principles and the attitude toward capitalism) at the level of all subjects; yet, when all participants were divided into samples, the relation remained significant only in the case of 29% of the samples.

The results clearly indicate an inconsistency in the results obtained for particular samples. The inconsistency is important, as even though the data was collected from a relatively homogeneous sample, there are still significant discrepancies to be found. Needless to say, we are not referring here exclusively to the obtained levels of significance (which should be treated very cautiously due to the relatively small size of particular convenience samples) but most importantly to the varying directions of the interrelations. The study conducted by Peterson and Merunka (2014) shows that a sample consisting exclusively of students is not the optimal solution, but it also proves that the method of their recruitment for the purpose of a study (without the 1st degree randomization) creates major problems related to producing diverse results. Obviously, this problem is not limited to students; it pertains to any non-random sample selection method.

Those in favor of conducting studies based on samples composed of students can argue that in the contemporary world, students represent a vast (and still growing) portion of the population of young people. True, it is difficult to argue with that. But let us stop for a second and focus on the "young" part of the above sentence. After all, psychology aims at discovering interrelations applicable to people and not to "young people." Meanwhile, it turns out that the age of the subjects can be a crucial factor in social science studies. In order to illustrate this problem, we will refer to the field experiment conducted by Ada Maksim and Slawomir Spiewak (2017). The researchers investigated the effectiveness of the classic social influence technique, i.e., the foot-in-the-door technique. A classic experiment devoted to this method (Freedman & Fraser, 1966) has been described in more detail in Chapter 3. Here, we will only briefly discuss its basic principle, according to which if one wants to make somebody more willing to comply with a rather difficult request, he or she should first ask for a similar but clearly a smaller favor. In the study by Maksim and Spiewak, in the control conditions (i.e., where the difficult request was formulated right away) a female experimenter approached a lone pedestrian to show him/her a detailed brochure on voluntary service opportunities available in the city where the study was being conducted. She asked the pedestrian if they would like to read the brochure and then take it home or give it to one of their family members. In the experimental conditions, the pedestrians were first shown a large sheet of paper with wishes for children from an orphanage and asked to sign it. Once the subject agreed to sign the sheet, the female experimenter would reach for the brochure and formulate the same request as the one used in the control conditions. More subjects agreed to take the brochure with them in the experimental than in the control conditions. Yet, the researchers had another agenda apart from replicating a classic foot-in-the-door effect. They decided to approach only those pedestrians who appeared to be either young individuals (up to, at a guess, 26 years of age) or elderly (over 60). The researchers assumed, similarly to the team led by Roberto Cialdini (Cialdini, Trost, & Newsom, 1995; Guadagno, Asher, Demaine, and Cialdini, 2001; Guadagno, and Cialdini, 2010), that the effectiveness of the foot-in-the-door technique results from our need to remain consistent in terms of our actions. They also assumed that this need intensified with age. If this were the case, the foot-in-the-door technique should be more effective when applied to the elderly as compared to young individuals. The results recorded by Maksim and Spiewak were completely in line with the above assumption (as seen in Table 7.2).

As evidenced by the study discussed above, the problem is not only that social psychologists predominantly use students as subjects in their studies. Perhaps a more severe problem is that, by selecting students as their subjects, they test their hypotheses exclusively on young people.

Table 7.2 Percentage of subjects who agreed to comply with the request to take the brochure

	Control conditions	*Experimental conditions (foot-in-the-door)*
All subjects	37.3%	82.7%
Young	65.4%	88.5%
Elderly	8%	76.9%

Source: Prepared by the author based on Maksim & Spiewak, 2017.

In the case of field experiments, we make decisions not only regarding the selection of the subjects, but we also choose a location and time of the study. It should be noted that these aspects are not entirely independent from one another. If we decide to conduct our study in a library, chances are that the people we will meet there will be of a different type than those we would meet in front of a football stadium. The people we meet in the city center late at night (leaving pubs and not necessarily sober!) are not going to be the same as those we meet at noon in a park.

As much as randomly selecting locations suitable for our studies and randomly selecting subjects who, first, would be included in the study on a random basis and second, would be randomly assigned to a particular group, may seem like a very tough challenge in the case of a field experiment, there are certain technical solutions that can facilitate this task. In order to take a closer look at how to use them, we will now describe a study, a replication of Stanley Milgram's "lost letter" experiment (described in Chapter 3), which we conducted with our team (in cooperation with Katarzyna Byrka). In the course of the study, we wanted to check how a typical Polish and a typical Jewish name written on an envelope affects the chances of a letter reaching its addressee.

As we needed to choose a "prototypically Jewish" surname to be written on the envelopes, we conducted a pilot study. This resulted from the specific historical background of Jews in Poland. Until WWII, they constituted a very large portion of Polish society (approximately 30%). Due to the war and the Holocaust, the Jewish community in Poland became almost non-existent. After the war, the remaining Polish Jews successively emigrated to Israel and other countries, and as a result, it is now estimated that there are only 10,000–20,000 Jews in Poland. This means that it is difficult to predict which surnames are considered typically Jewish by contemporary Poles, who most likely do not know any Jews personally. Therefore, we decided to conduct a pilot study. First, eight surnames of Jewish married couples were generated. The names were found in the interwar records of magistrates' courts for the city of Warsaw (from 1924 to 1947). The Jewish surnames found in the court records (such as Goldman, Rapaport, and others belonging to defendants or aggrieved parties – all for minor offenses) were matched with addresses in Opole (where the actual letters were meant to be delivered). Such addresses were presented to the respondents via Google Forms. Being widely accessible, inexpensive, and fast, this method enables the effective conduct of online surveys. Subjects participating in the pilot study (adults, non-academics) received a link to the web page presented in Figure 7.1.

There were 29 individuals who participated in the pilot study: 16 women and 13 men. The youngest respondent was 26, the oldest was 64. Goldbaum was voted the most prototypically Jewish surname, as 18 subjects declared that they associated the name very strongly with Jews living in Poland. Eventually, the following was put on the envelopes (in the Jewish variant) in the addressee's name field: "Stanisław and Sara Goldbaum."

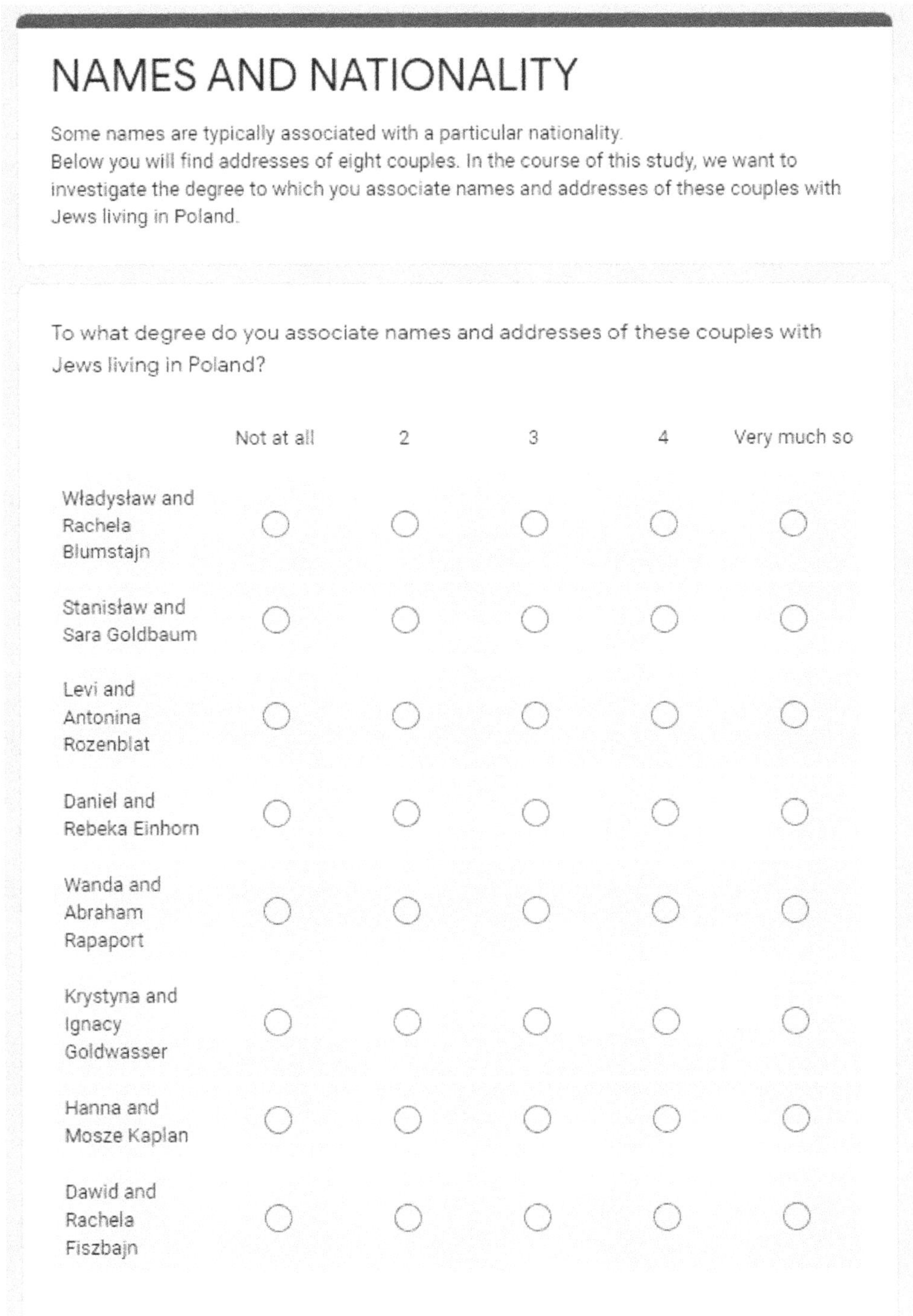

NAMES AND NATIONALITY

Some names are typically associated with a particular nationality.
Below you will find addresses of eight couples. In the course of this study, we want to investigate the degree to which you associate names and addresses of these couples with Jews living in Poland.

To what degree do you associate names and addresses of these couples with Jews living in Poland?

	Not at all	2	3	4	Very much so
Władysław and Rachela Blumstajn	○	○	○	○	○
Stanisław and Sara Goldbaum	○	○	○	○	○
Levi and Antonina Rozenblat	○	○	○	○	○
Daniel and Rebeka Einhorn	○	○	○	○	○
Wanda and Abraham Rapaport	○	○	○	○	○
Krystyna and Ignacy Goldwasser	○	○	○	○	○
Hanna and Mosze Kaplan	○	○	○	○	○
Dawid and Rachela Fiszbajn	○	○	○	○	○

Figure 7.1 A section of the survey presented to the subjects on the web page (here a translation from Polish).
Source: prepared by the authors.

The next step (crucial for the successful completion of efforts undertaken in relation to the execution of the field experiment) was to find reasonable assistants (we are intentionally not using the term "experimenters," as their role in the study was slightly different than in the case of a typical experiment). There is always a considerable risk involved in this step of the process; choosing even one inappropriate individual is often equivalent to ruining the work of a team of people and sometimes also measurable financial losses. Our experience dictates that it is advisable to search for candidates among dedicated students who have already proven to be reliable in the course of earlier research works and also among their friends from outside of the psychology and social science milieu. A properly constructed agreement providing for non-payment of the contractual remuneration (in the case of this study we could afford to remunerate the assistants) or fines in the case of abandoning one's tasks is important for smooth cooperation.

The role of the assistants in our study was to:

- manually address 4,000 envelopes (the number of envelopes we were going to plant on the streets of Wrocław);
- prepare the letters (print and seal);
- plant the letters early in the morning on particular days according to the prepared maps with an accuracy of 50 m.

As we wanted to ensure a completely random selection of the locations where the envelopes would be dropped, the first step was to create a database with all postal codes for Wrocław (around 4,705 postal codes). Using this database, we randomly selected particular streets where our letters were to be planted (2,000 letters addressed to the Goldbaums and 2,000 addressed to the Nowaks, and in each group there would be 1,000 envelopes with a stamp and 1,000 without a stamp). Next, we prepared a database including the following information: the particular location where the letter was planted, the day of the week, and the variation of the letter (Goldbaum/Nowak; stamp/no stamp). With Google Fusion Tables, we converted the database into maps, according to which the experimenters were to plant the letters in the designated locations on particular days. As the success of the entire undertaking depended on their reliability and devotion, they were provided with very detailed instructions on how to proceed (see Box. 7.1).

Box 7.1 The Lost Letter Study – an experimenter's guide

If you decide to work for us as an experimenter, you will become a member of our research team. Please read this guide carefully and think it over. Unreliable experimenters or experimenters who abandon their tasks prior to completion will be detrimental to the study and our efforts will be wasted. Also, no remuneration will be paid for partial completion of the task.

About the study

The Lost Letter Technique (LLT; Milgram, Mann & Harter, 1965) is a classic method for measuring attitudes toward particular social groups within a given population.

In this study, the use of LLT will consist of planting/scattering letters in public places , which are addressed either to a couple with a typical Jewish surname (Stanisław and Sara Goldbaum) or a couple with a typical Polish surname (Stanisław and Barbara Nowak). They will be "fake" lost letters. The actual address belongs to one of the organizers of the study. The letters may or may not have a postage stamp, depending on the experimental conditions.

The study will be conducted between November 17, 2012, and November 22, 2012, with the majority of letters being planted over the weekend. Each experimenter will be given 640 letters, which they will be required to plant. The letters will be delivered in folders, and it is important to take them out in the order they were packed in.

The table below will tell you how many letters must be dropped each day.

Day of the Week	*No. of Letters*
Saturday	180
Sunday	180
Monday	70
Tuesday	70
Wednesday	70
Thursday	70

On Friday evening (November 16, 2012), the experimenters will be given the letters for Saturday, a certificate regarding the execution of the study, the maps and their agreements.

On Saturday evening, they will submit a study report (a completed form and the maps) and will receive another batch of letters.

On Sunday, they will be given the maps and letters for the remaining days of the week.

Each experimenter will receive maps with the locations for each day of the experiment, where the letters must be dropped with an accuracy of 50 m. The maps will be generated based on postal codes and thus they will cover only a section of Wroclaw, not the whole city. Once a letter has been dropped, the location must be marked out. The maps must be returned after the study has been completed.

You must not be seen when planting the letters. You should start dropping the letters in the morning. At least 40% of the letters must be planted in indoor public locations: a shopping mall, a library, a post office, a tram or a café. In such locations, the distance between letters dropped on the same day must be at least 50 m and it must not be possible to see one letter from the location where another one was dropped. The letters are to appear to have been lost⋆.

I have read the experimenter's guide:.................................
Date and signature

⋆ Think about potential locations where you could possibly lose a letter – perhaps near an ATM when you go to reach for your wallet, at a bus stop while trying to find your ticket, by a poster pillar while searching through your pockets for a pen to write down the date of a concert – these would be optimal locations for dropping your letters.

Form to be completed:

Write down the number of letters you have dropped at locations belonging to the given category:

Day	*e.g., Saturday, November 17, 2012*
Shop	
Restaurant, café	
Bus stop, train station	
Tram, bus	
Shopping mall	
Other	

Mark these locations on the map in green.

The assistants received maps with addresses marked on them. Figure 7.2 presents a fragment of one of these maps.

The experimenters set out into the city equipped with sets of sorted letters (the purpose of sorting was to ensure compliance with the principles of 2nd-degree randomization – the random dropping of letters addressed to the Goldbaums and the Nowaks).

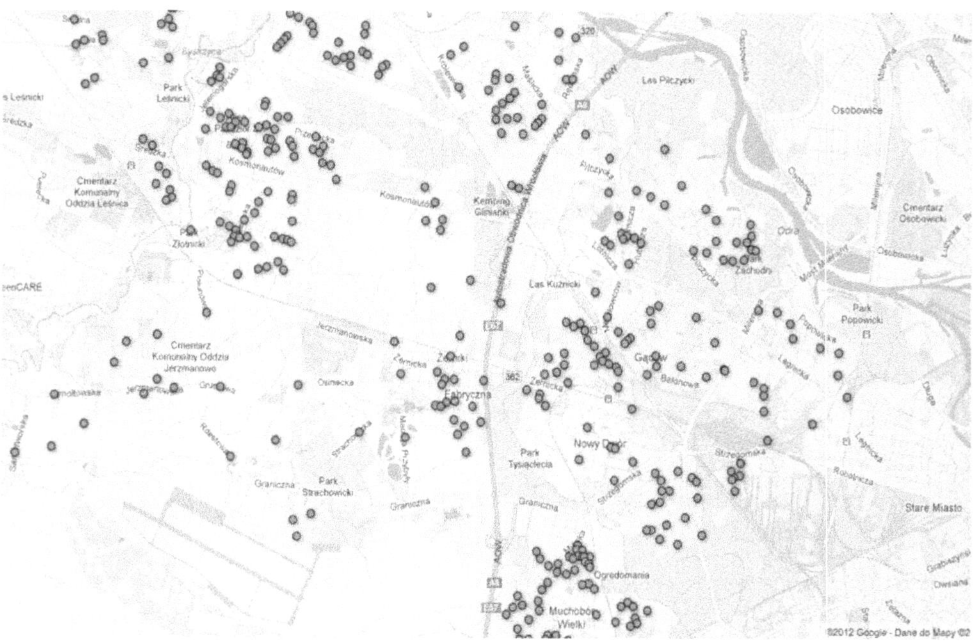

Figure 7.2 A fragment of map with 450 addresses marked.

As usually happens, not everything went according to plan and the number of letters initially planned to be planted in the course of the study was reduced by 120 (1940 letters with a stamp and 1940 without a stamp were planted), but it did not affect the quality of randomization (all randomly selected locations were covered).

The results demonstrated that the letters dropped with a stamp were much more likely to reach their addressees, which, needless to say, should come as no surprise. In total, out of 3,880 planted letters, 960 reached their addresses, which corresponds to 24.7%. Out of 1940 letters with no stamp, 132 were delivered to their addressees, whereas the figure for the same amount of letters with a stamp was 828 (6.8% and 42.7% accordingly). Table 7.3 presents the exact numbers of letters that reached their addresses under the given conditions.

The successful delivery rate was almost equal for letters addressed to the Nowaks and the Goldbaums. Needless to say, the small difference in favor of the Goldbaums, as demonstrated in the table, was not statistically significant.

The fact that a slightly higher number of letters with no postage stamp was successfully delivered to the Nowaks, whereas in the case of the letters with a postage stamp there was a slight advantage in favor of the Goldbaums, was purely coincidental.

In the course of the study, we also investigated the successful delivery rate exclusively for letters with no stamp on them but allowing for whether or not the finder purchased the required postage stamp. At this point, it must be explained that in Poland a letter with no postage stamp on it usually gets delivered with the addressee being charged for postage. Table 7.4 presents the numbers of letters reaching addresses in particular conditions.

It was also in this case that the results demonstrated no differences between the typical Polish and the typical Jewish surname in terms of the number of letters successfully delivered to their addressees.

It should be emphasized that the study in question is a good example to illustrate the amount of work put into the preparation of an experimental scheme as well as its precise execution if the researchers are to comply with the principles of 1st- and 2nd-degree

Table 7.3 Number of letters reaching addressees (based on name and presence of stamp)

		Stamp on the letter		
		No	*Yes*	*Total*
Surname	Nowak	72	401	473
	Goldbaum	60	427	487
Total		132	828	960

Source: prepared by the authors.

Table 7.4 Number of letters reaching addresses without stamps (based on name)

		Postage stamp put on the envelope by the subject		
		No	*Yes*	*Total*
Surname	Nowak	33	38	71
	Goldbaum	24	36	60
Total		57	74	131

Source: prepared by the authors.

randomization. At the same time, it should be noted that even though it is extremely laborious and expensive, it is still feasible, which should come as a certain consolation for the researchers who claim that randomization is always illusory (apparently it is not).

To recapitulate this chapter, it might be concluded that the "no pain, no gain" proverb proves, once again, to hold true. Obviously, one can always use convenience samples but the results these samples yield, even though they are easy to collect and calculate, are always going to be flawed. Only careful and precise randomization (to be taken into consideration both at the stage of designing the experimental scheme as well as the stage of its implementation) ensures credible data, from which meaningful conclusions can be drawn. At this point, it would also make sense to remind the readers that this approach is essential, particularly in the case of an experimental study, where random assignment of subjects to particular groups is simply definitional.

8 The effect of the social context of studies

A psychologist–researcher never works in a vacuum. His work is affected by a vast number of variables increasing with the decision to take their experiment outside of the laboratory and conduct it in a natural environment. Yet, it took many years and a considerable pool of "strange results" produced by researchers in the course of their studies for this knowledge to become widespread. Similar to the discovery of penicillin, which was invented, to some degree, thanks to impurities and the somewhat slovenly nature of Alexander Fleming (Fleming et al., 1946), today's knowledge of interferences affecting the experimental process and resulting from conducting the experiment in a specific social context is more or less related to anecdotal descriptions of experiments that did not work out, as their authors failed to factor in a number of interfering variables.

The story of experiments conducted by Elton Mayo in the field of organizational psychology exemplifies just that. Mayo was a psychologist who was responsible for studying the effect of both external and internal factors on the quality and organization of work, as well as productivity, at various companies (Mayo, 1949; Mayo and Lombard, 1944). In the period between 1924 and 1932, he supervised a large-scale study of factors affecting the productivity of personnel in Hawthorne, Illinois, near Chicago. The experiments were conducted in a Western Electric Company plant that manufactured electrical elements for the Bell Telephone System – a telephony magnate of that time. The subjects were female workers, whose job was to assemble devices made of small components along an assembly line. Their task was to assemble a finished product composed of several dozen small parts (from 26 to 52, depending on the complexity of the task), fasten them together with snap fasteners or small rivets, and verify the correct functioning of the finished product. According to precise calculations (Whitehead, 1938), the task required 32 movements of the right hand and 31 movements of the left hand, with 21 of those movements being carried out simultaneously with both hands. According to the researchers, the job required good short-term memory, the ability to visually discriminate objects, nimble and tough fingers, as well as good eye–hand and hand–hand coordination. Mayo and his associates were interested in a pool of variables that could affect the productivity of personnel working in such conditions (mainly female workers to be precise, as the tested sample consisted predominantly of women).

Thus, the researchers started introducing various changes in many areas, affecting the quality of the work. For example, they tested an alternative remuneration system (one that was more focused on the individual effort of each particular worker), they tested the influence of a modified system of rest periods, various shift start and end times, the introduction of Friday and Saturday afternoons off, the effect of making Monday a day off, as well as many other combinations of these factors. Each time, they would also establish a

DOI: 10.4324/9781003092995-8

control group for which the working conditions remained unchanged and whose members were asked by their superiors to work normally, as they would if there were no experiment being conducted (Roethlisberger and Dickson, 2003). The researchers were regularly surprised by the yielded results. As they had expected, the productivity of the female workers, for the most part, increased constantly but this result was observed both in the experimental group, where organizational changes were introduced, as well as the control group. In other words, significant changes within subjects were observed (consisting of a comparison of results for the same individuals at certain intervals) but no significant changes between subjects were observed (occurring between individuals from the experimental and the control groups). Since the effect size was considerable and relatively constant (observed over the course of 24 quasi-experiments), it was deemed important from a methodological perspective and so a search for its sources began. The researchers concluded that the effect was caused by the fact that the subjects knew that they were participating in an experiment and that their performance was being assessed by an external body (this assumption was also supported by the fact that the increased productivity was maintained also after the completion of the main part of the experiment and after restoring the previous working conditions – the female workers knew that their productivity was still being monitored and thus the effect was still there). It should be noted that throughout the last decades, the Hawthorne studies were often criticized (Adair, 1984; Steele-Johnson, Beauregard, Hoover and Schmidt, 2000), mainly for their methodological shortcomings but also due to the fact that the final productivity of the female workers might have been affected by completely different variables. Richard Nisbett went as far as referring to the Hawthorne experiment as an anecdote rather than an actual study; he also added the following: "Once you've got the anecdote, you can throw away the data," (Kolata, 2007). Nevertheless, the term "Hawthorne effect" was coined to describe a situation where the very fact of being aware of taking part in an experiment has a significant impact on the yielded results, regardless of the fundamental stimuli that the members of the experimental groups are subjected to (or the lack of the same in control groups).

The experiments conducted by Martin T. Orne (1962), whose work also had a significant impact on our understanding of the processes taking place in the course of psychological studies (particularly in the course of field experiments), yielded data that was concurrent with the results obtained by Mayo et al. The studies by Orne, aside from being methodologically advanced and providing intriguing results, have one additional quality: they are unusually simple and elegant. In one of his studies, in order to investigate the level of obedience of subjects to evidently absurd instructions given by the experimenter, Orne instructed the subjects to perform the following task: they were given sheets filled with lines of random numbers and they were asked to add all adjacent numbers. In order to complete this process, 224 addition operations were required for a single sheet. The subjects were given a pile of 2,000 sheets (which made it impossible to perform the task in a reasonable time frame), the experimenter would say "Get to work, I will be back in a while," and then he would leave the room and wait for the subjects to give up. The researchers were certain that after some time, the subjects would surely give up and resign from continuing the experiment. Surprisingly, after five and a half hours it was the experimenter who had to give up and put an end to the experiment, while at that point, the subjects still soldiered on and kept adding the numbers and experiencing only a slightly reduced pace of work (most likely due to fatigue). In their search for nonsensical procedures, the researchers decided to introduce another element to the task consisting of adding the numbers written on the sheet, an element that would make the entire endeavor pointless. Next to a table with 2,000 sheets with numbers, there was another one with small cards. The instructions were modified, i.e., the subjects were told that once they completed the adding operations for each sheet, they must approach the other table, read the instructions written on one of the cards, execute the instructions, and then continue adding up the numbers on the next sheet. Each card had identical instructions written on it: *Now, tear the sheet you used to add up the numbers into at least 32 pieces. Then, take another sheet with numbers and continue adding them up as before. When you are done, take another card with instructions, read and execute them. Work as quickly, precisely and as best you can.* As it turned out, even when it was made obvious that the required task was completely pointless, it had little impact on the behavior of the subjects; they worked in a very similar fashion as before and the few hours-long sessions involving adding up and tearing the result sheets repeated over and over again continued to take place. What is more, according to Orne there were no visible signs of impatience, irritation, or hostility towards the experimenter (who, in one of the variations, was present in the room with the subjects). Clearly, the subjects must have gained some sense of the whole. The interview conducted after the experiment revealed that the subjects came up with a rather good explanation of the reasons for which they were expected to destroy the results of their work, namely, they believed that they were taking part in a study designed to test their persistence.

The conclusion that comes to one's mind after reading the descriptions of Orne's experiments is simple. The very participation in a study sends the following signal to its participants: "this is an experiment, weird things will be happening, you do your thing, there must be some sense in it." An analogy for the underlying mechanism is found in the following proverb, present in many cultures: "If you do not know what you are spanking your child for – do not worry. The child surely knows," and thus one could say: "Even if you do not know what your study is about – do not worry, the subject will come up with something."

Perhaps the most comprehensive illustration of this mechanism was the anecdotal field experiment conducted by Orne, where the researcher sent his students into the streets and told them to ask randomly selected pedestrians to do five push-ups. Some subjects were asked to perform the task in a standard manner with the following words: "Would you do five push-ups for me?" while others were first informed that they were participating in a small and very brief experiment with the same question afterward. While in the former case the most common response from the subjects was the question "what for," in the latter it was "where?"

The problem with this study, though, is its anecdotal nature. Orne describes it as an illustration for the phenomenon rather than an experiment, and he does not even provide any figures that would demonstrate differences between particular groups. Additionally, this quasi-experiment was carried out during the 1950s and 1960s, i.e., over 50 years ago. Therefore, it should be debated whether the passage of time and (more importantly) the slightly different role of a researcher (or, more broadly speaking, a scientist) in society would affect its results. After all, if the global gross enrollment ratio was approximately 9.74% in 1970 (tertiary: ISCED 5 and 6) and now the figure is over 38% (2019, World Bank data), this fact alone could justify a conservative hypothesis regarding the less monumental role of a researcher and scientist and, thus, a potentially reduced impact of the experimental situation alone on the behavior of the subjects. In order to clarify all these doubts, we decided to conduct a study that would replicate the anecdotal story by Martin Orne in a controlled fashion.

In the course of our study, a female experimenter was walking in the vicinity of dorms at Wrocław's technical university and asked randomly selected pedestrians (every fifth pedestrian walking alone who did not see the previous interaction) to do five push-ups. Four different phrases were used to request the push-ups (their order was previously randomized).

- The first version, as in the basic variation of the study conducted by Orne, included no explanation and was phrased as follows: "Would you do five push-ups for me?"
- The second version (with explanation) was phrased as follows: "I am a 5th-year psychology student at Wrocław University, would you agree to take part in a brief experiment and do five push-ups for me?"
- The third version (clearly referring to one's internal motivation regarding their own contribution to science) was phrased as follows: "I am a 5th-year psychology student at Wrocław University, would you agree to take part in a brief experiment? This way, you can contribute to science and help me collect data for analysis."
- The fourth version (referring to one's external motivation and an external reward) was phrased as follows: "Would you do five push-ups for me in exchange for a bar of chocolate?"

A total of 80 subjects were tested using the above procedure (20 in each variation). The yielded results demonstrated a clear difference among particular groups: in the group where the request for push-ups was not substantiated in any manner, the majority of subjects refused to comply, whereas providing justification (regardless of its nature) generally modified the behavior of the subjects and persuaded most of them to do the five push-ups. The chart in Figure 8.1 presents the exact number of refusals and consents in particular groups.

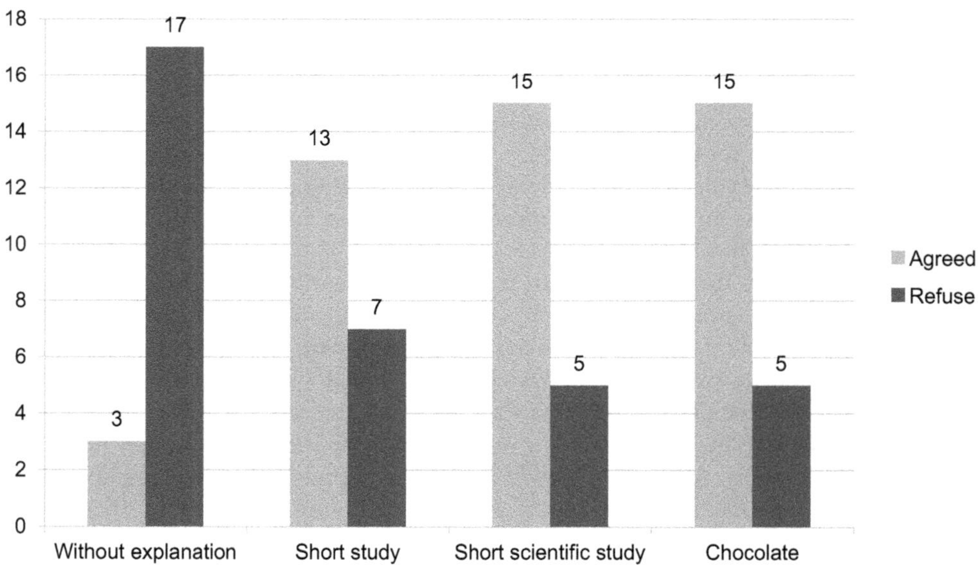

Figure 8.1 Number of individuals who agreed or refused to complete five push-ups depending on experimental conditions.

Source: prepared by the authors.

Our experiment demonstrated, rather convincingly, that (first) just being aware of the fact that a scientific study is being conducted affects the behavior of the subjects participating in the study and (second) the argument referring to one's contribution to science strengthens this effect even further. There is one more outcome demonstrated in the course of our study that should be noted: the role of external motivation and reward (the promise of a bar of chocolate). It should be also pointed out that subjects from the group where reference was made to one's contribution to science, without explaining how push-ups are relevant to that, very frequently agreed to comply with the request. This may call up certain associations with the classic experiment by Ellen Langer et al. (1978), described in Chapter 3 herein, on mindlessness and the effect of pseudo-justification on people's behavior. As a quick reminder, in the experiment conducted in a line to a copy machine, the experimenter's assistants first asked if they could use the copy machine by offering an actual explanation ("because I'm in a rush") or a mock one ("because I have to make copies"). Where photocopying five pages was involved, the level of compliance was similar in both groups. Ergo, perhaps even though the subjects can see no connection between doing push-ups and contributing to science, the very use of the phrase "I am conducting a study" serves as sufficient justification for the request made of them.

Another researcher who produced results that significantly modified our knowledge of the social world was Solomon Asch (1951). In his classic experiment, at least from the perspective of the history of psychology, Asch asked his subjects to assess the length of a standard line against three comparison lines. The results of his experiment (a high level of conformity to the group norm in the conditions of incorrect assessment of the lines) were justified by obedience to the created group norm. What is also interesting is that the researcher's own interpretation of the results was somewhat different from the prevailing one. According to Asch, it was notable that a considerable number of subjects did not succumb to the influence of the other members of the group at all and the majority of those who did only did so once or twice for every 12 trials (Asch, 1951). Yet today, this fact is often ignored, and what is emphasized is that (depending on particular experimental conditions) as many as three-quarters of subjects succumbed to what was clearly an incorrect assessment on the part of the group. The analyses of psychology textbooks conducted in 1990 (Friend, Rafferty, & Bramel, 1990) demonstrated that it was the prevailing interpretation of the results of the study (even though – let us emphasize – this is inconsistent with the intention of the author).

The conformity experiment by Asch is so well-known that describing it here would serve no purpose (besides, it was a laboratory experiment, and this book, at least in principle, does not deal with this type of experiment) but we feel that attention should be given to certain variations of this experiment, which were designed to test identical hypotheses only through the application of slightly different experimental procedures and in a somewhat modified social and historical context. First, these variations clearly illustrate how questions asked by researchers 50 years ago are still relevant today. Second, they demonstrate the extent to which the social context can impact study results.

In 1996, Ron Bond and Peter Smith of the University of Sussex published a voluminous meta-analysis on the results of the replications of studies by Solomon Asch conducted over the last decades (Bond & Smith, 1996). They analyzed 133 studies conducted in 17 countries worldwide. The following general conclusion can be drawn from their analyses: since the 1950s, the level of conformity in studies replicating the experiment of Solomon Asch has been systematically declining. For instance, replications conducted on British university students in the late 1970s (Perrin & Spencer, 1980) revealed a significantly lower level of conformity with the opinion of the group than that indicated in the original study by Asch. This resulted predominantly from a different historical and cultural context. As pointed out by the authors, in the 1970s and 1980s, British universities were characterized by a much stronger tendency to challenge the *status quo* and show one's individualism than American universities in the 1950s. One should also bear in mind that the 1950s was a time when the notorious House Committee on Un-American Activities was conducting its investigations in the United States (Griffith, 1987). In the course of its witch-hunt, the committee targeted alleged members of the Communist Party hidden among various influential social groups in the USA (with a particular focus on politicians, artists, scientists, and journalists). At the same time, the committee wanted to instill the idea that the United States were threatened by Soviet infiltration in public opinion. Perhaps this was the reason why uniformity of views and conformity with the prevailing opinion of the group seemed to be so highly valued at that time. According to the aforementioned Stephen Perrin and Christopher Spencer, the study by Asch should be treated as a "child of its era" rather than a "hard and replicable phenomenon," and even though there is some reason in that claim, it nevertheless should be regarded as somewhat exaggerated. A meta-analysis encompassing 97 studies conducted in the USA demonstrated that even though the level of conformity displayed by the subjects has been on the decline, it is still there.

A very interesting (laboratory) study based on the scheme applied by Asch was published in 2005 (Berns et al., 2005). The researchers, who focused on identifying neurobiological explanations for conformity, conducted analyses using MRI (magnetic resonance imaging) technology. Their intention was to examine the brain activity of subjects as they were performing intellectual tasks (and as they were experiencing pressure from their environment, similar to the case of the original study by Asch). Thirty-two individuals were asked to rotate three-dimensional figures in their minds and as they were doing so, they were shown two figures in different positions and were asked if they were identical or different. At the same time, the subjects could see the answers given by the other four participants (who were, in fact, confederates). The experiment's results revealed that in a situation of conflict between a decision made independently regarding geometrical similarity (and, e.g., the decision to claim the figures are identical) and apparently different decisions made by the other participants in the study (according to whom the figures are different), there is a visible activation of those areas of the brain that correspond to perception and not of those that correspond to making informed decisions. Generally speaking, the subjects gave incorrect answers in 41% of the cases. Interestingly, the level of conformity with the answers given by the group was higher than it was in the case where subjects could see the decision made by a computer (in other words, conforming to a computer's opinion was not as important for the subjects as conforming to the group of peers). The results obtained by Berns and his associates were interpreted as indirect proof that information coming in from our social surroundings affects our perception of reality (in other words, depending on the opinion of the group, we actually perceive geometrical figures differently and they actually appear to be more similar or more different from each other than they truly are).

Another contemporary attempt at utilizing the experimental scheme suggested by Asch was a study during which his hypotheses were put to the test using a field experiment. The attempts were made in Wrocław in an unpublished study report (Grzyb, 2005).

The study was conducted on one of the main streets of the city. Only male subjects participated in the experiment. Randomly selected pedestrians were approached by a man holding a microphone, who asked them the following question: "Excuse me, do you have children?" If the answer was "yes," the man proceeded as follows: "I'm on television, and we are shooting some material on parents. Would you please walk toward the man with the camera and I'll explain everything in a minute?" The subjects were randomly assigned to one of two groups: in the first group, they appeared solo, while in the second group, they were accompanied by four other individuals who were taking part in a TV opinion poll. Regardless of the group to which they were assigned, the experimenter (acting as the journalist) would say:

> We are shooting a program on whether the residents of Wrocław hit their children. In a minute, we will turn on the camera and record your answer to my question, but before we do that, let us try it first without the camera rolling, does that sound OK to you? Good, let us start. Do you ever hit your child?

In the group where the subjects appeared solo in front of the camera, over 90% of them declared that they had never hit their children, while the others admitted that they had spanked their children on one or two occasions. The experimenter continued as follows: "Good, let us record it now, the camera is rolling," at which point the subject's answer was recorded, which essentially did not change (with the exception of sometimes being embellished with such elaborative phrases as "It is my opinion that ..." or "I wholeheartedly believe that ...," etc.).

It was a very different situation in the group that included the confederates. In this group, when asked to express their opinion without the camera rolling, the confederates would consecutively respond in the following manner:

Assistant No. 1: You know how kids are, sometimes they misbehave so badly that you simply have to spank them but only when it is absolutely necessary. Explaining things to children does not always work. Sometimes you just do not have the patience.

Assistant No. 2: It depends, I basically try not to but you know, gravity is at work and sometimes you need to put the sense back from the child's butt up into his head where it belongs. Sometimes it is the only way.

Assistant No. 3: Well, I have to admit that, occasionally, I do. When I keep telling him not to do something over and over again, and he still does it, I can't help but give him a spank. You know how kids are, they don't listen and this is what happens.

Assistant No. 4: True enough, I won't pretend to be a better person than I actually am, my son got a licking on several occasions. For getting home after his curfew, for poor grades, because he fails to apply himself to his studies. He took a beating at least a few times.

After these statements, it was time for the actual subjects, all of which, with no exception, admitted that they had hit their child "on one or two occasions."

At that point the experimenter would say: "All right, now that we know your opinions, we need to record them. OK, the camera is ready, let's do it. Three, two, one – the camera is rolling. Do you ever hit your child?" The experimenter's assistants would reply as follows:

Assistant No. 1: Never. Absolutely not. You mustn't. A child is vulnerable and nothing good will come out of it, even a slight slap can do harm, so no, never.

Assistant No. 2: My blood boils when I hear about parents hitting their children. This is reprehensible. Children become traumatized and those who are beaten will beat their own children in the future. This makes no sense.

Assistant No. 3: I think my hand would wither away if I were to raise it against my child. You mustn't do that, I agree with the other men here, nothing good will come of it. You need to explain things to your child, talk to him so that he understands.

Assistant No. 4: I have never hit my child and I never will. You need to be there for your child, spend time together, you need to be demanding but also giving. If you do that, the problems will be solved and there is no need for using physical punishment, that is my opinion.

Obviously, in this experiment, the researchers were mainly interested in the actual subjects' reactions to such a change in the opinions expressed by the other respondents. While the conformity previously observed with the majority of the group could result from the subject's actual opinion on the topic of hitting children (possibly facilitated by the opinions expressed by the other respondents), here a change in the content of the statement was evident. The results demonstrated that also in this case the group's norm was stronger than one's personal opinion as a vast majority (70% of subjects) declared "in front of the camera" that they had never hit their children.

This attempt to conceptually replicate Asch's experiment demonstrates several interesting phenomena. First, it proves that Solomon Asch had great intuition as a researcher; the phenomenon he discovered remains active and scientifically resonant to this day, even when given scenery that has changed significantly (in terms of both time as well as surroundings). Second, with the field experiment designed and conducted in the manner described above, we can also learn about the importance of the impact of normative social influence outside of the laboratory, i.e. in a real environment. Finally, careful analysis tells us that it would be advisable to conduct another experiment (preferably a field experiment) where the potential impact of self-presentation in front of a camera is eliminated altogether. For it cannot be excluded that the effect yielded by the experiment resulted from a peculiar conflict between the "private I" and "public I" experienced by the subjects.

Another experiment of fundamental importance for the development of the field of social psychology, designed by Stanley Milgram (1974) and referred to many times in this book, has been criticized on numerous occasions. Obviously, the criticism was due to the ethical aspect of the experiment: making subjects do things that led to a clear and significant deterioration of their frames of mind. Nevertheless, the criticism that pertained to the very experimental scheme used by Milgram or, to be more precise, its ecological validity, was equally important. As a reminder, ecological validity, broadly speaking, refers to the degree to which results obtained through the execution of a given experimental procedure can be related to actual phenomena in a non-experimental situation. In order words, the term refers to the correspondence between a situation acted out for the purpose of the study and a real situation that, at least potentially, could happen to the subject. Numerous critical voices (Bem & Lord, 1979; Orne & Holland, 1968) pointed to this aspect of the procedure prepared by Milgram. Researchers argued that due to the aspect of ecological validity (or the lack of it, to be precise), it is difficult to accept Milgram's results as a reliable measurement of the level of obedience to an authority figure that could be observed in a real-life situation (and not one created in a laboratory). It was claimed, e.g., that the subjects participating in the study received two contradictory signals: the screams of the learner who pleaded for the experiment to end and the absolute calmness and coolness of the experimenter, who seemed to be completely ignoring the fact that there was somebody in the adjacent room who was clearly experiencing strong physical pain. According to the critics (Orne & Holland, 1968), this could make the subjects doubt the authenticity of the pain they were apparently inflicting on the person in the adjacent room. Even though the post-experimental interviews conducted by Milgram demonstrated that only 16 of 658 individuals participating in his studies claimed that the person "at the other end of the electrical wire" did not actually feel any pain, some of the critics remained unconvinced.

There was also another group of critical remarks that partly pertained to the doubts as regards the ethical aspect of the study but that predominantly touched on its ecological validity (Baumrind, 1964). It was argued (and quite rightly so) that "in normal conditions, ordinary people are not asked to electrocute other people." It could be therefore concluded that the ecological validity of Milgram's studies was low, as it would be difficult to imagine an ordinary, real-life situation where we are instructed to physically hurt another human being (and, if that was not enough, to repeat it 30 times, each time with increased intensity).

Wim Meeus and Quinten Raaijmakers (1995) of Utrecht University decided to modify Milgram's procedure and transfer it into the sphere of "corporate reasoning." Thirty-nine individuals, both men and women, aged 18 to 55, participated in their first experiment. The subjects, as in Milgram's experiment, were recruited through an ad and they were remunerated for their participation in the study (they received 40 Dutch guilders, which was equivalent to USD 13). They were informed that the University's Department of Psychology launched a procedure to select candidates for several positions and that passing a special test was a part of that procedure. Passing the test, comprising 32 questions, was crucial for getting hired, while failing the test was equivalent to immediate elimination from the further stages of the selection process. The subjects were to ask the test questions. They received a package including the test (one question on each page) and basic information on the candidate (with emphasis on his or her status as unemployed). The subjects were taken into a separate room equipped with a system that enabled audio communication with the candidate (who was actually a confederate). As the experimenter was seating the subject down at his or her station, he would add: "This isn't exactly a rule, but the Department of Psychology uses the candidate selection procedure to investigate the relationship between stress level and the test results. The main question is this: does stress have a positive or a negative impact on one's performance, and if so, to what extent?" Additionally, the experimenter informed the subject that the candidate did not know about this aspect of the test; he also showed the subject a special list of negative comments (15 comments in total), which were to be communicated to the candidate at particular points during the test. Exemplary negative comments: "Your answer to question No. 13 was completely incorrect"; "If you keep on answering like this you are certainly going to fail"; "According to this test, the job you are applying for is too big a challenge for you"; "According to this test, it would be advisable for you to apply for a lower-level position." The subject could also monitor the level of stress experienced by the candidate on a special screen, which indicated the level of tension both verbally (from "normal" to "strong") and in numerical format (from 15 to 65).

The subject was informed that conducting this "test within a test" involved a certain risk for the candidate, as his or her answers may be affected by stress and consequently he or she may not get hired. Therefore, the experimenter explained, we must first ask for the candidate's permission. The experimenter would connect with the candidate and, in the course of a brief conversation, he would ask the candidate if he or she agreed to participate in a study on stress, but he would lie to the candidate twice in the course of the conversation (which the actual subject witnessed). First, the experimenter lied when he did not inform the candidate about the negative comments he or she would hear from the person conducting the job interview (he only told the candidate that he or she would be connected to instruments monitoring his or her levels of tension and stress). Second, the candidate was explicitly told that the study would not affect his or her chances of getting the job he or she was applying for (which was clearly inconsistent with what the "recruiter" had said earlier). Obviously, the candidate, i.e., the confederate, agreed to participate in the study.

As in the original experiment conducted by Milgram, the subject was instructed to escalate the negative comments throughout the study, while the "candidate" was instructed to object to the comments made by the subject (initially, he or she would claim that the answers were correct, and he or she would start to mutter incomprehensibly, and from comment No. 10 onwards, he or she would openly demand that the comments should stop). Subjects who wanted to withdraw from the procedure, similarly to Milgram's experiment, were encouraged by the experimenter to continue the experiment.

In the control group, subjects were told that the level of stress experienced by the candidates would be measured and that they could, if they wanted, induce it with negative comments (they received the same list as the subjects from the experimental group but they were not made to read out the comments included in the list).

The results of the experiment essentially corresponded with those obtained by Milgram in his studies. In the experimental group, 91.7% of subjects were completely obedient and completed the experiment by delivering all negative feedback provided in the list. None of the subjects from the control group did so (the average for the number assigned to the comment the subjects stopped at was 6.75).

Meeus and Raaijmakers also conducted other variations of this study (all of which were based on one of the procedures previously used by Milgram). For instance, they conducted a variation where the experimenter would leave the room and would not supervise the course of the study (the percentage of completely obedient subjects was 36.4% and the average for the number assigned to the comment at which point participation was terminated was 10.17). This effect also corresponded, essentially, with the results obtained 30 years earlier by Milgram.

The studies described in this chapter demonstrate that, in some cases, taking into account a change in the social context of a study brings about a fundamental change in its results (e.g., in the case of certain replications of studies by Solomon Asch), while in other cases, the same only confirms that the investigated phenomenon can also be analyzed by using a modified procedure and within a different context. Nevertheless, it is clearly evident that what affects the behavior of subjects in the course of an experiment is their very awareness of taking part in a study (knowing that their behavior is being observed and assessed). This is yet another argument in the discussion on the topic of conducting psychological studies related to withholding the objective from the subjects, or even the very fact that an experiment is being conducted.

9 Imprecise procedures as a source of error variance

Authors of empirical scientific articles offer descriptions of the course of their experiments. In most cases, such descriptions are included in a separate, dedicated section of the article titled "Method" or "Procedure." Essentially, the level of detail of the text in this section should be enough as to enable another researcher to independently replicate the described study, should they desire to do so. However, due to the limit on the number of words imposed by many journals, among other things, in many cases this is simply impossible. As it turns out, it is often enough the case that the outcomes of a study (particularly of a field experiment) are affected by details, and even minute deviations from the previously adopted scripts may entail severe consequences for the produced results. In this chapter, we will examine examples of such cases. First, by discussing studies where very slight changes in procedure prompted heavy modifications of the results, and second, by taking a closer look at the experimenters' assistants as individuals, as the overall result of the experiments depends on their own reliability and diligence. Apparently, minor lapses on their part can also completely change the outcome of a study.

Appropriate and precise training of experimenters' assistants is a crucial element of any field study. This is important, as it is not always possible to fully control the individual (most likely an undergraduate or a Ph.D. student) conducting a study in a natural environment. The importance of exercising such control is demonstrated by our frequent (often difficult) personal experience with individuals conducting experiments in an unreliable fashion. At this point it should be emphasized that such unreliability was not always due to ill will on the part of the students or hired personnel; in most cases it simply resulted from not paying enough attention to details such as the order of words in the formulated request, initiating the interaction precisely as instructed, or the more or less unnatural feel of the role-play (depending on the talent for acting a given person may have). In order to check how requests were actually formulated, we verified their wording by recording the utterances with a microphone hidden in the clothes worn by the experimenters. Obviously, the experimenters were aware of it, since we either told them that we needed the recordings to analyze the number of words uttered by the subjects or that we were measuring the time it took to formulate the request (to verify if there is a connection between this factor and the level of compliance displayed by the subjects). This verification was introduced, *inter alia*, in the studies designed to test the effectiveness of two social influence techniques: the involvement-in-a-dialogue technique (Dolinski, Nawrat, & Rudak, 2001; Dolinski, Grzyb, Olejnik, Prusakowski, & Urban, 2005), and the even-a-penny-will-help technique (Cialdini & Schroeder, 1976).

DOI: 10.4324/9781003092995-9

In the study in question, a female experimenter pretended to be a volunteer collecting donations for an animal charity (to be used for purchasing dog food). Subjects were randomly assigned to one of the following four experimental conditions:

1 Monologue: Good day, I'm a volunteer for the "Mam Głos" Animal Support Association. I'm collecting funds for dog food. Would you support us with a donation?
2 Experimental Group 1 (monologue combined with the even-a-penny-will-help technique): Good day, I'm a volunteer for the "Mam Głos" Animal Support Association. I'm collecting funds for dog food. Would you support us with a donation? Even a penny will help.
3 Experimental Group 2 (dialogue):

   - o The experimenter: Good day, do you like animals?
   - o The subject: (responds)
   - o The experimenter: (I'm glad to hear that/That is a pity, depending on the response). I'm a volunteer for the "Mam Głos" Animal Support Association. I'm collecting funds for dog food. Would you support us with a donation?

4 Experimental group 3 (dialogue combined with the even-a-penny-will-help technique):

   - o The experimenter: Good day, do you like animals?
   - o The subject: (responds)
   - o The experimenter: (I'm glad to hear that/That is a pity, depending on the response). I'm a volunteer for the "Mam Głos" Animal Support Association. I'm collecting funds for dog food. Would you support us with a donation? Even a penny will help.

A total of 120 individuals participated in the study, 40 in each group, and half of the subjects were women. The female experimenter was told that the recordings would be used to measure the length of the interaction between her and the subjects (to test the differences between particular groups).

Essentially, the results confirmed the previously adopted hypotheses and both techniques proved to increase compliance (measured both as one's willingness to support the initiative and the average donation amount). Table 9.1 illustrates the percentage of compliance (the percentage of individuals who donated money) as well as the average donation amounts by group.

There are several problems evident in this study that should be pointed out. First, there is a correlation between the average donation amount and the standard deviation of the outcomes, which, in a way, makes it difficult to interpret the results of the variance analysis. Even though the directions of interrelationship are essentially confirmed (the average amount in the dialogue conditions is higher than in the monologue conditions, and the average amount in the even-a-penny-will-help group is higher than that in the control group), the measured differences fail to reach the level of statistical significance expected in social sciences.

Let us not forget, though, that what we mainly wanted to check was the degree to which the experimenter would adhere to the instructions she received. A detailed analysis of the course of the interactions revealed numerous deviations from the instructions provided. Sometimes additional words were introduced (e.g., the interaction was initiated by

Table 9.1 Number of individuals who donated money and average donation amounts

Involvement in a dialogue	*Even a penny will help*	*Average amount [PLN]*	*Standard deviation*	*Number of individuals who donated money*
No	No	3.5000	1.64317	6
	Yes	1.4714	0.57302	14
	Total	2.0800	1.35825	20
Yes	No	2.7692	1.30664	13
	Yes	4.0833	2.76495	24
	Total	3.6216	2.42030	37
Total	No	3.0000	1.41774	19
	Yes	3.1211	2.54910	38
	Total	3.0807	2.22321	57

Source: prepared by the authors.

the phrase "Excuse me" or the phrase "I have one question" was added in the dialogue conditions), while in other cases onomatopoeias affirming the views presented by the subject (in the dialogue conditions) were used. Most importantly, we failed to establish a specific pattern of occurrence for these additional elements representing deviations from the previously prepared script.

Therefore, one can claim that the main outcome of the conducted experiment was demonstrating the degree to which lack of strict control over the actual conduct of the experimenters in the course of a study can disturb the results produced.

In another experiment, we investigated how a small change in the way of asking for a donation for the benefit of an NGO affects the chances of receiving money. For many charitable organizations, donations collected in the course of public fundraising events (on the street, at a supermarket, at cultural event venues) constitute a vital source of funding. Whether or not such a fundraiser is successful depends on a number of factors. One of them is the effectiveness of the person asking for donations or, to be more precise, their ability to delicately overcome the resistance experienced by the person being asked for the money.

For several years now, the literature on social influence has been producing an increasing number of works focused on making people compliant by reducing their resistance to a request. The Alpha and Omega strategies described by Eric Knowles and Jay Linn (2004a, 2004b) has changed the perception of social influence processes, particularly in the context of charity-oriented activities. Costs of giving and not giving help had already been discussed (e.g., Piliavin, Piliavin, & Rodin, 1975; Piliavin, Rodin, & Piliavin, 1969) but it was the introduction of the notions of the Alpha and Omega strategies that changed the perception of social influence processes.

Eric Knowles refers to the application of the Omega strategy as concentrating on reducing the resistance to granting a request. According to Knowles, there are many ways to reduce said resistance, e.g., through verbal anticipation. In their study, Elyria Kemp and Elizabeth Creyer (2007) encouraged students to go to the concert hall by anticipating their resistance through the use of the following phrase in their advertisement: "You might think that the symphony is dull and boring …." As it turns out, this phrase increases the likelihood of students participating in the classes when compared to other groups for which this phrase was not included. In another example, attempts were made to make students believe that an increase in tuition translates to higher quality of classes. When arguments to this effect were preceded with the phrase "I know you won't want to agree with this, but ..." the average approval for the presented arguments increased significantly.

According to Vera Corfield (1969), each situation where social influence is being exerted by a real person increases the feeling of insecurity and suspicion in the subject. After all, it is almost on a daily basis that we have to deal with situations where granting a seemingly trifling request leads to escalation and then being faced with the choice to either refuse (and perhaps feel bad about it) or grant a request, which we find difficult and inconvenient. Social influence practitioners make wide use of the knowledge of techniques used to influence one's behavior with a particular focus on the foot-in-the-door technique (Freedman & Fraser, 1966). As a reminder: according to this technique, in order to increase the probability of a subject granting a difficult request, one should first ask for a small favor. Even though this technique proved to be effective according to a number of psychological studies (e.g., Dillard, 1990; Schwarzwald, Bizman, & Raz, 1983), other studies demonstrated that it was not effective or that its effectiveness was related to other factors (Burger & Guadagno, 2003; Scott, 1977). One reason for this method being effective may be the experience of a large number of people who know that granting an easy request may prompt the asker to formulate another, much more demanding, request. Thus, it should come as no surprise that virtually all languages of the world feature proverbs and bywords illustrating similar situations. For instance, in the USA and in Great Britain, people say: "give someone an inch and they'll take a mile," while in Germany or in Poland the proverb is: "give someone a finger, and they'll take the whole hand."

Numerous studies that we have conducted in the paradigm of a field experiment demonstrate a certain trend among the reactions of individuals inquired on the street. Actually, it has become increasingly difficult to even initiate a study there, as it already is to attempt to formulate any request to which potential subjects could respond with "no, I don't want to, thank you, goodbye." It seems that such a reaction could result from the anticipated escalation of the initial request and, by the same token, the desire to terminate the interaction as quickly as possible (and also, undoubtedly, from the fact that there is an increasing number of all sorts of pesterers on the streets).

Therefore, it appears that ensuring a potential subject who is already in the initial stage of the interaction that no such escalation will take place may be an effective tool for reducing their resistance to engaging in conversation. This phenomenon would also correspond with the notion of the Omega strategies proposed by Knowles. The mechanism could be as follows: upon hearing a small request, the subject may suspect that it only serves as an introduction to the underlying, and more substantial, request. As a result, the subject becomes reluctant to grant the first, small request. Therefore, if the subject learns, already at the onset of the interaction, that there will be no escalation and that the small request will be the only one made, they will be more willing to grant it. This would be consistent with the Omega strategies, as described by Knowles, designed to reduce one's resistance to undertaking an action, particularly the so-called anticipation of resistance. A declaration of no further escalation could take the form of the following phrase being added after the actual request: "This is the only request I am going to make."

The study (Grzyb & Dolinski, 2017) was conducted by two female volunteers, who were 20-year-old undergraduates. For the duration of the experiment, they became associates of the "Fields of Hope" campaign for the benefit of juvenile hospice patients. All collected donations were transferred for the benefit of the campaign and any activities were undertaken with the approval and full knowledge of the fundraising foundation.

The subjects were randomly selected from among pedestrians at the market square in Wrocław and in a large square by a shopping mall. The sex and estimated age of the subjects were controlled. The selected subjects were randomly assigned to one of the two groups: the experimental group (where the phrase "this is the only request I am going to make" followed the request) and the control group (where a standard donation request was made). In both groups, the request was formulated as follows:
The control group:

> Good day, I'm collecting funds for the "Fields of Hope" Hospice Foundation to improve its operations. Would you join our cause and make a donation?

The experimental group:

> Good day, I'm collecting funds for the "Fields of Hope" Hospice Foundation to improve its operations. Would you join our cause and make a donation? This is the only request I am going to make.

If the subject decided to make a donation, the volunteer would move the money box closer to them and once the money had been put into the box, the volunteer would thank them and wish them a good day. In the event the subject refused to make a donation, the volunteer would also thank them and wish them a good day.

A total of 106 individuals participated in the study (59 were women). The subjects were assigned to one of three age ranges (up to 25, 26–45, and over 45). The sex of the subjects had no influence on their willingness to make a donation. It was a somewhat different story with their age: even though the connection was not statistically significant, it was observed that donations were made most frequently by subjects from the "over 45" age group.

Donations were made considerably more frequently by individuals when the request was followed by "this is the only request I am going to make" (55%) compared to the subjects from the control group (15%).

As demonstrated by the experiment, simply adding the phrase "this is the only request I am going to make" (which, importantly, is rather natural and feels almost necessary) caused a considerable increase in the number of people who agreed to grant it. It should be noted though that the study in question did not factor in a measurement of compliance (the dependent variable dichotomous in nature, as the person either agreed or did not agree to help). An ideal solution would be a study designed in such a way as to verify compliance using a quantitative variable, e.g., the amount donated by each person. As we were unable, due to technical reasons, to plan the experiment in such a way as to precisely verify the amount of the donations made by the subjects (the charity we were working with in the course of the experiment was using their own money boxes, which prevented the installation of the type of coin-counting mechanism described in upcoming sections of this book), we decided to modify the experimental scheme. On the one hand, we wanted to elicit information from the subject just on their willingness to help, while on the other hand we wanted information on the subject's willingness to make a sacrifice. In other words, we wanted our measurements to be taken not only at the level of the nominal variable but also at the level of the quantitative variable. For this purpose, we entered into cooperation with an organization that supports inmates by sending them Christmas cards, and used the reaction to a request for help addressing and writing out these cards as the main dependent variable in our study.

The study was conducted by a female experimenter aged 21. In two city parks, randomly selected individuals were approached and (in experimental conditions) exposed to the following request:

> Good day, could I ask you for just one favor? I'm a volunteer for this organization that helps inmates re-enter society. Among other things, we send them postcards. You know, so that they do not feel completely alone. Would you help me with that? I need you to take some of the postcards to write them out; the text is already prepared, you only need to copy it. How many postcards would you be able to write out? This is the only request I am going to make.

In the control conditions, the request was formulated without information on the fact that it would be the only request made. Having learned the decision made by the subjects, the experimenter would record their declaration and would inform them that they, in fact, had participated in a psychological experiment. Those subjects who declared their willingness to write out postcards received a leaflet with the email address of an actual charity, which they were told to contact in order to receive addresses of particular inmates. This was the end of the interaction.

A total of 80 individuals were tested under two sets (experimental and control) of conditions. Half of the participants in each group were women.

First, it was verified whether the use of the this-is-the-only-request-I-am-going-to-make technique alone changed the decision to help or not. The effect was statistically significant. The experiment also tested the influence of the sex of the subjects on their decision to grant the request. Even though women were somewhat more willing to help, the effect was not statistically significant. Next, we examined how the assignment to the experimental group as well as the sex of the subjects affected the size of the help declared (the number of postcards the subjects declared they would write out). A two-way analysis of variance was used. Even though the effect of belonging to a particular experimental group on the size of the help declared did not achieve the conventional level of significance expected in social sciences, it was very close to this level (at $p = 0.057$). Both the main effect of sex as well as the interaction between sex and belonging to a particular experimental group were statistically insignificant. Table 9.2 presents the reactions of the subjects, as well as the average number of postcards they declared they would write out.

Table 9.2 Reaction to the request and average size of help declared (number of postcards), depending on group and sex

Condition	*Sex*	*Average*	*SD*	*Refusal*	*Consent*	*No.*
The only request	Female	1.75	2.653	10	10	20
	Male	2.65	5.143	12	8	20
	Total	2.20	4.065	22	18	40
Control	Female	1.25	3.093	16	4	20
	Male	0.30	0.733	16	4	20
	Total	0.78	2.270	32	8	40
Total	Female	1.50	2.855	26	14	40
	Male	1.48	3.816	28	12	40
	Total	1.49	3.349	54	26	80

Source: prepared by the authors.

The outcomes of the second experiment confirmed the results obtained in the course of the first one. The second experiment also demonstrated that adding the phrase "this is the only request I am going to make" makes it more probable for the subject to agree to help. Additionally, the experiment also corroborated the hypothesis regarding the increased help the subjects agreed to give in "the only request" condition (a larger number of Christmas postcards that subjects declared they would write out). Even though the difference was below the level expected in social sciences, it was very close to it, while the effect size was at least average.

The phrase used to inform the subjects that the request they were about to hear was going to be the only one that would be made was intentionally introduced in the above described studies (we expected the phrase to affect the reactions of the subjects). Let us note though that in many cases, the individual conducting an experiment can utter this or a similar phrase spontaneously, without even realizing that its presence might be of fundamental significance! Undoubtedly, other phrases that seem completely unimportant can also substantially modify subjects' behavior.

What is more, one should bear in mind that in the case of the two experiments mentioned above, we were dealing exclusively with controlling verbal communication, while non-verbal communication was ignored altogether. Numerous studies (Burgoon, Guerrero, & Floyd, 2016; Knapp, Hall, & Horgan, 2013; Siegman & Feldstein, 2014) demonstrate the importance of gestures, both mimic and pantomimic, for interpersonal communication. They turn out to be particularly important from the perspective of the rules of social influence. For we cannot be entirely certain that the female experimenter did not perhaps touch the subjects' shoulders, more or less consciously. However, this gesture, as Nicolas Guéguen and Jacques Fischer-Lokou (2002) demonstrated in the course of a very interesting experiment, proves to be an effective social influence tool. The researchers observed that previous analyses tested the effect of a gentle touch to the subjects' body (usually their shoulder) on their compliance, being understood as granting rather small requests. For instance, Jacob Hornik (1987) demonstrated how touch can increase the chance of eliciting a pedestrian's consent to complete several items on a survey. Other researchers (Lynn, Le, & Sherwyn, 1998), in the course of an experiment positioned somewhere on the border between social psychology and marketing, examined the effect of a waiter's touch on the amount of the tip he receives (evidently, touch was an effective tool for increasing tip amounts). As noted by Guéguen and Fischer-Lokou, these were rather trifling requests that, as a matter of fact, are granted semi-automatically, or without a second thought. These two French researchers wanted to know how touching the forearm of a subject could affect their willingness to help, when the request was actually substantial.

They decided to use an animal, a dog to be precise, for the purpose of their experiment. The researchers did not specify its breed (perhaps it was a mixed breed), yet, based on the description provided, one can assume that it resembled a large Labrador-type dog: it weighed approximately 40 kg and was visibly hyperactive, as it constantly wanted to play and was always trying to break the leash while occasionally and unexpectedly jumping up on passers-by. The experimenter's assistants (a woman and a man, both approximately age 20 and wearing jeans, trainers, and shirts) would stand (in half of the conditions it was the man and in the other half, the woman) on a street, in a city with 100,000 residents in France, and they would ask randomly selected pedestrians for a favor. They would explain to the subjects that they needed to purchase something from the pharmacy across the street but unfortunately no dogs were allowed in the pharmacy. Therefore, they asked the pedestrians to watch their dog for 10 minutes so that they could go to the pharmacy and buy the items they needed. In half of the cases, they formulated their request while simultaneously touching (for at least one second) the subject's shoulder. If the pedestrian agreed to grant the request, the experimenter's assistant would walk across the street, enter the pharmacy, and then return to conduct debriefing, i.e., to tell the subject that they had taken part in a study.

The experiment was conducted on a group of 120 individuals (60 in each group) and 67 of them were women. The results demonstrated that the touch modified the subjects' behavior. While in the "no touch" group, 21 out of 60 individuals agreed to watch the frisky dog (35%), the figure was 33 (55%) in the "touched" group. The observed effect was statistically significant.

By the same token, it is evident that even small gestures, which are considered deviations from the instructions and sometimes go unnoticed by researchers (and which are sometimes performed unintentionally by the experimenters' assistants) can have real influence on the outcomes of field studies. Such gestures might include the aforementioned touch, tone of voice, style of speaking, looking at the face of the individual asked for a favor, and a number of other variables affecting the outcomes. At the same time, descriptions of the method found in journals do not always allow us to clearly picture the very course of the study. Even in the case of the above-quoted article by Guéguen and Fischer-Lokou, we have no certainty as to what breed of dog was used in the study. The description fits the suggested Labrador-type dog but a cheerful Doberman is also a possibility. It does not take a cynology expert to know that the social perception of both of these breeds is very different. A few years back, we conducted an experiment during the course of which we asked people to express their judgment about the individuals presented to them in pictures. For this purpose, we used the Katz and Braly (1933) adjective scale where, as far as the pictures were concerned, the manipulation was exerted by the presence of a dog and its breed. Some pictures presented only the individuals to be assessed, while other pictures featured an individual with a dog: either a Labrador or an AmStaff (American Staffordshire Terrier, a breed considered dangerous). It turned out that the company of a dog affected the assessment of the person in the picture to a considerable extent; the description ranged from rather positive (with the Labrador) to rather negative (with the AmStaff).

It should be noted that the above analyses lead us to the conclusion that in reality, particularly in the case of field experiments, we should be able to fully control the course of a study, preferably through the use of audio–video recording equipment capable of capturing the interactions. The technical and legal aspects of this approach will be discussed in Chapter 15 but at this point let us focus on the following question: how to prepare the recording?

It should be pointed out that with the so-called Internet revolution and the shift towards the Internet-based publication system on the part of a considerable share (if not virtually all) of world-class psychology journals, entirely new possibilities have emerged for supplementing standard research reports with additional materials, such as raw data from the study and additional instructions, but also – more importantly from the perspective of our considerations – materials documenting our experiments.

Interestingly, numerous journals, both traditional and open-access journals, promote this approach (e.g., *Social Psychological and Personality Science*, *Frontiers in Psychology*, *PLOS ONE*) by suggesting that certain parts should be moved from the main body of the text to the "Supplementary Materials" section or that the text should be simply supplemented with certain details (e.g., pictures illustrating the course of the experiment). What is more, in the process of submitting their text to a journal, authors are asked if certain data (e.g., the elements described above) can be made accessible through open-access repositories, so that other researchers might use them. In the event a researcher does not accept this choice, for any reason, they may opt for another solution: providing a declaration stating that said materials would be rendered available to interested parties upon request. However, it is important to note that researchers must also declare that this shall not infringe any personal interests of, e.g., the individuals in the pictures. Apart from the obvious advantage, i.e., accessibility to full documentation and the ability to identify alternative explanations for the obtained results (or the lack of such results), enjoyed by those who wish to replicate particular studies, an additional benefit resulting from this solution is the certainty that the researcher is not hiding anything while presenting his results.

Submitting such detailed data appears to be a particularly recommendable procedure, especially in the wake of the infamous scandal featuring Diederik Stapel, which we discuss in more detail in Chapter 12.

10 Variables that are (usually) omitted in the experimental procedure and that affect the outcomes of the experiment

There is no doubt that a large number of factors, as well as their interactions, affect one's behavior at a given point in time and at a given location within the social and physical sphere. At the same time, a researcher conducting an experiment focuses on merely a few of such factors and sometimes on just a single one. This results simply from the logic behind the plan for the experiment as well as the limitations in terms of conducting a given study. It is also worth noting that the researcher has no control over many of the variables that affect the subject's behavior. Obviously, some of them, at least potentially, are measurable and their results could be factored in during the final analyses but a significant portion (one may even venture to say that a majority) of these variables, due to technical, ethical as well as methodological reasons, cannot be measured. The technical reasons include such situations where we are unable to measure a variable since, e.g., we might not have suitable tools at our disposal. For example, in studies of the so-called culture of honor (Nisbett & Cohen, 1996), one might expect that the concentration of testosterone in one's blood might be a factor affecting the behavior of male subjects but, due to the lack of appropriate medical and laboratory facilities, we are unable to verify this. As far as the ethical reasons are concerned, there is a whole category of questions (or, to speak more broadly, measurements) that might make the subjects feel uncomfortable. One can easily imagine studies from various areas of psychology, in the case of which the current level of one's satisfaction derived from their sex life or (in the sphere of evolutionary psychology) the current phase of the menstrual cycle in women would be the variable that, at least theoretically, affects the outcome of the study. Nevertheless, in many cases such questions cannot be asked precisely for the sake of the mental well-being of the subject or respecting the researcher–subject relation standards. The final area includes methodological reasons. In some cases, the very measurement of a variable in subjects may interfere with the internal accuracy of the study (e.g., in social influence studies), the very fact that we ask a subject to answer a question might make this subject, as expected in line with the foot-in-the-door technique, more willing to grant the following request, i.e., the one being a fundamental part of the experiment (Freedman & Fraser, 1966).

From the perspective of this book, it must be also emphasized that a field experiment should be considered a special type of a psychological study, where the spectrum of interfering variables is particularly broad. In this chapter, we will examine a number of variables that, even though they seem to be of minor importance and not indicative of serious problems from the perspective of the measurement of the dependent variable, prove to be significant modifiers of outcomes of field experiments.

As indicated by some research, even subtle details of the adopted scheme can affect the results of an experiment, even those that the vast majority of researchers would not even

DOI: 10.4324/9781003092995-10

consider controlling. This is exemplified by the experiments carried out by Daniele Marzoli and Luca Tommasi (2009) in Italian discos. The researchers ventured a very interesting project. As scientists focused on the study of a strictly physiological aspect of human existence (to be precise, the asymmetry of the cerebral hemispheres), they decided to illustrate this phenomenon, not with the typical tool, i.e., functional magnetic resonance imaging carried out in strictly controlled laboratory conditions, but with a field experiment. They devised a series of innovative experiments through which they intended to investigate the reactions of subjects to a request (e.g., for a cigarette) directed into their ears. As their focus was on the above-mentioned asymmetry of the cerebral hemispheres, the researchers formulated a hypothesis according to which a request uttered in somebody's right ear would be more effective than the same request directed to somebody's left ear (due to the general preference to use one's right ear when listening to verbal stimuli) (Bryden, 1988; Kimura, 1961). Yet, the researchers faced an interesting problem methodologically speaking, namely: how could they plan the experiment in such a way as to make sure the request is directed to a particular ear of the recipient in a natural way, i.e., without causing confusion on the part of the subject? Marzoli and Tommasi decided to conduct their experiment in noisy locations, where the only way to communicate effectively is to speak directly to the other person's ear: at discos.

First, the researchers observed regulars at discos located in Pescara and Chieti, paying particular attention to the following three aspects: the sex of the speaker, the sex of the recipient and the ear (left or right) to which the message was being directed to. The results demonstrated a clear preference for the right ear: 72% of all messages were directed to the recipients' right ears. This preference was clearly present in all communication configurations (a male speaker communicating his message to a woman, a female speaker communicating her message to a man, etc.) with the exception of a situation where a male speaker communicated his message to another man. In this case, the effect was not observed (to be more precise, there was a certain dominance of the messages directed to recipients' right ears but as there were too few of such conversations, they were not considered statistically significant).

In the following stage of their research program, Marzoli and Tommasi proceeded with the experimental part of the study. For the purpose of the experiment, they hired a young girl whose task was to approach randomly selected women and men at the same discos and mutter an incomprehensible utterance while standing in front of the recipient. When the recipient leaned forward and moved their ear closer to the speaker (in order to be able to hear what the confederate was saying), the girl would ask for a cigarette. Having received an answer to her question, the confederate would walk away and record the sex, the ear (left or right), as well as the decision of the subject. The results, yet again, demonstrated a preference for using one's right ear (in 58% of the subjects) but the expected level of statistical significance was achieved only in the case of female subjects. No connection was found between the "choice of ear" and the chance of receiving a cigarette.

In the third study of the series (also conducted at a disco, yet this time only in Pescara), the experimenters' assistant approached randomly selected individuals (88 women and 88 men) and, while randomly assigning them to particular experimental conditions, asked them for a cigarette by directing her request to their right or their left ear. The results (unsurprisingly) demonstrated that the girl was given a cigarette more frequently by men than by women (even though this effect was not statistically significant). More interestingly, a distinctive "ear effect" was observed: the assistant's request was granted significantly more often when directed to the interlocutor's right ear. The effect was statistically significant both in the case of male and female subjects. When women were asked for a cigarette, the request was granted in 31.8% of the cases if directed to the right ear and in 13.6% of the cases if directed to the left ear; the figures were 45.4% and 25% for men, respectively.

Obviously, the study is interesting predominantly for individuals concerned with the physiological aspect of the nature of our functioning but it also demonstrates a very important methodological problem: the role of seemingly unimportant variables in field studies. For it should be noted that the dependent variable used by Marzoli and Tommasi is, in a way, "a natural" dependent variable in studies conducted in the area of broadly defined social influence. At the same time, no information is found in descriptions of experiments in this branch of psychology on the ear to which the request was directed even though, as the above-mentioned experiments prove, this may affect the outcome of the study.

The precise location where the experiment is being conducted is yet another variable that, for the most part, is omitted in descriptions of experimental studies conducted in natural conditions. When referring to the location of their experiments, researchers usually state "on one of the town's streets," "in one of the squares," or "in a park." As it turns out, the very site where the study is being conducted can have a major impact on the results.

Another factor that is relatively infrequently described in the "Method" or the "Procedure" section is the clothing worn by the experimenters or their assistants acting as subjects. In most cases, the description is limited to "assistants of the experimenters/confederates were wearing casual clothes," while there may be a significant difference between the "casual clothes" of a university student and those of an employee of an exclusive store offering high-quality cosmetics. In order to investigate the effect this difference might have on study results, we conducted an experiment designed to verify the impact of the clothes worn by a female experimenter and of the props she was holding in her hand on the willingness to give help as declared by the subjects.

The experiment was conducted in an underpass close to a major public transport passenger transfer center in Wrocław. The subjects included randomly selected pedestrians (every fifth adult who did not witness the preceding interaction). The subjects were assigned to particular experimental groups based on the previously established randomization procedure.

In each variation of the study, a young woman, aged 24, approached a pedestrian using the underpass and expressed the following (in each case identical) request: "Excuse me, would you please buy me a tram ticket?"

Independent variables included the clothes worn by the experimenter and the payment card she was holding in her hand (to suggest an earlier attempt to purchase a ticket with the card; each interaction took place within approximately two meters of a ticket machine).

In the first variation of the experiment, the subject was approached by the experimenter wearing casual clothes (i.e., a black coat, blue jeans, a pair of black sneakers, and a rucksack). In another variation, the woman was more dressed up (she was wearing a black jacket, a white shirt, a short, black skirt, heels, and a black purse). It should be noted that this outfit was also categorized as "casual but more so for an employee of a boutique or customer service point. In two other variations of the experiment, the researcher was wearing more or less formal clothes and was holding a payment card in her hand.

When the given subject declared their willingness to help (i.e., to purchase a ticket) or refused to help, the experimenter responded by saying that she just found a valid ticket in her pocket and thanked them for the help.

Two independent observers assisted in the study. Their task was to assess the age of the subjects and pay attention to the occurrence of any other factors (interfering variables that could affect the subjects' willingness to help the experimenter). The assistants were positioned in such a manner as to remain hidden from the pedestrians, so that they would not become suspicious and have, at the same time, a good overview of the interaction.

In total, 160 individuals participated in the study (40 individuals in each of the four experimental groups). The exact same number of men and women was examined in all experimental conditions. The average age of the subjects (as assessed by the observers and averaged out based on their assessments) was 33.16 ($SD = 13$).

It was demonstrated that the outfit of the experimenter had a general impact on the subjects' decisions to help her out; subjects were slightly less willing to help the girl when she was dressed in a more elegant fashion. Nevertheless, the most interesting results were recorded when we simultaneously factored in the effect of the sex of the subjects and the manipulation through the outfit. In the case of female subjects, elegant clothes clearly reduced the experimenter's chance of receiving help, while it was the other way around in the case of male subjects. They were more willing to pay for the ticket when the experimenter was dressed elegantly. Table 10.1 presents the number of individuals who were willing to give help depending on the outfit of the experimenter and the sex of the subjects.

No effect of the presence (or absence) of the payment card in the experimenter's hand on the subjects' willingness to pay for the ticket was observed.

Another aspect worth highlighting is the specific configuration of the results of the experiment: the sheer effect of the type of outfit on the willingness to give help was characterized by the greatest effect size, when the sex of the subjects was taken into account in the analysis. One may even venture to say that from the perspective of the entirety of the study results, these effects cancelled each other out. In the case of female subjects, the more formal outfit resulted in a reduced willingness to give help, while it was the opposite in the case of male subjects. This shows us, yet again, how subtle an effect of control

Table 10.1 Number of individuals who agreed to help or refused (depending on the outfit of the experimenter)

Number					
Sex			*Agreed to Help*		
			No	*Yes*	*Total*
Woman	Outfit	Casual	8	32	40
		Elegant	30	10	40
	Total		38	42	80
Man	Outfit	Casual	21	19	40
		Elegant	11	29	40
	Total		32	48	80

Source: prepared by the authors.

variables (in addition, affecting the results of the study in various interactions) we are dealing with in the case of a field experiment. What is more, many of those variables are incredibly difficult to control because, as in the above-mentioned case, they interact with other control variables and generate a substantially greater number of possible combinations of effects affecting the ultimate results of the study.

The site of the study is yet another variable that authors of scientific articles usually describe rather perfunctorily in the "Method" or the "Procedure" section of their reports. In most cases, experiments are conducted on streets, in squares, at campuses, i.e., in crowded locations, where conducting a study is, for this reason, facilitated (the time between consecutive interactions with subjects is reduced). Yet, location descriptions rarely provide detailed information on the objects found near the square or the street where the study was conducted. As it turns out, the type of such objects can have a significant impact on the results of the experiment. Nicolas Guéguen, a French psychologist, is an example of a researcher who, in his works, analyzes the role of the location of the study as well as its effect on the results (particularly, albeit not exclusively, from the perspective of altruistic behavior). His research demonstrated, *inter alia*, that young women are more willing to disclose their telephone number to a man when the request is made near a florist (as compared to identical requests made near a confectionery or a shoe store) (Guéguen, 2012). In the course of another study conducted by Lubomir Lamy, Jacques Fisher-Lokou and Nicolas Guéguen (2015), the experimenters investigated how the neighborhood of the location where the subject had the opportunity to help a person in need affected the subject's decision to give help. In this study, 192 subjects participated (50% of which were women). The experimental procedure pertained to a situation where the subject had the opportunity to voluntarily help a young woman. The woman, wearing a clearly visible leg brace, was walking along the pavement with a crutch in one hand and a bag of candy in the other. At some point (when she was approximately 5 meters from the subject walking from the opposite direction, who had been randomly selected from the pedestrians), the woman dropped her bag of candy and tried to pick the pieces up while struggling to keep her balance. The researchers wanted to know what her chances of receiving help would be (picking the candies up or in the form of a verbal offer to pick them up) when the candy was dropped in one of four locations: in the control location (in the street far from any public building), or in the vicinity of a hospital, a church or a florist. They also investigated the effect of the sex of the subject on his/her decision to give help.

Their results demonstrated that sex had no effect on the subjects' willingness to help the young woman. Nevertheless, there were clear differences in terms of the reactions of the subjects depending on the location of the experiment. Subjects were most eager to help in the vicinity of the hospital (91.6% of the subjects) and in the proximity of the florist (87.5%). The response rate was different near the church (75%) and in the street located far from any of those sites (68.7%). The researchers claimed that the differences were caused by the associations related to particular locations. In the pilot study, they proved that a florist, for a vast majority of people, is associated with love while a hospital makes people think of helping others, which might have spurred the subjects to help the person in need. Yet, since the associations related to these locations may vary in particular cultures, we decided to conduct a slightly modified version of the above-described experiment in real Polish society.

We introduced certain changes in the very experimental scheme. The first modification consisted of changing the dependent variable, which was replaced with a verbal request for financial help in a difficult situation. The second modification consisted of adding one more location, where the subjects (as expected, according to the hypotheses) should be less willing to grant the request. We believed that a site located near a discount store would meet the above condition, mainly because people with no money to buy alcohol frequently operate near discount stores, where they ask pedestrians or customers of the store to "spare some change" (in most cases, their request is either ignored or refused). The third modification consisted of introducing a factor into the experimental scheme based on the sex of the person asking for help. The last element that differentiated our experiment from the French original was investigating several demographic variables: the exact age, education, and marital status of the subject. Obviously, we also used their sex as the control factor. The subjects were asked to complete a survey with questions regarding these aspects following the interaction and after it was explained to them that they were participating in a psychological experiment.

The study was conducted by two experimenter's assistants, a woman and a man, both aged 25. They were both neatly dressed: the woman was wearing a blue, knee-long dress, a cornflower blue jacket with short sleeves, and blue, low-heeled sandals. Her hair was tied in a ponytail. The man was wearing beige trousers, a jacket, a blue shirt, and leather shoes. He had short, slicked back hair. The experiment was conducted in four locations in Wrocław:

- near a church,
- near a hospital,
- near a discount store,
- near a florist at one of the main squares in Wrocław.

The experimenter's assistants randomly selected and approached every fifth passer-by who did not witness the previous interaction and asked him or her for help (the pedestrians were assigned to a particular group based on a previously established randomization procedure). They made the following request:

> "Excuse me, I am sorry to bother you but I have a problem. My wallet and my documents got stolen and I do not have the money to get back home. I would rather not hitchhike and I was wandering if you could buy me a ticket or give me PLN 3 so that I could buy one."

As the pedestrian, who had been asked for help, was reaching for their wallet or a bus ticket, the two people were approached by the experimenter supervising the whole process from a distance. The experimenter thanked the subject for help and informed him or her that they were participating in a psychological experiment. He also asked the subject to complete a survey regarding his or her age, education, and address, and ensured that the data would only be used for the purpose of the study. Each experimenter's assistant questioned 16 individuals in each location.

A total of 128 individuals took part in the experiment (half of the group were women). Table 10.2 presents the number of people who were ready to give help in each location, taking their sex into account.

Table 10.3 presents the number of people who were ready to give help in particular conditions taking into account the sex of the experimenter's assistant.

Table 10.2 Number of individuals who agreed to help or refused (depending on the location of the experiment)

Number						
				Outcome		
				Agreed to Help	*Refused to Help*	*Total*
Location	Church	Subject	Woman	13	3	16
			Man	12	4	16
		Total		25	7	32
	Hospital	Subject	Woman	14	2	16
			Man	9	7	16
		Total		23	9	32
	Florist	Subject	Woman	10	6	16
			Man	8	8	16
		Total		18	14	32
	Discount store	Subject	Woman	0	16	16
			Man	3	13	16
		Total		3	29	32
Total		Subject	Woman	37	27	64
			Man	32	32	64
		Total		69	59	128

Source: prepared by the authors.

Table 10.3 Number of individuals who agreed to help or refused (depending on the location of the experiment and the sex of the experimenter's assistant)

Number						
				Outcome		
				Agreed to Help	*Refused to help*	*Total*
Location	Church	Assistant	Woman	11	5	16
			Man	14	2	16
		Total		25	7	32
	Hospital	Assistant	Woman	12	4	16
			Man	11	5	16
		Total		23	9	32
	Florist	Assistant	Woman	13	3	16
			Man	5	11	16
		Total		18	14	32
	Discount store	Assistant	Woman	2	14	16
			Man	1	15	16
		Total		3	29	32
Total		Assistant	Woman	38	26	64
			Man	31	33	64
		Total		69	59	128

Source: prepared by the authors.

The statistical analyses showed a strong effect of the location where the request for help was made; the subjects were most willing to help if asked for support near the church (78.1%) and near the hospital (71.9%), whereas significantly fewer subjects were willing to help near the florist (56.3%) and the lowest number was recorded near the discount store (9.4%). All these differences were statistically significant. We also investigated the impact of the sex of the experimenter's assistant and the sex of the subject on the willingness to give help: both effects turned out to be statistically insignificant. What was relevant, though, was the interaction between the two factors. Female subjects were approximately equally willing to help both the male as well as the female assistant, while male subjects were more willing to grant the request made by the man than by the woman. The other variables (age, education, and marital status) had no impact on the willingness to give help.

There are at least two ways of looking at the outcome from the perspective of methodology of a field experiment. The first pertains to the specific problems caused by replication of studies in other countries (or, to speak more broadly, in other cultures). Clearly, the vicinity of a florist, which positively affected subjects' willingness to give help in the French study, was not as effective when the experiment was replicated in Poland. It was quite the opposite with the church. No significant difference in the number of people willing to give help as compared to the control group was recorded in the course of the original French study, whereas in Poland, the vicinity of the church was where the highest number of subjects who agreed to give help was recorded (although some of the differences obviously might come down to the different operationalization of the dependent variable). Therefore, one might venture to claim that the replication of experiments that were originally conducted in a different culture entails the need to factor in cultural specificity during the design stage of the experimental scheme, as well as for the very operationalization of variables.

Another important finding resulting from the experiment is the extremely low (close to the so-called floor effect) number of subjects willing to give help in the vicinity of the discount store. It seems that the low result may be due to the fact that we frequently meet people asking for change in specific locations: by railway stations, main city squares, and discount stores or supermarkets. One of the possible explanations for this phenomenon is the representativeness heuristics (Kahneman, 2016; Kahneman and Tversky, 1972; Sotirovic, 2016). If we meet somebody asking us for change in certain locations, we tend to believe that this person is trying to con some cash out of us and we are not really interested in the reasoning behind this person's request. We have noticed that in Wrocław, where we work and conduct most of our field experiments, the market square and Solny Square – two sites located close to each other and characterized by heavy pedestrian traffic – are some of the worst locations for conducting field experiments. As it turns out, in the case of these two locations, the most common reply to any request (and even to an attempt to verbalize a request) is "no." Obviously, another possible reason conducting field experiments in these two locations is difficult is that people we meet there are simply in a hurry (which is not the case in parks or other walking areas).

Another aspect worth noting, while analyzing the replication of the French study, is the different response from pedestrians near the florist (87.5% in France and 56.3% in Poland). Needless to say, questions as to the reasons behind the observed difference emerge: are florists located differently in Poland and France? Or, perhaps, did the two florists used in the two countries differ in terms of their surroundings, to such an extent that it affected the results of the experiment? Maybe the results were affected by the fact that we chose, for the purpose of our study, a florist located in Solny Square in Wrocław? Of course, there is no answering these questions but we should definitely keep them in mind when considering replicating studies based on a field experiment as well as their sensitivity to contextual variables.

Yet this is not the only factor that often goes unnoticed when conducting field experiments. Even though "Method" or "Procedure" sections often provide a more or less accurate description of the location where the experiment was conducted, they rarely include information about the weather at the time of the experiment. One can learn about the extent to which the weather affects our lives by, e.g., analyzing election results in many countries. There is a large body of research (e.g., Gomez, Hansford, & Krause, 2007; Lewis-Beck & Stegmaier, 2014; Persson, Sundell, & Öhrvall, 2014)) showing that the weather has a significant effect on election results as well as voter turnout. Some researchers have even attempted to precisely calculate how a certain amount of rainfall translates into decreased voter turnout (the meta-analysis by Gomez et al. demonstrates that 2.5 cm rainfall translates into a 1% reduction in voter turnout; paradoxically, rain turns out to be a better predictor of voter turnout than snow, as the same amount of snowfall results in just a 0.5% reduction in voter turnout).

So can such factors as a cloudy or a sunny sky affect the results of experimental studies? The aforementioned French social psychologists, Guéguen and Lamy (2013), attempted to verify just that. Their study included 464 individuals (243 were women) aged between 20 and 50, according to the estimation, randomly selected from among pedestrians.

Two women and two men aged 20–21 played the role of experimenters' assistants. They were all wearing jeans, t-shirts, and trainers; they were also holding bags in their hands. When they saw an individual meeting the randomization criteria (i.e., walking by themselves, in the desired age range, not talking on the phone, etc.), they would wait until the subject came within a distance of approximately 3 meters and they would "accidentally" drop their glove, pretending not to have noticed losing it, and continue walking. Two observers, positioned approximately 50 meters from the site of the experiment, were asked to record whether the subjects picked up the glove or informed the male or the female assistant in any way about the lost item. If the subject failed to do so within 10 seconds, the male or female assistant would stop and "realize" that they had lost their glove and they would go back to pick it up. The weather was the independent variable in the study. The researchers would always conduct their experiment between 9 a.m. and 1 p.m. but would choose either cloudy (but with no rain) or sunny days. The researchers tried to control other variables that could potentially affect the results, e.g., ambient temperature (ranging from 20 to 24 degrees Celsius). To verify the accuracy of the manipulation, each day pedestrians (not the ones who participated in the actual study) were asked about their opinion on the weather that day (using a scale of 1 through 9, where 1 represented a very cloudy day and 9 a very sunny day). The experiment was conducted only on those days for which the average score was not higher than 3 (for cloudy days) and not lower than 7 (for sunny days).

The results demonstrated that on sunny days, 65.3% of the subjects spontaneously helped the person who lost their glove, while on cloudy days the figure was 53.3% (the result was statistically significant, even though it must be clearly said that the significance resulted predominantly from a very large sample size; the effect itself was not particularly strong, with Cohen's $d = 0.244$).

When analyzing the experiment, one has to appreciate the interesting results as well as the diligence exercised by the researchers in terms of describing the conditions in which the experiment was conducted. The results themselves are also valuable, particularly from the perspective of social influence studies. Factoring in the current weather when designing studies is an interesting idea, even though the significance of this factor will surely vary depending on the location and circumstances of the experiment.

Another problem described predominantly by Robert Rosenthal (1966, 2002) is the so-called confirmation bias, to which we referred in Chapter 3. Even though the meta-analyses show that this effect is incredibly subtle and difficult to replicate (Barber et al., 1969), it should be assumed that it does affect study results. The authors of the Experimental Psychology (Kantowitz, Roediger III, & Elmes, 2014) textbook describe EBE (Experimenter Bias Effect) as not only a deliberate violation of the experimental scheme (e.g., by fabricating results or rejecting those subjects who behaved inconsistently with the adopted hypotheses) but predominantly as unintentional changes in one's behavior, as a result of which some subjects (e.g., belonging to a particular experimental group) are actually treated differently by the experimenter's assistant than the remaining participants in the study. They point to a number of factors that may affect the way subjects behave, such as a slightly modified tone of voice when reading out the experimental instructions, a different distribution of accents, different mimic and pantomimic stimuli in the case of various experimental groups, etc. Obviously, such problems can be solved through the use of the double blinding procedure, which has been known in experimental psychology for quite some time and makes the experimenter's assistants – at least theoretically – blind, i.e., they do not know the hypotheses adopted for the purpose of the study or to which experimental groups particular subjects have been assigned. The problem is that if subjects are rather good at anticipating the experimental hypotheses (Weber & Cook, 1972), the experimenter's assistants, frequently recruited from among students or graduates of psychology, are certainly going to be even better at it.

An interesting solution to this problem is to conduct the experiment in such a manner as to reduce, as much as possible, the risk related to the occurrence of the EBE. One can assume that since, as demonstrated by the above-quoted Barber et al., the effect occurs irregularly, it is relatively difficult to foresee, and its impact may be difficult to measure, it can be eliminated by "dilution." For it seems that even if the effect does occur, it will apply to one or two of the experimenter's assistants. They can unintentionally affect the results of the study only when they represent a significant portion of the total number of the assistants (e.g., 50% or 25% of all the assistants). The greater the number of the assistants, the lower the risk of affecting the results. Therefore, some researchers hire dozens or even over a hundred assistants for the purpose of conducting their experiments, where each assistant handles only a few, several at most, interactions with the subjects.

This method was applied, among others, by Meineri and Guéguen (2011) in their study intended to test a modified variation of the foot-in-the-mouth technique, originally described by Daniel Howard (1990). The author claimed that before we ask anyone for a favor, we should first ask this person about their frame of mind. If the person replies that they feel well (and this will be their response in the Anglo-Saxon culture) and if we respond by stating that we are glad to hear that, the person will be more willing to grant our request. In later studies (e.g., Dolinski et al., 2005) it was demonstrated that the subject matter of the conversation is not that important and that the dialogue itself, and not its content, is what matters. Meineri and Guéguen decided to verify the effectiveness of this phenomenon in the course of performing a telephone consumer survey regarding the local newspaper, *Le Télégramme*. In the experimental conditions, the interaction proceeded as follows:

> "Hello, I'm a student at the technical college in Vannes. I hope I'm not disturbing you, am I?"

Here the interlocutor would respond, and the assistant would say:

> "You probably know the regional daily paper, *Le Télégramme*, at least by name. Well, for our studies, we are carrying out a survey on this newspaper. Would you have a few minutes to answer by phone? There are only yes-or-no questions, so it should go very fast."

In the second group, the experimenter's assistant did not ask if he was disturbing the subject and only expressed his hope that this was not the case (did not engage in a dialogue with the interlocutor). In the control conditions, the assistant would ask the subject to take part in the telephone survey right away.

The results demonstrated clear differences between particular groups. In the group where a dialogue was present, the interlocutors agreed to take part in the survey much more frequently (25.2%) than in the group in which the assistant only said that he hoped he was not disturbing (19.1%), or in the control group (17.3%). What we find most interesting about this study, though, is the way in which the problem of the potential EBE was solved. The study included a total of 1,791 subjects who were inquired by as many as 105 experimenter's assistants (which translates into 17.6 individuals per one assistant). It appears to be a very interesting methodological procedure. As we have already mentioned, the EBE is incredibly subtle and difficult to control, therefore, the procedure applied by Meineri and Guéguen is a specific "insurance policy" purchased by the researcher. Even if EBE does occur in the course of the study, it will not affect the entirety of the results in a significant manner, as the "EBE-contaminated" experimenter will only affect 1.5% of the subjects.

To summarize the studies described in this chapter, there are several aspects to highlight. First, a field experiment, when conducted in natural conditions, will inherently be a "high-risk study" as far as the influence of the confounders on the outcome is concerned. The location of the experiment, the weather, the time of year, small mimic and pantomimic gestures, a specific personality of the experimenter – all these factors (and many others) can affect the results of the study. Consequently, conducting a field experiment requires the preparation of a very thorough documentation of its course, which must be rendered available to other researchers who would like to replicate the experiment. This issue remains relevant not only to field experiments; after all, descriptions included in articles on laboratory experiments also rarely provide details regarding the experimenter or the confederate (such as their height, general appearance or speech pace). The above-mentioned results, even though they illustrate the problem from the perspective of a field experiment, can undoubtedly also be considered a signal for researchers conducting their experiments in a laboratory: the aforementioned factors can have real influence on their results.

Second, one should remember the specific methods that can be applied to reduce the influence these factors can have on results obtained in the course of a field experiment. A very precise randomization (both of the first and the second degree) or a large number of experimenter's assistances used in the course of the study are simple yet effective methods, the use of which enables the elimination (or at least reduction) of interference with a field experiment.

11 Studies conducted via the Internet perceived as being in a natural environment for numerous actions of contemporary man

Despite major doubts as to studies conducted on-line (e.g., Krantz & Dalal, 2000), they seem to be an important trend in contemporary psychological studies, particularly those in the area of social psychology. Michael Birnbaum (2000) presented a wide spectrum of arguments both in favor of and against Internet studies. Objections include, primarily, sample representation issues. In most cases, it is believed that a sample obtained in the course of an on-line study is strongly biased towards young and well-educated individuals characterized by an above-average material status. Yet the analyses carried out by John Krantz and Reeshad Dalal indicate that this is not necessarily true (perhaps it was in the year 2000 but ten years later the situation has changed as the Internet has become much more accessible). In reality, samples obtained through on-line studies were far more diversified than commonly expected and they did not differ significantly from those selected in a traditional fashion. It should also be noted that when using the term "average man," we are referring to an individual randomly selected to participate in an experiment through a full randomization procedure. Nevertheless, as the practice demonstrates, this method of randomly selecting individuals to be included in samples used in psychological studies is very rare, which makes on-line studies even more appealing. After all, a well-controlled sample picked up over the Internet will offer a better reflection of the general population than a sample composed exclusively of 2nd-year psychology students (surely, the former will be more diversified than the latter).

However, here we are referring predominantly to demographic variables. Meanwhile, it is also possible that on-line samples and those selected outside of the Internet will vary in a more profound manner. For example, it is commonly believed that Internet users recruited to participate in studies have more hang-ups and are more prone to depression than average people (Gosling, Vazire, Srivastava, & John 2004). Robert Kraut et al. (2004) demonstrated that even though there are certain differences in terms of extroversion and communication skills between average Internet users and individuals not included in that category, these differences do not prevent conducting meaningful on-line studies. In other words, just as in the case of off-line studies, we usually get a sample that is biased in some manner. In survey-based studies conducted outside of the Internet, the fraction of inaccessible individuals, i.e., those who refuse to take part in the experiment, is a major problem. It is estimated that this fraction may represent up to 60% of the randomly selected sample (Kołakowska, 2005). It is a similar case with on-line studies, and the above-mentioned analyses by Kraut indicate that even though both methods yield biased samples, the difference between them is minor.

In recent decades, studies conducted via Amazon Mechanical Turk (commonly referred to as MTurk) or any of its local counterparts have become particularly popular

DOI: 10.4324/9781003092995-11

in the field of psychology. Such studies are based on a rather simple pattern – an on-line platform is used to gather a group of users who declare their willingness to perform a task against a small fee (e.g., they agree to fill out a questionnaire or select pictures from among a set of several photographs presenting particular animals). A researcher promises to pay a specific fee for the performance of the task (e.g., USD 1 for a ten-minute task), the platform charges a commission (approximately 10%), and the potential subject either accepts or does not accept the proposed conditions. There are several advantages to conducting studies in this manner. This method enables quick access to a large sample and feedback is received quickly, it offers a chance for a relatively "good sample," i.e., it is heavily diversified and including individuals characterized by varied psychodemographic parameters, and it is relatively inexpensive (Mason & Suri, 2012; Reips, 2000). Obviously, predominantly the researcher will care about the "quality" of the sample, namely, the extent to which it manages to avoid being biased and corresponds to an off-line sample. Research demonstrates that the demography of MTurk users is very similar to that of the real world (Ipeirotis, 2010). As compared to the American population, MTurk users are slightly younger and have fewer children but their income is very similar. Joseph Goodman, Cynthia Cryder, and Amar Cheema (2013) conducted very interesting studies designed to verify samples obtained through the use of MTurk in terms of personality traits. They demonstrated that even though, in many respects, it is impossible to identify systematic differences, there are a few variables to indicate that samples picked up through this platform are different, e.g., its users were less attentive when exposed to experimental stimuli (which resulted in reduced power of the experiment) and more willing to search for the correct answers using web search engines, while their attitude towards money was closer to the approach typical of students than that of the entire population. It was also observed that their self-esteem was reduced and they were less extroverted.

Krantz and Dalal took their analyses even further in order to verify the credibility of on-line studies. They compared experiments that had been conducted over the Internet since 1995 with experiments designed to investigate identical phenomena in the conventional manner (e.g., the paper-pencil method). Their data clearly indicated a strong correspondence between results produced with different methods.

Nevertheless, more recent research brings about serious doubts as to whether individuals participating in on-line studies are actually desirable subjects. It is true that in some cases the point may be to examine a sample that is as diversified as possible, but in other instances researchers may want to, e.g., compare vegans to people eating predominantly meat, or amateur marathon runners to people who hardly walk at all. As individuals who agree to participate in on-line studies, for the most part, do so for the money, it is possible that, at least in some cases, they will mislead the researchers by untruthfully claiming that they meet the applicable recruitment criteria. Jesse Chandler and Gabriele Paolacci (2017), while conducting survey-based studies related to state education testing through the MTurk platform, asked their subjects at the end of the study if they were parents or legal guardians of autistic children. In 50% of the cases, subjects were simply asked the question, while in the other 50% of the cases it was suggested that the researchers were trying to determine participants' eligibility for another study. In the former case, 4.3% of the subjects gave a positive answer to the question and as many as 7.8% did in the latter case. In another experiment, the authors asked the subjects about their sexual orientation. In control conditions, 3.8% of subjects identified as homosexuals. In experimental conditions, the researchers asked if subjects were homosexual at the very beginning of the study, which made the subjects prone to believe that homosexuals were wanted for the studies. It turned out that as many as 45.3% of MTurk workers claimed to be homosexual. In subsequent experiments, the researchers demonstrated that the tendency to lie increases in subjects along with the increase in the remuneration promised for participation in the studies.

Another problem with experiments conducted via the Internet is how to effectively motivate subjects not only to engage in the study but also to remain engaged over its entire duration. Indeed, one may assume that for some of the subjects, their participation in the experiment is simply about having a good time (which is not an issue in itself but it becomes an issue if "having a good time," which can mean different things to different people, is the sole purpose for participating in the experiment). Some subjects may discontinue their participation in the experiment before it is complete (the percentage of individuals who do so is usually higher compared to studies conducted in the real world). It is much easier for somebody on their computer in their own home to quit than for a person who would have to leave a laboratory and inform the experimenter about their decision to quit. Therefore, it should come as no surprise that for various reasons (fatigue, boredom, a visit from a friend, etc.) as many as several dozen percent of subjects participating in on-line studies quit before reaching the end of the experiment. Zhou and Fishbach (2016) conduct their own on-line experiments, which demonstrate fascinating consequences of this attrition. In one such experiment, the participants were asked, depending on the conditions to which they were randomly assigned, to imagine that they were using eyeliner or an after-shave lotion and then they were asked about their body weight. Surprisingly, imagining using eyeliner reduced participants' body weight when compared to imagining using an after-shave lotion! Why? Could it be that a magical and virtually effortless way to lose weight was discovered? Unfortunately, no. Quite simply, imagining using eyeliner was so difficult for many of the male participants that a fair share of them quit before they reached the end of the experiment. As a result, ultimately, there were more women in the eyeliner conditions and since, generally speaking, women weigh less than men, there was a difference in the body weight reported by the subjects in both conditions. In another experiment, subjects were asked to recall and describe 12 (in conditions A) or 4 (in conditions B) happy moments they had experienced in the previous year. Subsequently, they were asked to determine the level of difficulty of their task. It turned out that recalling and describing 12 events was the easier task! Why? Because as many as 69% of the subjects who were asked to recall and describe said 12 happy moments quit in the process of doing so. This, presumably, left the group with only those individuals who were so satisfied with their lives that recalling 12 happy moments was not a problem for them. Another paradox? Yes, and perhaps the most amusing of them all. When people with precisely defined opinions on open access to firearms (or on the need to restrict access to firearms) are asked to express their views and present arguments in favor of their approach, their opinion should, as a result of that, become solidified. This is completely obvious! To verify this, Zhou and Fishbach surveyed opinions held by their subjects regarding this matter and then asked them to substantiate their views. Next, the researchers again surveyed the subjects' opinions on the matter and it turned out that the average approach of all participants had shifted towards opting for restricting firearm accessibility. Why? Those who support open access to firearms are generally less educated than their opponents and they find it more difficult to provide arguments supporting their views. As a result, they quit the experiment before reaching the end more often than those who believe that the right to own firearms should be restricted. Evidently, attrition is a very serious problem for on-line studies.

However, there are many ways to encourage participants to follow study instructions in a conscientious and reasonable manner. One way to do so is to provide feedback once the participant has shared their e-mail address, while another is to reduce the feeling of anonymity on the part of the participant by involving the same individuals in a number of studies, e.g., in the paradigm of repeated measurements (Skitka & Sargis, 2006). Another method, applied by a Polish website for on-line studies, is to switch from financial remuneration (paid by transfer) to points, which participants collect and can exchange for material prizes. With this solution in place, each individual asked to fill out a questionnaire (or to participate in any other study) is required to provide a validated postal address in order to receive the selected prize. This greatly reduces the risk of setting up numerous fake accounts that may serve as bots to the benefit of one individual.

One should also bear in mind that, apart from the apparent methodological complications (which, as described above, do not hinder the study process as much as is commonly believed), there are many benefits resulting from conducting studies over the Internet. Intriguing data on this matter was published by Brian Nosek, Mahzarin Banaji, and Anthony Greenwald (2002). They demonstrated, among other things, that on-line studies can be conducted more efficiently (with an automated data collection and compilation process) in a more comfortable manner, at least for the researchers (at a convenient location and time), and – what is also important – at a lower cost than experiments conducted in the real world. The above-mentioned authors present, e.g., results of studies conducted on a mind-boggling, from today's perspective, sample of 2.5 million people. Of course, this generates more consequences as, e.g., the available statistics and analytic tools are ill-suited to handle such sample sizes (to put it simply – with such a large sample, every difference will be statistically significant); yet, this problem can be solved through the use of other statistics (e.g., based on assumptions other than zero-hypothesis testing or referring more to effect size than to the classical *p* figure). Additionally, it should be noted that conducting studies on-line eliminates a number of interferences from the experimental process that are present in conventional studies. There is no fear (or at least it is reduced) of being judged by the experimenter, which is a major issue in the case of conventional studies (Rosenberg, 1965). As subjects can remain completely anonymous in the course of on-line studies, also in terms of their visual contact with the experimenter, the fear of being judged is significantly mitigated. What is more, the effect the expectations of the researcher have on the result of the experiment is reduced (Rosenthal, 2002) as it becomes possible to effectively separate the creator of the experimental scheme from the data collection process. Moreover, the randomization of participants is much easier in the case of on-line studies, because subjects can be assigned to particular experimental conditions through the use of a computer-sampling frame.

Michael Birnbaum and Ulf-Dietrich Reips point to a vital advantage that on-line studies have over conventional ones when they refer to the ecological validity of studies conducted over the Internet (Birnbaum, 2000; Reips, 2000; Reips and Birnbaum, 2011). One should be aware of the fact that in the case of studies carried out in the real world, particularly in laboratory conditions, it is often believed that being in a new environment the subjects are unfamiliar with and the new situation they find themselves in affects their behavior. There is no such risk in the case of studies conducted over the Internet, as subjects participate in the experiment while sitting in their own chair in front of their own computer. What Birnbaum and Reips emphasize is a greater possibility of reaching those groups that are weakly explored in conventional studies, such as people with impaired motor functions or disabilities.

Another argument in favor of this proposition is the fact that a significant share of the activity of contemporary man has moved to the Internet. We buy on-line (on-line auction sites, on-line stores), we socialize on-line (social media), we work on-line (home office tools, specialist social media), and we seek sexual partners and new friends on-line (e.g., on Tinder). Today, there is hardly an area of our life that does not have its reflection (or its complete counterpart) on the Internet (White & Selwyn, 2013). It seems that, for the most part, this is beneficial to the quality of our everyday life, even though some may criticize this approach (Frith, 2013; Nilsen & Pavel, 2013). Nicholas Carr, in his essay titled, "Is Google Making Us Stupid?" (2015), analyzes the effect that using not only Google products but modern IT technology in general has on the way we function. Carr claims that as we have gained easy access to large volumes of information, we (as Internet users) have lost the ability to analyze it in depth and verify the accuracy of the information. To describe the current situation, he uses the following metaphor: prior to the "Google revolution," we were scuba divers in the sea of words. Now we zip along the surface like a guy on a Jet Ski.

To conclude: on-line studies have numerous and substantial advantages as well as numerous and substantial disadvantages and limitations. Therefore, we believe that it is not a question of deciding whether on-line studies should be considered an alternative for those conducted in the real world, rather we believe they should be carried out in parallel to conventional studies.

From the perspective of this book, the possibility of using the Internet for the purpose of investigating human behavior is particularly important. A typical social psychology problem, for example, is the relation between our declarations as to our behavior and our actual behavior. One of the most famous studies designed to verify this problem is the already mentioned iconic experiment by LaPiere (1934), in the course of which the author asks about room availability in hotels for a Chinese couple visiting the USA (a detailed description of the experiment can be found in Chapter 3, which is devoted to the history of field experiments). The problem still persists though, as it was addressed, *inter alia*, in the vital text by Roy Baumeister, Kathleen Vohs, and David Funder (2007), which criticized the direction in which psychology was heading and claimed that the discipline was becoming "a science on self-descriptions and finger movements." Therefore, it should come as no surprise that researchers who use questionnaires try to verify the extent to which the results collected using them can be applied to predict subjects' actual behavior. This procedure was used in the study conducted by Michał Bilewicz et al. (Bilewicz, Winiewski, Kofta, and Wójcik, 2013), which was designed to verify the extent to which results obtained using scales that were intended to test the level of anti-Semitism could be used to predict one's willingness to make donations to a charity related to Jewish culture in Poland. In the course of the experiment (Study 2), Bilewicz and his colleagues asked participants to complete a number of questionnaires (testing, *inter alia*, "traditional" as well as "modern" anti-Semitism, the level of authoritarianism, the Bogardus social distance scale, the feeling of injustice, one's faith in conspiracy theories, etc.). At the initial stage of the study (conducted over the Internet), its participants were told that they would receive a small amount as remuneration for their taking part in the study, which they would then be able to donate to charity. Once they had filled out the questionnaires, they were given the choice of making their donation to an organization established for the purpose of preserving Jewish or Polish historic monuments. The researchers deemed it to be a behavioral measurement of a pro-Jewish vs. an anti-Jewish approach. The results demonstrated that the level of anti-Semitism revealed in the questionnaires showed it was an accurate tool for predicting the behavior of the subjects (their unwillingness to donate their remuneration to a pro-Jewish organization).

It should be noted though that in the study conducted by Bilewicz et al., the subjects were not actually asked to donate their money. At no point in the course of the study were they given the choice to either "keep the money or give it to somebody else" (a charitable organization in this case), as they were not offered the option of keeping the money, rather they could only decide which of the indicated charitable organizations to support. One can assume that this fact significantly affected their decision, similar to the case of the "Dictator" or "Ultimatum" games as popular experimental instruments in economics, which we discussed in Chapter 4.

Therefore, there are reasons to assume that if the study by Bilewicz et al. was modified in such a manner as to present the subject with a choice, "you can either keep the money or donate it to charity (a pro-Jewish or other charitable organization)," the results might have been very different.

The sequence of events could be another aspect affecting the results. In the study conducted by Bilewicz and his colleagues, the participants were first asked to fill out a number of questionnaires, where they expressed their attitude towards Jews, and then their willingness to donate PLN 1 to a pro-Jewish charitable organization was tested at the end of the experiment. One could reasonably expect different results if the order of these elements were reversed.

Therefore, we decided to design and conduct such an experiment (Byrka, Grzyb, & Dolinski, 2015). For this purpose, we used a Polish platform for on-line studies, i.e., Ariadna, which is a local version of the concept behind MTurk. The panel has approximately 100,000 registered users aged 14–70. From among these users, one can randomly select a sample using virtually any parameters. As we have already mentioned, the difference between Ariadna and MTurk is that there is no money involved in the settlements between the panel and its users. Instead of an account with cash in it, individuals who agree to complete the surveys receive points, which are then assigned to their accounts and can be exchanged for material prizes (e.g., a new TV). In the course of our experiment, we decided to take advantage of the point assignment mechanism and offer our participants a chance to donate their points to a charitable organization established to preserve historic monuments, split into two groups: one for a charity to protect Jewish historic monuments and the other a charity to protect Polish historic monuments.

Although 769 individuals participated in the study, the results of seven of those individuals indicated that they might have been dishonest when completing their questionnaires (their results differed by three standard deviations from the remaining data), so only data from 762 individuals were accepted for final analysis. Once subjects had logged into their accounts on the platform, they were informed that, as usual, they would receive points for participating in the study. They were also told that, should they agree, their points could be donated to an organization for the preservation of historic monuments. The wording of the communication was as follows:

> As in the case of every study carried out through the Ariadna panel, you will be awarded points for your participation. Yet this time, if you desire to do so, you can donate your points to an organization for the preservation of historic monuments. Make your choice:
>
> Yes, I would like to donate my points No thank you

Figure 11.1 A banner with information on the beneficiary organization participants may donate their points. Source: archive of Tomasz Grzyb.

Half of the subjects (randomly selected) received the above communication at the beginning of the study, while the other half received this at the end of it (this is how we hoped to measure the extent to which completing a set of questionnaires regarding an open-minded attitude toward Jews would affect the decision of the subjects).

Additionally, subjects were presented one of four images containing information on the beneficiary organization (the subjects, unlike in the experiment conducted by Bilewicz et al., were not able to choose which organization to support – the choice was either to keep the points or donate to an organization already chosen). In the picture presented to the subjects, there was a façade of a building with the Star of David and a caption that reads: "Association for the Preservation of Jewish Historic Monuments" (Figure 11.1).

In the other three groups, we juggled with including the Star of David (it was removed using photo editing software, in two experimental conditions) and the word "Jewish" was replaced with "Polish." As a result, the following groups were formed: combinations of "Association for the Preservation of Jewish (or Polish) Historic Monuments" with or without the Star of David. The entire experiment was based on a 2 × 2 × 2 scheme (donation at the beginning vs. end of the study; Jewish vs. Polish historic monuments, the Star of David present or absent).

The basic task of the subjects was to fill out a number of questionnaires, most of which pertained to one's attitude toward Jews. Since this part of the study is not what we are most interested in at this point, we will only describe it very briefly (we will not address the results of the scales, we will only comment on how their completion affected one's decision to donate their points). We used the following scales:

- The scale of pro-social tendencies (Kasser & Ryan, 1993): seven statements that subjects are asked to grade using a scale of 1 to 7 (from "completely unimportant" to "very important"). An example statement is: "How important is it to you to: help others make their lives better; devote your time and money to charity."
- The scale of modern racism ("Modern Racism", McConahay, 1986): the original scale referred to blacks. In our version, we modified the statement so that it referred to Jews. Example statements are: "Recently, Jews have been doing, economically,

better than they deserve to," "Anti-Semitism has ceased to be an issue in Poland." The entire scale included six statements, and answers were given on a five-point scale (degrees ranging from "I firmly disagree" to "I firmly agree").

- The social distance scale (Bogardus, 1925): a scale based on the classic Bogardus statements, designed to measure level of distance on the following seven statements: Mark "yes" as your answer if you would be willing to accept: "Banishing Jews from you country"; "Jews being employed in the same company as you." Each time, the subject could answer "yes" or "no."
- Subtle prejudice scale (Pettigrew & Meertens, 1995): we adopted eight items from the original scale, four pertaining to cultural differences and similarities, and four pertaining to emotions. Example statements are: "How different from you/similar to you do you believe the Jews living in Poland are … In terms of the values they pass onto their children? In terms of the language they speak?" In the area of emotions: "How often did you … Feel sympathy for the Jews living in Poland? Feel resentment towards the Jews living in Poland?"
- The scale of specifically Polish anti-Semitism and the scale of faith in Jewish conspiracy (Bilewicz et al., 2013): this scale consisted of 12 statements. An example statement is: "Please indicate the extent to which you agree with the following statements: Jews want to play a decisive role in international financial institutions; Jews meet secretly to discuss matters which are important to them."

For all of the above-mentioned scales, where there was no Polish counterpart we used a translation prepared by people who were proficient in both Polish and English. Such translations were then back-translated into English by other individuals, and then both versions, i.e., the original and the back-translation into English, were compared. All scales achieved satisfactory psychometrical indices.

The results demonstrated no statistically significant differences between one's willingness to donate points awarded for participation in the study and their assignment to any of the experimental groups. Therefore, for the sake of the clarity of the message, we combined all groups with the "Jewish" condition (either the Star of David present or information on the Association of the Preservation of Jewish Historic Monuments) into one and compared it with the control group (the Association for the Protection of Polish Historic Monuments and the image without the Star of David). Subsequently, we examined the differences between the individuals, in both groups, who were asked to decide on the donation before vs. after completing the questionnaires regarding their attitudes toward Jews.

The result was that if the request was made after the questionnaires had been completed, in the case of both the "Jewish" group and the "Polish" group, the probability of making the donation to the organization established to preserve historic monuments increased. The chart below illustrates the differences as proportions (Figure 11.2).

It should be noted that the results demonstrate two important aspects. First, when people are not asked to merely decide on the distribution of money that does not belong to them (as was the case in the original study by Bilewicz et al.) but are requested to donate an asset that is actually theirs (points in our study that can be exchanged for prizes), very few decide to make the donation, and there are hardly any systematic, inter-group differences among those who do. Second, the decision to make the donation is clearly affected by the task the subjects were asked to perform earlier. Obviously, in our case, it would be difficult to make predictions as to the effect of the content of the questionnaires. After all, differences were also present in the "Polish" group (to be precise, the differences were even more evident than in the "Jewish" variants). Perhaps, the foot-in-the-door effect was one

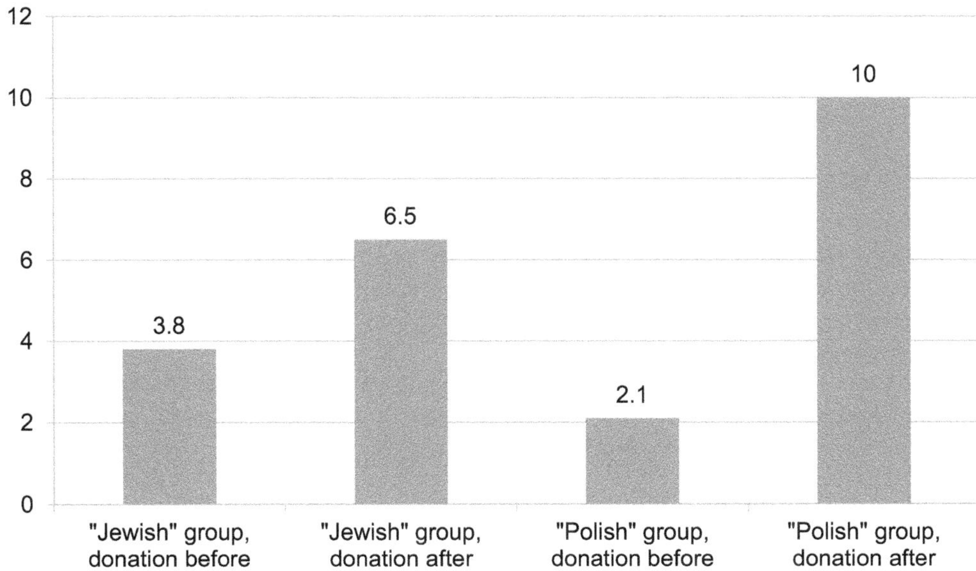

Figure 11.2 Percentage of people who donated points awarded for their participation in the study by group.
Source: prepared by the authors.

of the reasons we observed these differences (Freedman & Fraser, 1966). Nevertheless, it is clearly evident that the very moment the request is made affects the results of the study.

It should be also noted that, depending on the viewpoint adopted, the procedure we used might be considered a field experiment with the Internet space acting as the field. Of course, our subjects knew that they were participating in a study "of some sort" but it is unlikely for them to consider the request to donate their points as part of the study (the Ariadna panel itself offers the option of donating one's points to NGOs, e.g., the Polish Humanitarian Action, and thus the donation request was, most likely, not a surprise to the participants).

Another field experiment that we conducted over the Internet was a replication of the "lost letter" experiment by Stanley Milgram, which we have already described in this book (Milgram et al., 1965). This time, we intended to use a "lost e-mail" instead of a "lost letter" (Stern & Faber, 1997). The procedure we applied was as follows: we randomly selected 3,000 addresses from the database housing the e-mail addresses of all students at the University of Social Sciences and Humanities (over 17,000 addresses in total). The pool was split into two groups, each of 1,500 e-mail addresses. The first group received an e-mail sent from s.goldbaum@az.pl and signed by "Stanisław and Sara Goldbaum," whereas the other group received an e-mail sent from s.nowak@az.pl and signed by "Stanisław and Barbara Nowak." In both cases the content of the e-mail was identical:

> Hi there,
>
> I guess your telephone number has changed, because we were unable to reach you. Thus, I am writing to inform you that, unfortunately, we will not be able to attend your wedding. We still have to meet, though, to talk about all sorts of important things.
>
> Please write us back as soon as possible! You simply must!
>
> Stanisław and Sara Goldbaum (or Stanisław and Barbara Nowak)

Obviously, we wanted to see how many of the recipients would respond to the e-mail by perhaps writing back to inform the sender that the e-mail did not reach its intended recipient.

After one week, the same recipients got another e-mail, this time sent from an e-mail address belonging to the University, with the following wording:

> Hi there,
>
> I am a fifth-year student and I am collecting data for my MA thesis. You either already are or soon will be collecting data for your thesis, so you surely understand my situation. I am pressed for time and I am sending this request to every kind soul I can reach ☺. I am expected to turn in a completed thesis by 12/12 and my advisor is really pushing me ☺.
>
> Please fill out the survey available here (link), it will take you 15 minutes (I've checked, I'm not making this up :P). For you, it will only be 15 minutes of your time – for me, it will be a lifesaver!!
>
> Thanks a bunch,
> K.B.

The link redirected participants to questionnaires similar to those that were used in the course of the studies related to the donations for the preservation of Polish and Jewish historic monuments.

As you can imagine, only a few individuals responded to the "lost" e-mail. Only 78 individuals (0.053%) responded to the lost e-mail sent by Mr. and Mrs. Goldbaum and 67 (0.044%) responded to the e-mail sent by Mr. and Mrs. Nowak.

There are several factors that could have contributed to such a low response rate. First, students rarely use "standard-issue" university e-mail addresses to communicate and thus they do not check the inboxes for those e-mail addresses on regular basis, which might have affected the results of the experiment. Second, even though we tried to make sure the letter was written in such a manner as to stay under the radar of anti-spam filters (or at least those used by the university), there is a risk that personal filters used by students for their browsers or e-mail clients identified our message as spam. Third, as our experience tells us, the most common reaction to an unsolicited e-mail is to ignore it and not look for its sender (after all, the message could be some sort of a test designed to verify whether the e-mail address is still active and conducted in order to launch a phishing attack or carry out another malicious plan of a crafty hacker). To conclude, the lost e-mail method failed to meet our expectations, which, obviously, does not mean that it is not suitable for re-deployment after certain modifications have been made. Perhaps it would be a better idea to use a social media profile to send out a message clearly intended for somebody else (instead of e-mail, which has been losing its popularity among young people).

So the question remains: Should the Internet also be considered a "field" from the perspective of our reflections on field experiments? And the answer is it most certainly should. This is where a significant part of our life takes place, this is where we search for opinions on matters that are important to us, and this is where we become the objects of more or less planned marketing strategies. We are not referring here exclusively to on-line stores but also (and perhaps predominantly) to social media portals (such as Facebook, Twitter, or YouTube). Today, these locations are becoming a new arena of social influence. And if this is the case, they should also be the next target location for conducting research on social influence, including as field experiments.

12 Publication of results

Perspective on Psychological Science is one of the most influential psychological journals out there (in 2019, its five-year *Impact Factor* was 6.39). One of its characteristics is that aside from articles supported with studies (or any other data) it also allows publication of texts that could be referred to as "program" articles. These are articles in which authors investigate changes in psychology as a field of study, analyze trends and directions of its development, and diagnose potential problems that might impede its development. The article by Robert Cialdini from January 2009, with a significant title "We have to break up" is an example of such a text (Cialdini, 2009).

The title proposed by Cialdini is an obvious reference to a "goodbye letter" addressed to one's partner (typical of teenagers) and constructed around typical key phrases such as: "IT'S NOT YOU, IT'S ME," "WE'VE BEEN DRIFTING APART RECENTLY," "I ONLY WANT THE BEST FOR YOU." Cialdini uses the exact same phrases, but in this case they address social psychology understood as a field of study. The author points to three – as he puts it, essentially positive – fundamental changes that took place in psychology in the last couple of decades, while pointing to their specific "side effects," affecting the variant of experimental studies he likes to design and conduct the most, i.e., field experiments. The three changes are: (1) cognitive revolution (understood as a focus on cognitive variables as factors explaining human behavior); (2) the expectation to publish a series of studies in major scientific journals (this fundamental problem is discussed in the following chapter); and (3) the popularization of mediation analysis as a statistic tool for data analysis. In a very brief text (in its printed form the whole work consists of two pages), Cialdini explains why these three changes cause a downturn in the popularity of field experiments, while referring to a phenomenon that could be called publishing economics. If the probability of publishing an article on the conducted research depends on the degree to which the expectations of editors and reviewers are met, and if they expect that: (1) cognitive aspects are allowed for in explaining particular behaviors; (2) a series of research to validate the existence of the described phenomenon is presented; (3) analyses are carried out in search of the mediators of the described phenomenon; the researchers carrying out field experiments have absolutely no chance of being successful. First, behavior is the most typical dependent variable (investigated) in field experiments. Additionally, in most cases, behavior is perceived as a dichotomy (somebody donated money, agreed to sign a petition, replaced the old light bulb with an energy-efficient one – or not). With the dependent variable defined in such a manner, it is difficult to include this in the experimental procedure, e.g., verification of cognitive predictors of a given behavior (in any case, it would be very problematic). Second, as claimed by Cialdini (2009), even though the very expectation of auto-replication of obtained results is praiseworthy,

DOI: 10.4324/9781003092995-12

it is significantly easier in the case of a survey-based study than in the course of a field experiment. As the above-quoted author puts it, just obtaining approval from the relevant ethics committee to execute a field study takes as much time as a series of laboratory experiments (obviously, conducting a laboratory experiment also requires approval from an ethics committee, yet in most cases it is less complicated and less time-consuming). Not to mention the duration of the study itself (which quite often – just as a theatrical play – requires lengthy preparations related to the experimenters, the confederates, the observers, and other individuals involved in the experiment). It should be emphasized that the author of the article does not criticize the very notion of the need to replicate research, he only points to the fact that replication entails very different consequences for the researchers working in a laboratory setting versus those who choose to carry out their studies in a natural environment. The third element – the expectation of mediation analysis – is also very difficult to perform in the case of field studies. Participants in such experiments (hotel guests, passers-by, customers shopping in a supermarket) do not have any special interest in providing additional data, which would enable such mediation analysis. From their perspective, they have already done their job (e.g., they hung their towel on the peg after a single use, they helped a girl walking on crutches collect scattered papers, they put on a plastic glove while picking their bakery products). They will not, for example, complete a survey that would allow us to evaluate their need for cognitive closure (Webster & Kruglanski, 1994) even if we truly support the idea of mediating the willingness to give help through this variable. Obviously, subjects could be asked to fill out a survey after the main experiment and surely some of them would agree to do so. The problem is that only some (or even a small few) of all the subjects would be willing to grant such a request. What is more, these individuals would represent, at least in some cases, only a "section of just one section." In the experiments designed to test whether people are willing to stop and help a girl walking on crutches collect papers scattered by the wind in certain experimental conditions more than in others, we can approach them once they have already helped her and ask them to fill out a survey. Some will probably agree to do so, others will not. But what about the individuals who decided to walk past the girl without stopping to help her? Even if we chase them down and approach them with a request to fill out the survey, they will almost certainly refuse to do so. The results obtained from the survey will not be of much use to us. To be more precise: the lack of relevant data from the group that did not help will not allow us to conduct mediation analyses. (As a matter of fact, it will prevent conducting any meaningful statistical analyses). Unfortunately, the "no mediation, no publication" rule is increasingly popular among reviewers and editors working for journals.

All these factors clearly affect the probability of publishing results obtained through field experiments. Even Cialdini himself (2009) claims that throughout the last 15 years, he did not manage to get any of his articles describing field studies published in the major (perhaps even the most prominent) journal devoted to social psychology, referred to repeatedly in this book, i.e., *Journal of Personality and Social Psychology* (*JPSP*). What is interesting though is that in the same period, the journal featured articles authored or co-authored by Cialdini but devoted to studies conducted with other methods (e.g., Goldstein & Cialdini, 2007; Griskevicius et al., 2007; Jacobson, Mortensen, & Cialdini, 2011). A similar phenomenon was observed by Miles Patterson (2008), who analyzed another well-known journal, i.e., *Personality and Social Psychology Bulletin*, by checking the proportion of articles published in the journal containing data that could be considered a measurement of actual behavior. The results were very straightforward. Although in 1976 any measurement of behavior was considered a variable (dependent or independent) in approximately 70% of presented studies, in the period between 1996 and 2006 (such as the samples used by Patterson), the proportion was no more than 25%. Therefore, a phenomenon very similar to that observed by Cialdini and evidenced by his example, which we discuss in Chapter 1, is evident. In his text, Patterson also points to another aspect: a decreasing interest, among researchers, in the so-called unfocused interaction, i.e., specific interactions among people (or, speaking more broadly, between the sender and the receiver of a message) that occur even though they are not reflected in the verbal or nonverbal communication between them (Goffman, 1963). It should be emphasized that a significant share of measurements in studies conducted as field experiments pertain to such interactions, e.g., in the studies by James Fisher (1992) devoted to the effectiveness of road signs or studies on the duration of eye contact between strangers (Kleinke, 1986).

What are the consequences of the above-mentioned phenomena? According to Cialdini (2009), at this point and from his personal perspective, they are not particularly significant, as they do not affect his scholarly achievements as a retired professor. Nevertheless, they have a significant effect on young people at the onset of their scholarly careers in social psychology, who are very much interested in writing good (i.e., "published" and "quoted") articles. Some scholars complain about a pathological (in their eyes) phenomenon, where they are forced by their employers to produce measurable achievements in the form of the Global Impact Factor of their publications, as well as a constantly increasing Hirsch index from year to year (and most importantly, they are expected to write and publish numerous texts affecting these parameters). The "*publish or perish*" slogan applies to probably all major universities around the world. Even though there have been suggestions as to how to counteract this trend (e.g., in one of his interviews, anthropologist Robin Dunbar suggested that it would be a good idea to introduce a "total limit of texts," i.e., one would be allowed to publish no more than 20 texts throughout their entire career and thus with each subsequent article one would think twice about whether this particular text is worth publishing), at this point there seems to be no consensus on the horizon that would enable the introduction of such a restriction. As a result, Cialdini has declared that he stopped accepting Ph.D. candidates not because he has no desire to conduct studies or work as a scholar but because of his concern over their situation. As he does not wish to conduct studies other than field research with the Ph.D. candidates, and these do not give young scholars a chance to develop their careers.

Perhaps the best illustration of the potential consequences of all the processes described herein is the biggest scandal in the field of social psychology of recent years: the case of the "prodigy" of the discipline, Diederik Stapel. He was born in 1966 and therefore he was in the prime of his professional career by 2011, the winner of numerous prestigious awards (including the Career Trajectory Award he received in 2009 from the Society of Experimental Social Psychology), the author of an impressive number of widely quoted articles published in the best international journals, a professor of social psychology, and the dean of the School of Social and Behavioral Science at Tilburg University; yet he became the blackest sheep overnight. At the end of August 2011, three young scholars reported their suspicions to university authorities regarding alleged data fraud by Stapel. The accusations were treated very seriously, a committee was appointed to investigate the case, and the outcome of this work was soon made public. The results were shocking. From the investigation, it was proven beyond any doubt that the vast majority of analyzed articles used data that were either tweaked (e.g., by removing those individuals who acted inconsistently with the adopted hypotheses from the database or by pumping the database, adding participants to the point where the results become statistically significant) or fabricated altogether. At the end of the day, it was proven that Stapel had published 55 articles containing partially or completely fudged data (including a very widely read text which demonstrated that vegetarians are less selfish than meat-eaters). Numerous ideas for changes to be introduced into the field of social psychology in order to prevent similar cases from occurring in the future were presented, starting with measures aiming at verifying the internal publishing policies of the most widespread (and the most prominent) psychological journals and going as far as the statistical procedures designed to verify the accuracy of the presented data.

The way Stapel himself tried to explain his misconduct and the fraud he committed was very symptomatic of the whole case. He said (in the daily newspaper, *Brabants Dagbladt*):

> I failed as a scientist. I adapted research data and fabricated research ... I put my field, social psychology, in a bad light. I am ashamed of it and I deeply regret it ... I did not withstand the pressure to score, to publish, the pressure to get better in time. I wanted too much, too fast.

There is no intention on our part to defend Diederik Stapel, as nothing justifies scholarly dishonesty or plain fraud (let us not forget that Stapel actually embezzled huge amounts of money he had received in the form of research grants for his work), but we should reflect on his words. Or, to be more precise, on the extent to which the system that expects "great results" (results that support the proposed hypotheses, which are perfectly replicable and enable constant breakthroughs in the discipline) is to be blamed for provoking such pathological conduct. Let us be perfectly clear on this: our intention here is not to remove the responsibility from the fraud, but we believe that the reasons it was profitable for Stapel to commit fraud for quite a long period of time (55 articles questioned by the committee investigating his case date as far back as 1996) should be thoroughly analyzed. A special term was even coined for this procedure. The psychologists commenting on the case often said that Stapel simply conducted very specific desk research.

Jarosław Klebaniuk (2012) claim that one of the reasons for which Stapel's fraudulent misconduct remained undetected for such a long time, paradoxically, was the integrity of his fellow scholars. Simply put, those who consider data fraud unimaginable would never suspect their closest colleague or co-worker of committing it. Obviously, it would be very difficult to rule out such a possibility, but it seems that we should be a little concerned by the vision of the world where, by default, we act in a reversed manner. In other words, we don't suspect that someone who has had their study results published had used data collected in a dishonest manner or fabricated data.

Dishonesty or untruthfulness about published data does not always result from dishonesty on the part of the author of the publication. In some cases, the situation is much more complex. It may, for example, be related to the very nature of the field experiment being used as a research method. When considering the inherent threats of conducting field studies, we must not forget one more element: a high level of complexity of such experiments related to the number of logistical elements to be taken into consideration. In reality, conducting a field experiment resembles, to a certain extent, preparations for a play. One needs to take care of the makeup, the costumes, and the set design (with their performance, the experimenter's assistants have to make the audience believe the story they want to present to them and "immerse" them in the procedure of the experiment).

This means putting trust in a group of people – the experimenter's assistants, the organizers of the study and, generally speaking, one's co-workers. Unfortunately, sometimes this trust can be undue. We can learn this from the story of Nicolas Guéguen, a scholar who worked predominantly in France and described field experiments in almost all of his articles.

We described several of his studies in this book as they are extremely innovative and make use of very interesting operationalized variables. Sometimes, Guéguen and his colleagues use very interesting methods to deal with methodological problems (e.g., hiring a large number of experimenter's assistants in order to minimize their individual effect on the result). Therefore, we were particularly saddened and concerned by the articles published in 2019 in the *International Review of Social Psychology*, which called into question a series of texts authored or co-authored by Guéguen (Darnon & Klein, 2019). The whole story begins a little earlier, in 2017. At that time, Nicholas Brown and James Heathers (2017) published a very meticulously conducted analysis of works co-authored by Guéguen, which led them to believe that the results presented in these works were improbable to say the least. The authors of this analysis thoroughly investigated averages and standard deviations, as well as the distribution of variables, and noticed that these elements differed significantly from those usually presented in studies in the field of social psychology. It was a similar case with the size of the effects. Despite the fact that in psychology the observed effect size is usually somewhere in the region of Cohen's d =.43 (Richard, Bond, & Stokes-Zoota, 2003), in the articles analyzed the value was approximately 1, which is unlikely given the rather subtle manipulation methods. On top of this, Brown and Heathers pointed to other suspicious elements. For example, in the case of many experiments the response rate was 100%, which means that, for example, all passers-by approached on the street agreed to grant the request made by the experimenter's assistant. Interestingly enough, these situations took place exclusively in those groups where manipulation was applied. In their text, the authors claim that it was in 2015 when they reported their doubts to the French Psychological Society (SFP, for its initials in French), which acknowledged that their discoveries required Nicolas Guéguen's response. Unfortunately, no information or explanations were provided despite numerous requests made over the period of 18 months. As reported by Brown and Heathers: "At one point Dr. Guéguen sent a thick envelope containing details of 25 field studies that had been carried out by his undergraduates, none of which had any relevance to our questions."

As a result, Brown and Heathers decided to make the case public (up to this point their actions were limited to requests for explanations addressed to Guéguen as well as his employers). Following their publication, some journals (e.g., the above-mentioned *International Review of Social Psychology*) decided to take measures as regards the articles being the subject of the analysis conducted by Brown and Heathers. These actions resulted in expressions of concern. It should be noted that they do not call for retraction, they are simply expressions of concern and doubts. It should be also noted that they refer to selected texts authored or co-authored by Guéguen, not all of his scholarly achievements. Nevertheless, the very fact that the journal expressed its concern was a significant event also in the sense that certain individuals showed up with "behind the scenes" information on how studies conducted by Nicolas Guéguen looked. Brown and Heathers were contacted by a former student of Guéguen, among others, who described how the experiments were conducted in a brief e-mail:

> I was a student in an undergraduate course on [a social science field] … The university where Dr. Guéguen teaches has no psychology department … As part of an

> introductory class entitled, "Methodology of the social sciences," we had to carry out a field study … This class was poorly integrated with the rest of the course, which had nothing to do with psychology. As a result, most of the students were not very interested in this class. Plus, we were fresh out of high school and most of us knew nothing about statistics. Because we worked without any supervision, yet the class was graded, many students simply invented their data. I can state formally that I personally fabricated an entire experiment, and I know that many others did so too … At no point did Dr. Guéguen suggest to us that our results might be published.

As more information about doubtful results emerged, more scholars wanted to investigate the works of Nicolas Guéguen. One of them was Hans Rocha Ijzerman, who sent an analysis covering six texts to the editors of the *International Review of Social Psychology* in September 2019. Based on his findings, he suggested that two of the analyzed texts should be retracted, two should be corrected, and an expression of concern should be made in relation to the remaining two texts. The journal decided otherwise: an expression of concern was issued for five of the texts and one text was corrected. Other journals also took action in terms of potential steps involving texts by Nicolas Guéguen (including *Psychology of Music* and the *Scandinavian Journal of Psychology*) even though, as reported by Brown and Heathers, these were not excessively vigorous.

Currently (as of August 2020), the most severe and the most visible consequence of making the doubts regarding the works by Nicolas Guéguen public is his almost complete withdrawal from publication activities. Nicolas Guéguen has removed his Google Scholar profile (even though his articles are still available through the search engine). Since 2017, not many texts authored or co-authored by Nicolas Guéguen have been published (only a few can be found, whereas in the past he would publish as many as 20 articles a year).

It is clear that the case has not yet been closed, which means that it is too early to make any judgments about Nicolas Guéguen's guilt or the extent to which he should be held accountable for scientific misconduct. However, we would like to use this lamentable story to demonstrate a problem that we believe is typical particularly of field experiments and that was clearly illustrated in the letter written by Nicolas Guéguen's former student, which we quoted earlier. As we have already mentioned, works associated with conducting a field experiment are much more complex and require the involvement of a greater number of people than in the case of a laboratory experiment or a survey-based study. This also means that there are more links in the chain that can simply break. The trust put in the experimenter's assistants can be abused or minor mistakes can be made throughout the procedure, which consequently may lead to unreliable or even misleading results. Needless to say, we are not suggesting that these aspects relieve the scholar of all responsibility but quite the opposite. What we would like to do is emphasize that the field experiment, by nature, requires greater discipline and order from scholars conducting such an experiment, as well as greater control over the individuals who actually conduct the experiment. This is particularly important in the event a scholar remains in an asymmetrical relationship with the individuals performing the experiment, e.g., when such individuals are the scholar's students. For it may happen that such students, while accurately anticipating the hypotheses to be verified through the experiment, will try to please their professor and provide him with results that have little in common with reality but that meet the expectations of the scholar. Whereas the scholar, as a scientist convinced of the accuracy of their predictions, may gladly accept such results. We are not attempting to decide who is more to blame in such a situation. What we are trying to point out is that such situations must be prevented. The only reasonable solution we can see is to exercise extreme caution with regard to the procedure and the people involved, but most importantly with regard to our own expectations in terms of results. If something is too good to be true (e.g., the effect size exceeds Cohen's $d = 1.0$ following the application of relatively subtle manipulations), it most likely is not true. Thus, we should treat it with extreme caution.

We need to realize that as scholars, we cannot be doubtful, a priori, of the truthfulness of each article we read. We cannot become prosecutors constantly searching for a conspiracy, dishonesty, or fabricated data. It is only when we assume that results are reliable and that they have been presented in a reliable manner that we can cumulatively grow our knowledge of particular phenomena. Metaphorically speaking, it is only in this manner that we can build the edifice of science using bricks in the form of scientific articles. We will never be able to build it if we are subjectively convinced of the falsehood of these bricks. On the other hand, if we assume that the bricks are true, the whole building will not collapse even if it turns out that in a few cases we were gullible and that we were tricked. Obviously, the goal is to have as many true bricks and as few false ones as possible.

Therefore, it seems that the greatest share of responsibility for the future of social psychology (and particularly for whether or not there will be more false bricks in its structure in the form of various pathologies, such as those described above, as well as other types of pathologies) lies within the publishing policy of the most prominent and the most prestigious journals. One of the fundamental issues is their approach towards the publication of data illustrating null results. That being said, we do not necessarily believe that this should entail the establishment of special journals devoted exclusively to publishing studies in which the level of statistical significance expected for social studies ($p < .05$) is not achieved. Incidentally, there is such a journal, called the *Journal of Articles in Support of the Null Hypothesis*, and it was established by Stephen Reysen in 2002 (it is issued twice a year, but unfortunately – and understandably – the journal is not listed in the Journal Citation Report, JCR). The change that could actually make various types of pathological conduct in science less appealing should consist of making mainstream journals more open to the publication of studies that, even though they are correct from a methodological and statistical perspective, do not carry stunning or spectacular results. It even seems that such changes have already taken place in some journals.

One of the most famous decisions made by journal editors is that announced in two editorials in *Basic and Applied Social Psychology* (*BASP*) by David Trafimow and Michael Marks in 2014 and 2015, respectively. Both texts (Trafimow, 2014; Trafimow & Marks, 2015) indicated and then announced the changes that *BASP* editors were introducing in terms of editorial requirements regarding articles submitted to the journal. The editors announced that due to serious doubts about the value of study results based on NHSTP (Null Hypothesis Significance Testing Procedure), they expect scholars to refrain, within the transition period, from quoting testing results in their articles, for studies carried out in the field of psychology, along with figures such as p, F, and t values, as well as any other tests based on H_0 testing, and any such reference would be prohibited following the transition period. There were many doubts concerning the use of NHSTP, a major one being "*p* hacking" practiced by some of the scholars. The process consisted of designing study schemes in such a manner as to make sure the "*p*" parameter was below 0.05 at all costs (in most cases by means of increasing the number of tested individuals). Let us rephrase this: BASP does not accept specification of the *p* parameter, which means that null hypotheses cannot be rejected or confirmed and one is not allowed to use the following phrases, which used to be particularly important for psychology: "the difference between the groups was statistically significant," "a significant main effect and a significant interaction effect were achieved," "the relation between the variables was statistically significant." The editors have taken a very similar approach for data presented in the form of confidence intervals on results; as they claim, these are not free from some of the inherent flaws of NHSTP. They are slightly more sympathetic to results based on Bayesian statistics (but they are far from being enthusiastic about their use). To sum up, virtually no texts that have "Results" sections based on any statistics containing statistical inference procedures shall be approved for publication in *Basic and Applied Social Psychology*. This does not mean that such texts cannot be submitted to *BASP*; nonetheless, even if such texts are approved for publication, the editors will expect the author(s) to remove any results from statistical tests included in the text.

The editors encourage authors to provide descriptive statistics as well as effect size measurements (i.e., statistics that basically ignore sample size and focus on the variance percentage explained by the factors analyzed over the course of the study). They also indicate that due to the increasing stability of descriptive measures, along with the increase in the sample size, they will, as of now, expect slightly larger sample sizes than usual. They add, though, that they are willing to adopt a flexible approach to this expectation in justified cases and they actually do just that. We can testify to this personally, as our experimental studies featuring relatively small samples have been approved by the journal (Dolinski & Grzyb, 2016; Dolinska, Jarzabek, & Dolinski, 2020).

What is interesting is the final section of the second text declaring the end of the transition period and prohibiting publication of measures related to statistical inference. In that section, the authors state that contrary to what one could expect, the new rules will not make it easier to have one's article published in BASP compared to other journals: "after all, statistically significant results are no longer needed." Against all appearances, they warn it will be more difficult to have one's text published. Up to this point, in some cases, achievement of statistically significant results could be perceived as a decisive factor in terms of publishing texts suffering from methodological flaws. Now, according to Trafimow and Marks (2015), authors will have the opportunity to focus on designing and conducting well-thought-out and methodologically correct studies, instead of focusing on obtaining "good" results through null hypothesis testing.

Trafimow and Marks also announced that they expected other journals to follow their lead and also drop the requirement of including NHSTP results. Even though this expectation did not come true, in recent years we have certainly witnessed a more vigorous discussion in the field of social psychology regarding various aspects of publishing. Sometimes, studies of various types of factors improving one's chance for publication in major journals are conducted (which certainly proves, once again, the truthfulness of the "publish or perish" slogan). For example, Shaul Shalvi and his colleagues decided to check if the time of year that a text is sent to an online system (in most cases) used for submitting proposals for publication affects the decision of editors regarding its approval (Shalvi, Baas, Handgraaf, & De Dreu, 2010). The scholars focused on one of the most prestigious journals in the field of psychology: *Psychological Science*. They analyzed the month that 575 articles were submitted to this journal for the period between 2003 and 2006. The conclusion was that although the vast majority of texts were submitted in the summer months (June and

July), no such pattern was confirmed for articles actually approved for publication. This means that in all actuality there is a lesser chance of being approved for publication during the summer season compared to a situation where the article is submitted at another time of year (or at least that is the authors' interpretation of the data they collected, and they coined a catchy name for the effect identified that suggests how to proceed: "write when hot, submit when not"). Clearly, one could attempt to interpret the effect achieved by the authors of the text in various ways, one of the most obvious being the one related to the scholars' work schedule (assuming that most scholars are also academics). It is common practice to use at least a couple of the initial weeks following the end of the academic year for "closing any unfinished business," that is, *inter alia*, for describing earlier results and completing unfinished articles. Therefore, it is only logical that it was in June and July when an increased number of texts were submitted to *Psychological Science*. Nevertheless, the authors failed to confirm the existence of this pattern in the case of another major journal: *Personality and Social Psychology Bulletin* (*PSPB*). The scholars analyzed 1,811 texts submitted to *PSPB* during the period between 2003 and 2006 and they failed to identify a pattern similar to the one observed in the case of *Psychological Science*. The number of articles sent differed between particular months, but in the case of *PSPB* there was a decrease in the winter months rather than an increase in the summer months. The authors tried to identify the reasons for such differences in patterns of results, in terms of the number of articles submitted to and published in both journals, by analyzing the slightly different desk rejection policies of *Psychological Science* and *Personality and Social Psychology Bulletin*, yet their analyses seemed to predominantly demonstrate one element: a prevailing desire to have one's article published in top journals, which almost makes scholars look for a way to "crack the system" in order to – presumably – improve their chances of seeing their name printed in the best scientific journals worldwide.

Recently, another issue has spurred serious debate: journals for which authors have to pay to get published. The model seems simple: up to a certain point, authors used to write their texts without any fee, other scholars would review these texts, also on a *pro bono* basis, while editors (scientists) would run the journal, also without receiving, in most cases, any remuneration for their work, while the reader was expected to pay for access to an article (in most cases USD 30–50 for a single article or USD 200 for an entire issue). There was also an option to subscribe to the journal for slightly over USD 1,000 per year (with most subscribers being institutions). Obviously, the above-mentioned prices caused a significant drop in readership and thus it was suggested that the authors of the texts cover the costs (e.g., editorial staff, printing preparation, etc.). As a result, the Open Access model came into being, where the author of the article is responsible for the entire workload related to the text as well as any costs associated with preparing the text for publication (we deliberately refrain from using the word "printing," as the majority of contemporary journals are not printed anymore and are available only in their digital versions). What also needs to be emphasized is that these amounts are quite substantial. The publication fee in the leading Open Access journal, i.e., *PLOS ONE*, amounts to USD 1,495 (although discounts are available), whereas in the case of the quite prestigious *Frontiers in Psychology* (at the time of this article its JCR Impact Factor was USD 2,067), depending on the article type (e.g., an original article, a review, a case study report, a commentary), the fee ranges from USD 490 to USD 2,490. Evidently, the fees are rather high, particularly for scholars from less wealthy countries. To be honest, it must also be said that this model generates significant revenue for the owners of such journals. *Frontiers in Psychology* alone (which constitutes only a part of a larger Frontiers holding company that publishes numerous other journals) has already published 50,000 articles. If one assumes (optimistically) that on average USD 1,000 was paid for each article, the income from that single journal alone has reached USD 50 million (paid mainly with taxpayer dollars, obviously, as the cases of individuals paying for publication out of their own pockets are extremely rare or virtually non-existent). Needless to say, there are costs to be covered, but one way or another the above figures are impressive. As the essential purpose of this book is not to trace pathological conduct in scientific milieu, let us leave this issue without further comment, even though it should be said that it merits broader discussion among scholars.

Let us deal with another problem that might turn out to be a major trap for scientists. Aside from rather respectable journals offering the opportunity to publish one's articles in the Open Access system (virtually all journals offer this possibility), a great number of other publications have emerged that offer scholars a chance to publish their works in a journal with a remarkable name, including such words as "Global," "World," "International," "or Advanced." Since 2010, roughly speaking, many of us have been receiving e-mails with similar content, something along the lines of: "My name is John Smith and I am an editor for *The Biggest Universe Review of All Psychologies*. I have come across your article entitled (the title of one's most recent article would be entered here) and I can tell that you are a true expert in your field. I would like you to consider publishing your works in our journal." Obviously, most of us would at least visit the website of the journal. In most cases it would turn out that the quality of the website (as well as the quality of the English language used on the page) would deviate quite substantially from what we would expect of a professional journal (and the fact that the journal used a gmail.com domain for its e-mail account would also tell us that something was not quite right). Thus, here is our first encounter with so-called predatory journals.

This phenomenon intensified around 2008 and experienced a boom in 2012 (Butler, 2013). When one considers studies on the phenomenon of predatory journals, Jeffrey Beall is the name that immediately comes to everybody's mind across the globe. Since roughly 2008, this librarian and researcher from the University of Colorado Denver has become the main tracker, investigating shady scientific journals focused predominantly on charging authors publication fees for publishing their works in the Open Access system. It should be pointed out that these journals charged substantially less – in most cases the fee ranged from USD 100 to USD 200 and thus their offer seemed very attractive to less affluent scholars outside of the major, international academic centers. Beall has even prepared a special set of guidelines designed for individuals who consider publishing their work in a not-exactly-reputable journal, guidelines that could be titled: "How to identify a predatory journal?" In his guidelines, Jeffrey Beall has pointed to the following elements:

1 Check whether the journal has an address (not just a website but an actual postal address) and avoid journals that you can only contact exclusively through a contact form available on their website.
2 Check the individuals named as members of the editorial board. Do your know any of these names? Are you familiar with any of their works? Are they real experts? Does the journal list their affiliations and have you heard of these institutions? You can contact the members of the editorial board and ask them about their experiences with the journal. You can ask them (and the question would not be

completely unfounded) if they know that they are listed as members of the journal's editorial board.

3 Check whether the journal provides clear information on the type and the amount of publication fees, in some cases this information is provided only once the text has been approved for printing.
4 Use caution when you are invited to publish your works or join an editorial board.
5 Read the articles previously published in the journal. How would you grade their quality? Have you heard of their authors before?
6 Verify the journal's review procedure. Is it an actual review or just a gimmick?
7 Check whether the journal is a member of any widely recognized associations for Open Access journals (e.g., Directory of Open Access Journals or Open Access Scholarly Publishers Association).
8 Use common sense, just as you would do when buying things online. If something appears too attractive, consider this an argument against it.

Another aspect worth examining is the thematic scope declared by the journal. As an example, we can use a typical spectrum declared by one of the journals (*International Journal of Humanities and Social Science Review, IJHSSR*): Anthropology, Archaeology, Business Studies, Communication Studies, Corporate Governance, Criminology, Cross-cultural Studies, Demography, Development Studies, Economics, English Literature, Education, Ethics, Geography, General Studies, History, Human Studies, Industrial Relations, Information Science, International Relations, Law, Linguistics, Literature, Library Science, Media Studies, Methodology, Philosophy, Political Science, Population Studies, Psychology, Paralegal, Performing Arts (Music, Theatre, and Dance), Public Administration, Religious Studies, Sociology, Social Welfare, Statistics, Translation Studies, Visual Arts, Women's Studies, and so on ("and so on" are the actual words used at the end of the description of the journal's thematic scope as provided on its website). Apparently, it seems that virtually any text would fit into this very broad spectrum of topics.

The last item that Beall suggests checking is the Impact Factor (IF) of the given journal. Interestingly enough, despite the high prestige associated just with having an Impact Factor, a number of journals found on the Internet declare they have an IF (and it is often very high). The problem lies in the fact that it is very common for journals to use the Impact Factor parameter instead of the JCR (Journal Citation Report) Impact Factor. Simply put: in many cases the declared IF is just plain false. Sometimes it is a fake, another factor designed to imitate the actual Impact Factor. As it turns out, there are approximately 30 companies worldwide specializing in awarding such factors (Jalalian, 2015) which, in most cases, have nothing to do with the actual reach of the analyzed journal. Instead, they have catchy names (such as Real Time Impact Factor, IRB Impact Factor, Total Impact Factor, etc.). Additionally, they reach impressive values (for psychology) ranging from 3 to 7 (depending on the current level of insolence of the given journal). In August 2016 we even saw, on the website of a certain journal, a very high IF calculated at 3.25 for 2016, which, technically speaking, is impossible but even more so impressive.

Of course not all journals should be treated equally. What is more, there is no single, set, and clear-cut method that would allow us to categorize journals as predatory. For several years, Jeffrey Beall was the administrator of a website with a list of journals (and in some cases entire publishing houses) that could be labeled as suspicious to say the least. In time, a specific community has grown around this list and its members exchanged information on new predatory journals seeking (mainly) young scholars searching for quick and easy publication opportunities. Numerous individuals would ask about particular journals and there were discussions devoted to qualification criteria for a particular category. Beall was not inflexible in his opinions – in many cases he would change his mind and come to a conclusion that labeling certain journals as predatory would be an exaggeration. As a matter of fact, the criteria he used were also a subject of disputes among scientists; some claimed that Beall's criteria were arbitrary (Misra, 2016), even though they did not question the very problem related to Open Access journals. An interesting voice in this discussion comes out in the article written by John Bohannon (2013) and published in *Science*. In this article, the author described his experiment consisting of sending a completely ridiculous article on molecular biology to 304 Open Access journals. Everything in the article was made up by its author, starting from the scholar's surname and his affiliation up to the result of the studies: the discovery of a new, lichen-based anticancer medicine (the results described in the article did not support such a conclusion, the studies were conducted incorrectly, and the text suffered numerous gaps and shortcomings). Bohannon claimed that the article suffered from "such obvious gaps and flaws that it should be immediately rejected by each of the journals."

This author created his list of Open Access journals based on the list of predatory journals composed by Beall and that of the Directory of Open Access Journals (DOAJ) (167 journals were included in the DOAJ list, 121 in the list composed by Beall, 16 were included in both). The article was submitted to all these journals and Bohannon subsequently waited for the decision of the editors.

In 157 cases the text was approved for printing, 98 journals rejected the article, and the remaining 49 did not make their decision by the time Bohannon decided to close his study. According to the author, in 60% of cases there was no reviewer present in the editorial process. Only in 36 cases did he receive, from the reviewers or the editor, information on any problems with the text and its scientific shortcomings (even though in 16 of these 36 cases, the article was ultimately approved for publication despite unfavorable reviews). Bohannon noticed that among the journals that approved the text for printing, there were those associated with very prestigious publishing houses, such as Elsevier, Sage, Wolters-Kluwer, as well as esteemed universities. The most critical review (which rejected the article) was issued by *PLOS ONE* (it was also the only review which pointed to actual ethical problems associated with the studies being described).

From the perspective of Beall's initiative, we should also examine the results comparing the approval and rejection decisions among journals from both of the above-mentioned lists. Around 45% of the journals from the DOAJ list approved the article for printing, whereas the figure was 82% in the case of journals from Beall's list. The latter figure can be interpreted as either a confirmation of the accuracy or inaccuracy of the criteria adopted by Beall. After all, 18% of the journals labeled as predatory rejected the text, which could mean that almost one-fifth of the journals listed by Beall were erroneously included in the list (Davis, 2013). In any case, the problem in Beall's list is not valid any more, as it has ceased to exist as of January 15, 2017. Initially, there was some speculation on the reasons for this decision (it is known that Beall had received threats and that he had faced legal action on a regular basis). Beall's publisher reported that the website was closed due to "threats and politics" (Straumshein, 2017). At the same time, numerous voices emerged claiming that the date that Beall's list was shut down was a bad day for the world of science and that all necessary efforts should be made to keep it alive (Spears & Spears, 2017).

Why are we focusing on this threat so much? Predominantly because a scholar who conducts field experiments, discouraged by the problems with publication in "normal" journals, may, in an act of desperation, decide to submit their article to a clearly predatory journal. This would be a bad decision. Field experiments are too important for social psychology to let them be pushed to such periodicals.

To recapitulate the chapter devoted to publishing results of field experiments, one could venture so far as to point out the following general observations. First, publishing articles in good journals is, generally, a laborious undertaking, and the workload is even greater in the case of individuals who conduct field experiments. Second, there has recently been a lot of criticism of the publishing system in the field of psychology, and certain events have taken place that have revealed pathological conduct in this respect. Third, events such as the Diederik Stapel scandal have brought about a serious discussion as well as changes in terms of the policy of some of the journals, consisting of being more open to null results as well as non-mainstream methods of data analysis (even though so far it is difficult to tell whether this is actually true or just a claim). Fourth, and most importantly, there is a saying that is popular in psychology (and also perhaps in other fields of science): "editors are just like other people, only more so."

What does this mean for us in practical terms? Let us not give up, let us engage in a dialogue with editors, and let us present our arguments. The worst thing a scholar can do once their text has been rejected is conclude that "they failed to appreciate the quality of my work" and send the article, with no changes made, to another journal. Additionally, let us not neglect the importance of the cover letter, as this is where we can explain to the editor why we believe our text is important and worth publishing. And even if we do not improve our chances for approval by stating in the cover letter that we have, for a number of reasons, chosen a field experiment as our study method despite all the inherent problems and the increased workload involved, we might, at least, put a smile on the editor's face.

13 Replications

When the text entitled "Estimating the reproducibility of psychological science" was published on August 28, 2015, in *Science*, i.e., arguably the most prestigious journal to publish one's article in, it could be safely assumed that it would echo far and wide in the scientific milieu – and it did. In fact, discussions regarding the importance of the article announced by the Open Science Collaboration (a group of over 270 authors, including the undisputed leader, i.e., Brian Nosek) are very much alive to this day.

Let us recapitulate the most important facts: Nosek et al. (Open Science Collaboration, 2015) replicated 100 experiments and correlational studies published in three very important and prestigious psychological journals (*Psychological Science*, *Journal of Personality and Social Psychology*, and *Journal of Experimental Psychology: Learning, Memory and Cognition*). The scholars applied a high level of standardization to the procedure (which was necessary in the case of such a large group of experimenters; most of them did not know one another and communicated predominantly via electronic means of communication). A special replication protocol was developed for each member of the team to follow – the protocol provided for the following stages:

- selection of a particular study to be replicated (depending on the capacity of the given team) from a randomly selected sample;
- contacting the authors of the original study in order to obtain all the materials necessary for replication;
- development of a new experimental scheme;
- submitting the scheme for review by the authors of the original study and the remaining members of the team;
- registration of the study on the OSF (Open Science Framework – https://osf.io) portal;
- replication;
- writing a study report;
- submission for a specific "audit" carried out by the remaining members of the team in order to assess the quality of the performed work.

The entire process was carried out with technical support from the Open Science Framework, an Internet platform for study management that collects data and enables full control over the study process. It should be noted that the OSF also enables you to manage the openness of particular elements of the process. In the same way, for the sake of transparency in science and studies, one can also make certain stages of a study (e.g., proposed hypotheses or sample selection methods) available for "viewing" by non-members. It is

DOI: 10.4324/9781003092995-13

yet another form of protection against various types of pathological misconduct (such as conducting the study long enough for the results to become significant, cherry-picking subjects and removing those whose reactions are inconsistent with the proposed hypotheses, or *post factum* modification of the hypotheses). Another advantage of the OSF is that it stores raw data for the project over a period of ten years following its completion, which makes things much easier for those who would like to replicate original studies, re-analyze their results or perform meta-analyses (Condon, 2016). Even though some of the functionalities offered by the OSF are criticized (e.g., it is said to be difficult to carry out exploratory studies within the procedure proposed by the OSF (Ioannidis, 2016)), it can be assumed that this method of conducting studies will be increasingly popular.

Using the OSF, Nosek et al. performed 100 replications of results described in the journals mentioned. Their results demonstrated rather clearly that a number of psychological phenomena currently present in the general scientific discourse are either difficult or simply impossible to replicate. While the average effect size in the original studies (the ones which were used as the basis for replications), measured with the r value, was 0.403 ($SD = 0.188$), the conclusion of the replications performed demonstrated the average $r = 0.197$ ($SD = 0.257$). As one may notice, the r value was significantly lower than that in the original studies. What is more, the analysis of the significance of the results also revealed quite drastic differences. While in the original studies, 97% of the presented results were characterized by $p < 0.05$, the same level was achieved only for 36% of the tested effects in the course of the replication studies. To summarize the results obtained by Nosek et al., one can conclude that despite the fact that materials were provided by the creators of the original studies, and maximum care was taken in order to follow the original procedures, a significant share of the performed replications failed to confirm the existence of the described phenomena (or illustrated these phenomena as significantly weaker than those presented in the original articles). Obviously, the above conclusion does not mean that the relations demonstrated in the original studies do not exist. The fact that author X demonstrated a statistically significant difference between groups in his study ($p < .05$) and author Y failed to demonstrate the same significance in the course of a replication (as $p > .05$) does not disprove the existence of the effect in question. Not only that, but one could argue that in the event the replication carried out by author Y demonstrated the same effect as the one obtained by author X but at a level of, let's say, $p < .06$, it should be considered as additional empirical support for the relationship originally demonstrated. One should remember that the critical value of .05 is only a matter of the adopted convention. As Jacob Cohen (1994) had already noticed several decades ago, in the article with a witty and symptomatic title "The Earth is Round ($p < .05$)," situations where the p value is slightly lower vs. slightly higher than .05 do not differ in terms of quality. Therefore, it is foolish, to say the least, that both situations often lead representatives of social sciences to different conclusions as far as results of their studies are concerned.

Let us be clear that such a situation was very rare for the replications of studies by Nosek's team. Therefore, it should come as no surprise that the publication of the replication studies generated quite a response from the scientific milieu (in September 2020 the article was quoted more than 5,000 times). Needless to say, there were quite a few critical voices that questioned numerous elements of the standardized study process proposed by the Open Science Collaboration (Anderson et al., 2016; Gilbert, King, Pettigrew, & Wilson, 2016). Nevertheless, the text published by Nosek et al. again demonstrated the incredibly important role of replication in the process of scientific cognition.

Bogdan Wojciszke, a Polish social psychologist, presented a very interesting methodological proposition several years prior to the publication of the works by the Open Science Collaboration (2011). He recommended the strategy referred to as Systematic Modified Self-Replication (SMSR), which he says "is identified as a basic way of planning and performing programmatic empirical research in contemporary psychology. The SMSR strategy consists of replication studies on the same effect performed by the same team of researchers, with a systematic modification and diversification of the studied samples, variables and methods of their measurements" (p. 44). There are a number of various restrictions associated with a single study. For example, it is not known whether a specific manipulation to which the independent variable was subject was crucial for the study (and if no such effect would be obtained if another manipulation were applied). It is a similar case with the measurement of the dependent variable. Would another measurement method yield identical results? There are many more similar restrictions. For this reason, Wojciszke recommends the use of SMSR:

> The strategy enables researchers to achieve at least the following goals: (1) showing reliability of a basic relationship of interest, (2) checking efficiency of manipulations and construct validity of measures employed, (3) increasing internal validity, (4) increasing external validity, (5) eliminating alternative explanations, (6) identifying moderators of the basic relationship, and (7) identifying mediators of the basic relationship.
>
> (2011, p. 44)

Since the example of SMSR application discussed by Wojciszke is based on a series of studies conducted by one of the authors of this book and his colleague, i.e., Richard Nawrat, we will look no further in an attempt to be original (especially as field experiments, to which this book is devoted, constitute a prevailing share of said series of studies).

In 1998, Dolinski and Richard Nawrat published their text, which introduced the notion of the "emotional seesaw" to psychology and described its applicability as a technique for social influence. Perhaps the best illustration of its application is the method used during interrogations of suspects based on the "good cop/bad cop" scheme, which has been used for ages by police all around the globe. The scheme is as follows: the "bad cop" interrogates the suspect, and he obviously uses various "memory enhancers," such as threats, shouting, and perhaps even his fists. The police officer plainly torments his victim, mentally and perhaps also physically. At some point, the situation changes radically as the interrogator is replaced by his colleague. This officer is kind and polite, and he offers coffee or a cigarette. How does the interrogated person react to this? Will he spill the beans?

While referring to certain, more general emotional functioning patterns, Dolinski and Nawrat assumed that even though fear mobilizes us, the effect of a sudden disappearance of the cause of this fear is demobilization. In the state of relief preceded by fear (starting the emotional seesaw), an individual should become more susceptible to influence exerted by others. Obviously, Dolinski and Nawrat did not intend to interrogate anyone (or torture, or threaten with death or long-term incarceration, for that matter); instead they decided to verify the thesis according to which the state of emotional seesaw increases a subject's compliance.

The researchers selected a location in Opole (Poland), where some of the pedestrians would cross a busy street in a spot where there was no crosswalk. When the pedestrian was almost across the street, he would hear a police whistle being blown (the whistle was actually blown by the experimenters), the usual reaction to which was looking around nervously in search of a police officer eager to issue a jaywalking ticket. There was no police officer; instead there was a young girl waiting for the subject on the pavement, and she would introduce herself as a university student and ask the pedestrian to fill out a survey. Even though it was cold and windy, and filling out the survey on the street was inconvenient, as many as 59% of pedestrians, in a state of relief, agreed to grant the student's request. This percentage was clearly higher than in two other conditions, where jaywalkers were asked to fill out the survey without first having heard the alarming sound of the whistle (46%) and where pedestrians were asked to grant the student's request while they were walking on the pavement, not crossing the street (41%). Thus, the experiment's result confirmed the emotional seesaw hypothesis. Still, the authors decided to auto-replicate this effect in the course of several other studies. The objective was not to merely demonstrate, once again, that the condition of emotional seesaw leads to greater compliance (although such an objective would also be reasonable). The first objective of Dolinski and Nawrat was to maximize the internal validity of their study, that is, to cause an increase in the effect size, which in most cases is achieved by improving the experimental manipulation (so that the difference between the experimental group and the control group increases) or by eliminating undesirable elements (which might impede the effectiveness of the manipulation) from the experimental procedure. In the above-mentioned study, the differences in compliance between the individuals in a state of relief and in a neutral state were small, which, according to the authors, resulted from lack of a clear signal that would indicate that the threat is no longer there. Perhaps some participants were not sure whether there actually was a police officer in the first place (perhaps they thought they did not notice the officer), others might not have heard the whistle, or perhaps they thought that the police officer blew his whistle at someone else, etc. Therefore, the following experiment was arranged in such a manner as to make sure the signal denoting the passing of the threat as explicit and occurring for all subjects at the same time. This time around, the subjects were drivers parking their cars illegally. From a distance, the driver, as he was approaching the car, would already be able to see a piece of paper the size of a parking ticket behind the windshield wiper. When the driver picked it up, it turned out that it was not a parking ticket – what a relief! – but a flyer for Vitapan, a fictitious hair growth stimulator or (in other conditions) a flyer designed to promote blood donation. At this moment, a male university student would approach the subject and ask him to fill out a survey that he needed for his MA thesis. This time, as many as 68% of the drivers who found a flyer promoting blood donation and 56% of those who found a Vitapan ad agreed to grant the student's request at a significantly higher percentage than in the group where the flyer was attached to the side window of the car, where it was already easy to tell from a distance that it was not a parking ticket (40% compliance when the flyer pertained to blood donation, 34% when it was an ad for the hair growth stimulator), or in the group where there was no flyer on the car (36%). The improvement in terms of the method used in order to manipulate the state of relief translated to the increased internal validity of the study.

Another purpose of repeating one's studies (with procedures modified in various ways) might be to eliminate alternative explanations for the primary effect. In the course of the above-mentioned two studies on the state of emotional seesaw, participants subjected to experimental conditions experienced relief preceded by fear, whereas participants subjected to control conditions experienced neither relief nor fear. Therefore, it is not certain whether the differences between these individuals resulted from the feeling of relief alone or from the fear itself. It would be completely reasonable after all to assume that intimidated individuals are more susceptible to social pressure than those who are not intimidated. It was also impossible to rule out that it was not the dynamics of the experienced emotions that mattered (fear followed by relief) but the very fact of experiencing positive emotions at the end, as these often make us more willing to help (e.g., Isen & Levin, 1972; Kayser, Greitemeyer, Fischer, & Frey, 2010).

In order to settle this, Dolinski and Nawrat conducted another study with participants who were drivers who parked their cars illegally, only this time around they created one more type of condition, where drivers would find a parking ticket behind the windshield wiper. Regardless of the content of the note, the driver was approached by a female university student with a request to fill out a survey (actually the PANAS measure of positive and negative emotions) immediately after picking it up. According to the results presented in Table 13.1, drivers who received a summons from the police, certainly still affected by fear, agreed to grant the request incomparably less frequently than the drivers experiencing relief (from the "ad behind the windshield wiper" group) as well as the drivers in a neutral state (from the "ad on the door" and "no note" groups). This way, the authors proved that an increase in one's susceptibility to social influence is caused by a sudden removal of the source of fear, not by fear alone.

Within the same study, an attempt was also made to eliminate alternative explanations for the results. The survey the drivers were asked to fill out contained, among other items, a section devoted to the measurement of the feeling of guilt and shame currently being experienced as well as positive affective states. As it turned out, the level of those two emotions did not differ in subjects under relief conditions and subjects under neutral conditions, even though these emotions visibly intensified in the " parking ticket" group. The above-mentioned distribution of results allowed the authors to eliminate the explanation for the increased compliance to social pressure based on the alleged increase in the feelings of guilt and shame. Moreover, the results provide no grounds for assuming that the fear-then-relief sequence leads to experiencing positive emotions, which, subsequently, activate the subject's willingness to help others.

Table 13.1 Percentage of subjects who consented to fill in the questionnaire and mean indexes of positive mood, guilt, and shame in particular groups

	Vitapan advert card behind wiper	*Summons to a police station behind wiper*	*Vitapan advert card attached to the door*	*No card*
Percentage of people who complied with the request	62 (31/50) *a*	8 (4/50) *c*	38 (19/50) *b*	32 (16/50) *b*
Positive mood	27.10 (4.65) *a*	23.75 (5.32) *a*	29.60 (5.18) *a*	28.37 (5.29) *a*
Guilt	1.19 (.40) *a*	1.75 (.50) *b*	1.21 (.42) *a*	1.25 (.44) *ab*
Shame	1.29 (.53) *a*	2.75 (.50) *b*	1.42 (.51) *a*	1.37 (.50) *a*

Source: *Journal of Experimental Social Psychology, 34*, p. 31. Copyright: Academic Press.

Note: The greater the positive mood, guilt, and shame, the higher the score. *SD* in parentheses. Percentage or means which do not share common subscript differ within one row at $p < .05$.

At this point it should be noted that, in a broader context, the elimination of alternative explanations is a vital element of research programs in the field of social psychology. This is because a large number of phenomena that interest social psychologists depend on a number of factors. And if a phenomenon has many causes, which may exist simultaneously, eliminating alternative explanations is necessary in order to determine which of the potential causes is actually responsible for the given phenomenon. What is more, it is quite often the case that various factors are postulated by various psychological theories pertaining to the same problem, and thus deciding which of the alternative explanations holds true is equivalent to deciding which of the competing theories is valid.

Many times in this book we have stressed that even though we are huge supporters of field experiments, at the same time we are perfectly aware of certain inherent limitations in such studies. It was also in the case of the series of experiments on the notion of emotional seesaw that Dolinski and Nawrat did not adhere 100% to the procedure, and the subsequent study was conducted in a laboratory, not on a street. This way, they intended to increase the external validity of their studies. As was already mentioned in Chapter 5, a study is considered externally valid when its results can be generalized for people and situations other than those actually tested. An increase in external validity can be achieved by repeating studies on other types of subjects and by using different manipulations of independent variables as well as various operationalizations of dependent variables. This way, the chance of generalizing the obtained relationship to other, untested situations and individuals increases. Low external validity is a frequent reservation about laboratory studies due to the fact that laboratory conditions are significantly different from what happens in real life (outside of the laboratory). There are no such concerns as regards the above-mentioned studies of the state of emotional seesaw, as they were conducted literally on the street. Yet this fact alone does not automatically translate to the satisfactory external validity of the studies. This is, for example, because in the studies we described the dependent variable was measured in an almost identical manner in all three experiments; in all cases subjects were asked to fill out a survey. Therefore, a completely different operationalization of the dependent variable was used in the subsequent experiment. The participants (this time, high school students) were asked to participate in a fundraiser held to benefit children at an orphanage. Initially the participants were told that the experiment would consist of testing several of their skills and abilities. The participants were randomly divided into three groups. The first group was told that it would participate in a study of the learning process, where they would be painfully shocked with electric current for each mistake they made. It could be assumed that having learned that, these individuals should experience fear. The second group was told the exact same thing, but after a while the threat was called off and the group was informed that the professor supervising the study had changed his mind and that they would take part in a completely different study on visual–motor coordination, where they certainly would not be electrocuted. In the same way, individuals from this group were introduced to an emotional seesaw state: fear then relief. Finally, the third group was told from the very beginning that they would participate in a visual–motor coordination study. As they were waiting for the experiment to start in the laboratory waiting room, the subjects completed a scale designed to measure their actual fear (State Anxiety Inventory). Once they were done with it, they were approached by a female university student (supposedly unconnected with the ongoing studies in any manner whatsoever), who asked them if they would agree to participate in a street fundraiser organized for the benefit of a local orphanage. It turned out that the participants experiencing relief, which was preceded by fear, agreed to grant the request much more frequently (75%) than those experiencing only fear (participants expecting electric shocks, 37.5%) or those in a neutral state (waiting for the visual–motor coordination study, 52.5%). Once again, the emotional seesaw turned out to be an effective tool despite changing the characteristics of the group of subjects, using a different experimental manipulation, and changing the type of operationalization used for the dependent variable.

Diversifying the operationalization of the same variable, dependent or independent, is a vital element of the SMSR strategy. It should be noted that, e.g., a manipulation consisting of scaring a driver with the fact that he got a ticket is associated with a feeling of financial loss. One could imagine that it was only the feeling of relief resulting from the realization that no financial loss would occur that led to kindness in response to a person asking us for a favor at the given moment. The experiment, where the emotional seesaw is manipulated in a completely different manner (the fear pertains to the prospect of receiving painful electric shocks) and where the dependent variable is of a different nature (the beneficiaries of the assistance provided are individuals that the subjects are not in direct contact with at the given moment and the assistance itself is to be given in the future) eliminates these doubts.

The aforementioned laboratory experiment had one more important objective, though. It should be noted that fear is a key element of the state of emotional seesaw. If the applied manipulations evoke the states as intended by the authors, the individuals waiting for electric shocks should be the most frightened, the individuals waiting for the visual–motor coordination test should be the least frightened, and between these two extremes there should be those individuals for which one expectation was replaced with another one (state of relief). As demonstrated in Table 13.2, fear indices for the three compared groups corresponded exactly with the expectations.

Testing the effectiveness of manipulation is an important element of psychological studies. It is usually very difficult to introduce a direct measurement of the effectiveness of manipulating the independent variable into field experiments. On the other hand, it is significantly easier, and in a way more natural, in a laboratory experiment. Another objective of this laboratory experiment was to identify moderators of the interrelation between the state of emotional seesaw and the increase in susceptibility to social influence. A moderator of an interrelation is a factor that dictates the occurrence of this

Table 13.2 Mean level of anxiety in particular experimental groups

	Females	*Males*	*Females and Males*
Waiting for an electrical shock study	54.700 (6.191) *a*	51.800 (6.084) *a*	53.250 (6.234) *a*
Waiting for an electrical shock study, then informed that a visual–motor coordination will be conducted instead	44.050 (6.004) *b*	42.050 (5.978) *b*	43.050 (6.000) *b*
Waiting for a visual–motor coordination study	35.550 (5.708) *c*	33.350 (3.937) *c*	34.450 (4.966) *c*

Source: *Journal of Experimental Social Psychology, 34*, p. 34. Copyright: Academic Press.

Note: *SD* in parentheses. Means which do not share common subscript differ within one column at $p < .05$.

interrelation or affects its strength. It would, for example, be very reasonable to assume that the feeling of guilt or shame acted as a moderator for the effect that the feeling of relief had on the compliance with social influence in the first three experiments. All participants in the field experiments described above committed an offense (jaywalking or illegal parking) and perhaps that is why the relief they experienced made them more receptive to other people's requests, as feeling of guilt and/or shame intensifies one's willingness to help others (Kelln & Ellard, 1999; Vallace & Sadalla, 1966). Therefore, in one of the aforementioned experiments (where the subjects were drivers illegally parking their cars) the participants were asked to complete a survey designed to measure the extent to which these emotions were experienced, in order to verify whether experiencing such unpleasant emotions plays a crucial role.

The potential influence of feeling guilt or shame on the effect a state of relief has on people's willingness to grant other people's request and follow other people's suggestions can also be tested through an experiment designed in such a manner as to make sure the subjects do not experience these emotions. In the laboratory experiment described above, the high school students did not do anything wrong (or at least not directly prior to hearing the request addressed to them). If the feeling of guilt or shame played the role of moderator for the interrelation in question, the state of emotional seesaw should not have produced results in this particular study. In actuality, it still worked, which demonstrates that feelings of guilt and shame are not determinants for the occurrence of this phenomenon.

Generally speaking, as Bogdan Wojciszke emphasizes, a search for moderators is an important element of the SMSR strategy, as it is equivalent to searching for the limits within which psychological patterns still apply, and discovering these limits is just as important as learning the patterns.

In a way, the most important stage of a program of empirical studies, as well as the SMSR strategy itself, is to identify the mediators of the examined relationship, where a mediator is defined as a process or a state mediating between the independent variable (the cause) and the dependent variable (the effect). A moderator, as discussed earlier, tells us when or in which conditions the relationship occurs and when it is strong/weak. A mediator tells us why the relationship occurs. As providing an explanation is the most important purpose of a theory, searching for mediators can be considered the most important element of a research program.

Why is it that the sudden disappearance of a threat and appearance of the state of relief cause an increased susceptibility to social influence? It should be noted that the experiments on the state of emotional seesaw discussed earlier do not provide us with an answer to this question, even though they allow certain possibilities to be ruled out (e.g., they demonstrate that feelings such as fear, shame, or guilt are not the cause).

Ellen Langer (1989; Langer & Moldoveanu, 2000) points out that in many cases, people operate in a mindless manner. She claims that most of the time this results from the fact that certain situations repeat themselves many times throughout one's life, and thus we pay less and less attention to those recurring events and act in an increasingly automatic and mindless fashion. This mindlessness, as interpreted by Langer, is motivational in nature: people do not feel like devoting their attention resources to their actions. Dolinski and Nawrat (1998) assumed that the state of mindlessness also occurs in the case of emotional seesaw, even though its nature is completely different. When a threat suddenly disappears, people are so preoccupied with thinking about what just happened (my God, my heart is racing!) and about what could have happened (what would have happened if

I had gotten caught) that they lack the mental (attention-related) and cognitive resources necessary to reasonably process the incoming information. As a result, processing this information becomes mindless and people automatically yield to requests made or pressure exerted by other people.

In order to verify this reasoning, the authors designed one more experiment based on the scheme of the study by Langer, Blank, and Chanowitz (1978), which we described in detail in Chapter 3. Even though in this case the experiment was not about letting somebody use a copy machine at first, the nature of the requests addressed to the subjects was as diversified as in the original study. In the experiment, two elegantly dressed, male university students were collecting money for children with disabilities in a street fundraiser. The students approached every tenth single passer-by and used the following phrase, while shaking their moneybox: "Sir/Madam, would you please give us some money?" These were the so-called "request-only" conditions. In actual justification conditions, the students would say: "Sir/Madam, we are members of the 'Students for Disabilities' organization. Would you please join our charity action because we have to collect as much money as possible to cover the cost of a holiday camp for children with mental disabilities?" Finally, in mock justification conditions, where the phrase is grammatically structured to resemble a justification but fails to provide any arguments, the students collecting money would say: "Sir/Madam, we are collecting money. Would you please give us some money because we have to collect as much money as possible?" The authors assumed that in normal conditions, people would be able to recognize the mock nature of the justification and would donate money as infrequently as in the "no justification" conditions.

As illustrated by Table 13.3, that was actually the case. Nevertheless, the scheme of the experiment also featured conditions of an emotional seesaw. In those conditions, the students carrying their moneybox addressed those individuals who heard a police whistle being blown while they were jaywalking. Dolinski and Nawrat assumed that in this situation, the subjects would be in a state of mindlessness and would not be able to process incoming information in a precise manner. Consequently, they would respond to the mock justification in the same way as they would respond to the actual one. The results presented in Table 13.3 fully confirmed these predictions and suggest that the

Table 13.3 Percentage of people who offered money, mean amounts of money given, and a tendency to seek additional information under each experimental condition

	Jaywalkers with whistle			*Jaywalkers*		
	Request only	*Placebo info*	*Real info*	*Request only*	*Placebo info*	*Real info*
Percentage of participants offering money (without asking any questions)	38.7 *a*	76.0 *b*	71.9 *b*	11.3 *c*	15.1 *c*	58.5 *b*
Mean amount of money given in Polish zl	.80 *b c*	1.65 *a*	1.48 *a*	.31 *c*	.55 *c*	1.53 *a*
Percentage of participants asking for additional information	20 *a*	8 *b*	–	49 *c*	57 *c*	–

Source: *Journal of Experimental Social Psychology*, *34*, p. 37. Copyright: Academic Press.

Note: Means which do not share common subscripts differ within one row at $p < .05$.

reason behind this increased susceptibility to social influence in a sudden relief situation is actually mindlessness, in this particular case associated with one's inability to use the operational resources of one's mind necessary to effectively defend oneself against pressure exerted by other people.

As evidenced above, with numerous replications of the first experiment, and with new elements being incorporated into the procedure and changes being made both in terms of the method of emotional seesaw manipulation as well as the method used to measure compliance, the authors became convinced that they had discovered a new social influence technique that had not yet been described in the psychological literature. They also demonstrated its effectiveness in further studies (e.g., Nawrat and Dolinski, 2007; Dolinska and Dolinski, 2014; Dolinski, 2001; for review see: Dolinski, 2001, 2016). For a number of reasons (also due to the self-fulfilling prophecy effect, which we discuss in Chapter 3), both laboratory (e.g., Szczepanowski et al., 2019) and field (e.g., Kaczmarek and Steffens, 2017, 2019) experiments conducted by other researchers seem to be particularly valuable from the perspective of documenting the psychological consequences of the state of emotional seesaw. One such experiment was conducted by Tomasz Grzyb long before any of us could have predicted that we would be writing this book together.

In that study (Grzyb, 2003), phone calls were made to individuals randomly selected from a phone book (a word of explanation for the younger section of our audience: prior to the cell phone era, phone books were printed with a list of landline phone numbers). Once the person answered their phone, the experimenter would ask the following question of the experimental group (featuring emotional seesaw induction): "Excuse me, have you lost your wallet today? See, because I found a wallet today and there was a slip of paper with your telephone number on it." As one can imagine, the person who answered the phone typically responded with fear, resulting from the conviction that they had lost their money and their personal documentation. Once the subject made sure, to his relief, that he had not lost his wallet, the experimenter ended the conversation with the following phrase: "Oh, I understand, it must be somebody else's wallet then. Well, I will keep trying. Goodbye." Several seconds later, another person that was not the experimenter who had just called, would call the same number. This caller would introduce himself as an employee of the "Mobilex" company (which was a fictitious company name) and would ask the person who answered, without giving any additional justification, to say the first and second (in the case of the easy task) or the fifth and sixth (in the case of the difficult task) digits of their phone number. The request was phrased as follows: "Good day, Sir/Madam, I represent the Mobilex company. Could you tell me the first and second (or the fifth and sixth) digits of your telephone number?" At this point, time was being measured and the response was recorded. Following that, the caller would add: "Thank you very much Sir/Madam. Have a good day. Goodbye."

In the control conditions, only the request to provide the given digits of one's telephone number was made, without the prior induction (and subsequent withdrawal) of negative emotion. Initially, the study covered 120 individuals, but after final verification only 110 people were included in the analysis (in the remaining cases it was suspected that the individuals who answered the phone were minors). For obvious reasons, detailed data on the analyzed sample cannot be provided, and only the sex of the respondents was controlled: 39 women were approved for the analysis (35.45% of the whole sample) and 71 men (64.55% of all participants). Grzyb proposed that if the assumption, according to which mindlessness is associated with a temporary inability to process information, effectively occurs in the state of emotional seesaw, it should result in an extended response

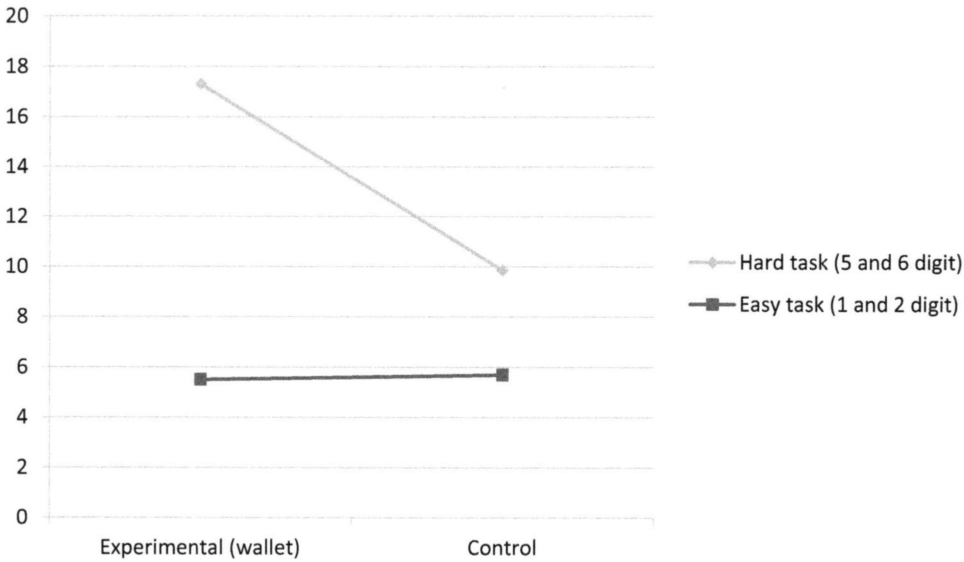

Figure 13.1 Time needed to respond to the question regarding telephone number depending on experimental conditions.

Source: prepared by the authors.

time, and this effect should be evident when the called individual was asked to provide the fifth and sixth digits of their phone number. When the called individual was asked to provide the first and second digits of their phone number, the response should have been automatic and not impeded by the state of emotional seesaw. Figure 13.1 clearly demonstrates that the results of this experiment were fully consistent with said proposition.

It is worth noting that this single and rather simple experiment not only produces interesting data on the mindlessness occurring during the state of emotional seesaw, but it also makes us more knowledgeable about other aspects of the phenomenon originally investigated by Dolinski and Nawrat. Grzyb managed to demonstrate that the physical presence of the person first inducing and then removing negative emotions is not required for an emotional seesaw state to occur. As it turned out, telephone contact was sufficient for this purpose.

Even though the emotional seesaw was originally designed as a technique for social influence, it also brings about important consequences in other areas of life, unrelated to social influence, due to the fact that it temporarily impedes one's cognitive functions.

Shortly after the initial articles on this subject had been published, Dolinski was contacted by the head of the German ADAC, one of the largest motorists' associations in the world. The gentleman had noticed, while reading an article describing the mechanism of the emotional seesaw, that he had encountered a similar phenomenon while analyzing the course of numerous traffic accidents in Germany. According to ADAC experts, a large portion of traffic accidents occur immediately after the driver has managed to evade a dangerous situation on the road. For example, the driver would realize, while overtaking, that oncoming vehicles travel much faster than he thought and, as a result, the side-view mirrors of both cars would graze each other. What a relief! He came within a hair's breadth of a head-on collision! According to the head of ADAC, this very moment, the one immediately after the driver feels relief as he manages to escape a dangerous situation uninjured, is critical. It is at this point when many accidents happen, as the driver, following a moment of intense mobilization caused by the presence of danger, falls into a state of mindlessness and, e.g., hits a truck parked on the shoulder. The apt observation made by the head of the German motorist's association should be appreciated. He was able to rationally apply the results of scientific studies to his line of work and, equally importantly, present a hypothesis on the psychological causes of (at least some) traffic accidents. It can be assumed that one of the reasons it was easier to do so was because the experiments, in the prevailing majority, were conducted in the natural subjects' environment, not in a laboratory. At this point, it should be added that it has only recently been proven experimentally (obviously through the use of a virtual environment) that, when drivers experience a state of emotional seesaw, one moment later, when the situation on the road becomes difficult, they react with delay and are unable to avoid an accident (Dolinski & Odachowska, 2018).

It is then clear that the replication of studies is absolutely crucial in science. Currently, the psychological milieu are, undoubtedly, perfectly aware of it. Bogdan Wojciszke (2011) noticed that while in 1965 only 10% of the texts published in the *Journal of Personality and Social Psychology* (*JPSP*) contained a description of more than one study, the share was 20% in 1975 and 48% in 1995.

As Wojciszke concluded his analyses in 1995, Grzyb and Steposz (2016) decided to verify the dynamics of the development of this trend. They analyzed 199 articles from the 2003 annual issue of *JPSP*, which contained descriptions of a total of 596 studies, 61.9% of which were experimental. Once they had calculated the number of studies per article, it became apparent that the trend identified by Bogdan Wojciszke had been maintained and had even been growing: from among 199 of the analyzed publications, only 46 (22.8%) described results of only one study. Table 13.4 presents exact numbers along with the percentage values.

As demonstrated by the above data, a single article from 2003 featured as many as six or even eight studies, and even though it was not the prevailing index (the median for the number of studies in the 2003 annual issue was 3), the tendency to demonstrate psychological phenomena by presenting a series of studies had become rather evident.

By comparison, Grzyb and Steposz (2016) performed identical calculations for the 2012 annual issue, where this effect was even more evident (Table 13.5).

Table 13.4 Number of studies per article published in *JPSP* (2003 Annual Issue)

		Frequency	*Percentage*
No. of studies in one article	1	46	22.8
	2	31	15.3
	3	45	22.3
	4	46	22.8
	5	21	10.4
	6	8	4.0
	8	2	1.0

Source: prepared by the authors.

Table 13.5 Number of studies per article published in *JPSP* (2012 Annual Issue)

		Frequency	*Percentage*
No. of studies in one article	1	22	15.9
	2	13	9.4
	3	27	19.6
	4	24	17.4
	5	33	23.9
	6	11	8.0
	7	2	1.4
	8	2	1.4
	9	1	.7
	10	1	.7
	12	1	.7

Source: prepared by the authors.

Table 13.6 Number of studies per article published in *JPSP* (2019 Annual Issue

		Frequency	*Percentage*
No. of studies in one article	1	23	22.6
	2	14	12.6
	3	16	14.4
	4	12	10.8
	5	21	18.9
	6	10	9.0
	7	6	5.4
	8	5	4.5
	11	1	0.9
	13	1	0.9

Source: prepared by the authors.

As evidenced by the above data, the number of articles in 2012 that described only one study was less than 16% (the median increased to 4). There were also texts describing truly extensive series of 9, 10, or even 12 studies.

For the purpose of writing this book, we also took a look at the 2019 annual issue (we were working on this book in 2020). Table 13.6 presents the results of our analysis.

To be honest, we expected the trend, which has been evidenced for years now, to increase. Therefore, we thought that there would be fewer articles that described only one empirical study than seven years earlier. Meanwhile, the number was higher than in the beginning of the 20th century. What is also interesting, even though the median was 4, just like before, is that the articles based on a single study were clearly the most frequent category.

Upon a more thorough examination of the content of the articles based on a single study, one may also notice that in virtually all cases these are non-experimental studies, predominantly conducted on very large samples, often of longitudinal nature. We also examined the number of subjects. It turns out that in 2019, the average number of individuals covered by one program (i.e., the number of individuals participating in all studies described in one article) was 3,924.5 (SD = 9,726.96). The lowest number of participants was 116, while as far as the highest numbers are concerned, in the top three articles these were 21,377, 38,376, and 90,651, respectively. We need to make one reservation here, namely: we did not include the study by Jackson and Gray "When a Good God Makes Bad People: Testing a theory of religion and immorality," in our calculations, as the data the scholars used was based on the number of books checked out from libraries. Let's just say that it was over one million.

Taking the above into consideration, it can be said that compared to previous years, there has been a growing trend to report a single, non-experimental study based on a very large sample.

We are far from claiming that such studies are redundant or faulty in terms of their methodology. Nevertheless, the large numbers of such articles published in *JPSP*, a leading journal in the field of social psychology, may be indicative of a gradual shift away from experimental studies in social psychology, while such studies have always been considered crucial for this discipline. Following this line of thinking, we are concerned that the methodology of social psychology is shifting toward asking subjects to complete various types of surveys. Let's see how consistent that is with what we have described in the initial chapters of this book: our field of science is becoming less and less interested in actual, not just declarative, behaviors.

On the slightly brighter side, it can be said that, at least in *JPSP*, publishing only one study in an article is still rather uncommon (articles based on a series of studies are still prevailing) and it almost never happens in the case of experimental studies. It should also be emphasized that for quite some time now, the strategy consisting of conducting a series of experiments has been typical when publishing the most momentous scientific discoveries. If we were to look back at the most important experiments in the history of social psychology, it would be difficult to identify such examples that were conducted only once, perhaps with the exception of the prison experiment by Philip Zimbardo (Haney et al., 1973; Zimbardo, 2007). Let's examine another milestone for the discipline of social psychology, namely the studies on obedience to authority by Stanley Milgram, which we have already mentioned several times in this book. The publication of the results of his experiments (Milgram, 1963, 1965), over the course of which Milgram demonstrated that in most cases people can be persuaded into electrocuting another human being sitting in an adjacent room with 450 volts, was not just a shock to the field of psychology. Shortly afterwards, Milgram's experiments were replicated by various teams of researchers (e.g., Bock & Warren, 1972; Kilham & Man, 1974; Shanab & Jahya, 1978). Every time, it was demonstrated that as long as the instructions to electrocute another human being were given by a figure of authority (a university professor), people would usually follow these instructions. Soon, scholars were trying to determine why this was the case (Milgram, 1974), and they started exploring personality factors that might modify the level of one's obedience (e.g., Fisher, 1968; Kaufmann, 1967; Mixon, 1972).

It should be noted, though, that prior to publishing his works, Milgram conducted 24 studies designed to verify the effect he had obtained in a variety of ways (e.g., Perry, 2013; Dolinski & Grzyb, 2020). Therefore, it can be said that before the scholar came to the conclusion that he was ready to announce the results of his experiments, he had verified these results in a variety of ways, while also looking for – as we would call them today – the moderators and mediators of the effect he described.

Obviously, Milgram did not verify all possible explanations. For example, Gilbert (1981) suggested that the procedure applied by Milgram could possibly be affected by the "foot-in-the-door" phenomenon (Freedman & Fraser, 1966), which we describe in Chapter 3. Gilbert notices that initially the subject was only asked to push a first button, which inflicted no pain on the person in the adjacent room. Subsequently, the subject was asked to push a second button, a third button, and so on. According to Gilbert, this gradual and consistent escalation of demands made by the experimenter might have affected the obedience displayed by the participants in the experiment. It was almost 50 years after the initial publications by Milgram that the studies designed to verify (and rule out) this possibility were conducted (Dolinski & Grzyb, 2016; Grzyb & Dolinski, 2021).

For ethical, practical, and methodological reasons, scholars would develop another procedure designed to test obedience. In their experiments, Virgil Zeigler-Hill et al. replaced electric shocks with strong acoustic stimuli, as they assumed that such a change would mitigate the feeling of guilt experienced by the subjects (Zeigler-Hill, Southard, Arche, and Donohoe, 2013). After all, electrocution is much more drastic than emitting loud sounds. Mel Slater et al. (2006) conducted a study where it was not a human but a virtual being (an avatar) that was electrocuted. The participants in the experiment would be seated in front of a screen displaying an image of a woman (the "learner"), which reacted, in real time, to the electric shocks delivered. In order to verify the accuracy of such an experimental setting, the scholars would also monitor various physiological parameters indicative of anxiety (e.g., heart rate, skin conductance response). Despite the fact that the subjects knew they were not electrocuting an actual human being, their bodies reacted in a manner indicative of their experiencing strong levels of stress.

Another idea for creating an ethically acceptable procedure in order to examine obedience was to assign unpleasant descriptors to relatively pleasant images (Haslam, Reicher, & Birney, 2014). To be more exact, the researchers prepared a series of 30 images sorted on the basis of their attractiveness (starting with the least pleasant to the most pleasant). As a result, the series would start with a picture of Ku Klux Klan members, followed by a picture of members of the Nazi party, followed by a picture of paramilitary groups, etc. The series would end with pleasant pictures, such as children playing in kindergarten, smiling seniors, and a picture of a family taking a walk. From among four negative adjectives, the participants were asked to choose the one that described the picture shown in the most accurate way. What is important is that as the experiment progressed, the pictures became more and more pleasant, whereas the adjectives remained negative, which resulted in the growing levels of discomfort experienced by the subjects. The creators of this procedure assumed that this discomfort would correspond with that experienced by participants in Milgram's original experiments. This experiment suffers from many methodological problems, but one deserves particular attention. While in Milgram's original experiment the participants felt they were hurting another human being (a man sitting in an adjacent room), in the procedure proposed by Haslam et al. it was only the participant who experienced discomfort. This is a fundamental difference between this and the original procedure designed by Milgram.

Similarly, Laurent Bègue et al. (2015) conducted a study based on a television game show. The participants were told that they were participating in a television show, and the authority figure was a TV star hosting the show. Like Milgram's original experiment, roles were randomly assigned and the punishment for each incorrect answer given by the "learner" was an electric shock.

However, Alex Haslam, Stephen Reicher, and Kathryn Millard (2015) used the so-called Immersive Digital Realism (IDR), a method that could be referred to as theatrical.

A key element of IDR is the role-playing performed by actors instructed specifically for this purpose. In the course of IDR-based experiments, actor–participants receive a certain share of necessary knowledge (they are informed that they are playing the role of subjects in a psychological experiment, but they receive no information on the purpose of the study or the variables being analyzed), and they are subsequently "immersed" in an environment resembling, as much as possible, the laboratory where Stanley Milgram conducted his original studies. Of course, it must be made clear that the method referenced as IDR by Haslam has actually been known in psychology for many years now and postulated as an alternative to misleading participants. It has been described by Herbert Kelman, for example, who pointed out that careful and precise communication of instructions to participants regarding the roles they are to perform produces promising effects in ethically dubious experimental schemes (Kelman, 1967). The importance here is that Kelman emphasizes the role of cooperation between the researcher and the participant in the experiment, which is crucial from the perspective of eliminating the temptation in the subjects to act according to the hypotheses. Martin Greenberg (1967) also voiced an important comment on the application of the role-play technique over the course of his successful studies regarding the relation between the order in which children were born and the way they act when faced with a threat.

On one hand, all these procedures, despite their differences, demonstrate a phenomenon of general obedience to figures of authority, even though Haslam, Reicher, and Millard all interpret identical behavior on the part of the subjects as evidence of completely different motivations. Therefore, one could argue that Milgram's discoveries have been replicated on numerous occasions. Nevertheless, there remain some major questions here, namely: what does it mean to replicate an experiment, and how is the notion of replication understood in the world of science? We devoted several years to studies on obedience (Dolinski & Grzyb, 2020), in which we used a device to deliver electric shocks that was a faithful copy of the equipment used by Milgram (see Figure 13.2).

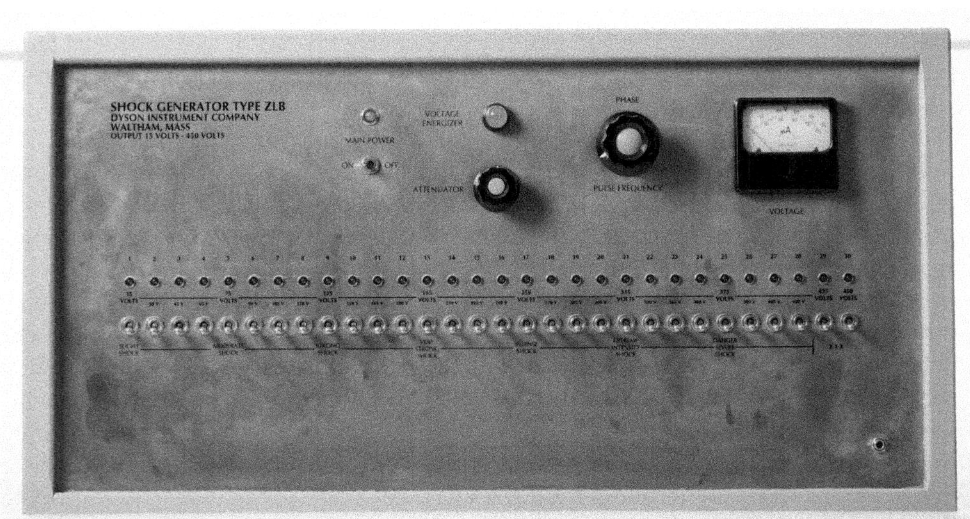

Figure 13.2 A replica of Milgram's original machine used in the experiments by Dolinski and Grzyb.
Source: photo by Michał Jakubowicz.

During one of the open lectures on the causes and consequences of general obedience in the contemporary world, Professor Dariusz Stola (the head of the Museum of the History of Polish Jews in Warsaw) asked us why we did not use a computer application, which would be more in the spirit of the 21st century. Although none of the several hundred subjects were ever surprised with the appearance of the apparatus, considering it to be a professional piece of fully functional equipment designed to generate electric shocks, the comment by the historian seems interesting. This could be expressed through a more general question, namely: is trying to maintain all standards of an original study, at all costs, actually equivalent to its replication?

It seems that the problem may pertain to another "scandal" exposed in social psychology: the matter of the facial feedback hypothesis (Wagenmakers et al., 2016). Let us recall the most important facts. In 1988, Fritz Strack, Leonard Martin, and Sabine Stepper published an article describing studies devoted to rating comic books in various conditions (Strack et al., 1988). The researchers asked the participants in the experiment to rate fragments of splash pages of "The Far Side" comic strip by Gary Larson. Strack et al. developed two conditions: one where the subjects were to hold a pencil in their mouth with their front teeth, and the other where subjects also held the pencil in their mouth but only using their lips (not using their teeth). As a result, the facial expressions in the first group (the one asked to hold the pencil with their teeth) resembled a smile (as the expression activated the *musculus zygomaticus maior*, i.e., the muscle which enables smiling), whereas the facial expression in the second group resembled the duck face typical of selfies (obviously, from today's perspective – luckily nobody knew what a selfie was in 1988). As it turned out, there was a significant difference between the two groups when their members were asked to rate how funny the comic strips were. Those participants who held the pencil in their teeth, having activated the muscles responsible for their ability to smile, rated the comic strips as funnier than those who were holding the pencil with their lips only. The results obtained by Strack et al. turned out to be incredibly important to a number of scholars (almost 1,500 citations of the original article) and strongly supported the facial feedback hypothesis, and its impact on our emotions (McIntosh, 1996; Strack & Neumann, 2000). These results, from a certain perspective, were also solid proof of the validity of the self-perception theory (Bem, 1972). Strack's results have even made it to the front cover of *Science*.

Surprisingly, in 2016, when Eric-Jan Wagenmakers et al. attempted to replicate the results originally produced by Strack and his team, the effect was not present. Over the course of 17 experiments conducted in various conditions, no correspondence was identified between their results and the results obtained by Strack et al. in their original experiments. Nevertheless, after a careful reading of the text by Wagenmaker et al., one is not entirely sure whether it does disprove the facial feedback hypothesis (even the authors of the article do not go so far as to make such unambiguous conclusions). However, the published text certainly demonstrates that a number of researchers testing a phenomenon in many laboratories simply opens a significantly broader perspective for drawing conclusions, particularly when one is dealing with such an elusive aspect as humor (one could debate whether the jokes in the comic strips would be equally funny to the subjects if the replications were carried out in the USA, Belgium, Canada, the UK, Italy, Spain, the Netherlands, or Turkey).

Some researchers (Bavel, Mende-Siedlecki, Brady, and Reinero, 2016) also noted that the cultural context in which replications are carried out must be taken into consideration. They referred to the Open Science Collaboration text described earlier in this chapter (100 replications suggesting a significant reduction in the effect size compared to the original studies) and re-analyzed their results. They examined the extent to which a change in cultural context might affect results of particular studies (and also the results of their replications). Bavel et al. used the notion of contextual sensitivity, and taking this into account they re-examined the effect size in particular replications. They identified an interesting pattern among the results: where a study was found to be sensitive to cultural context, the effect size for its replication was significantly reduced. The researchers also discovered that said pattern occurs in all areas of psychology they have ever dealt with, and its application is therefore not limited to, e.g., social psychology. Most interestingly, their conclusion does not suggest that the results obtained by Brian Nosek et al. (and their conclusions) should be criticized. The authors only point to the fact that the context of studies is extremely important when it comes to their replications. Again, this does not mean that attempts to replicate experimental procedures that are highly context-sensitive should be completely abandoned. On the contrary, it is in the case of such procedures that replications are crucial to understanding the extent to which a given phenomenon analyzed by the authors is universal. Moreover, the lack of a given effect on particular external conditions may be of fundamental importance in understanding the reasons for its presence in other conditions. In order to draw an analogy, Bavel et al. used an example from the field of biological sciences, where a connection was discovered between the level of humidity in a laboratory and the effects on genome studies. Needless to say, from this perspective the work environment of psychology researchers is far more complex. So even though we have selected a field of science where the social environment varies significantly in particular cultures, "the lesson here is not that context is too hard to study but rather that context is too important to ignore" (Bavel et al., 2016, p. 6458).

14 Areas where field studies have remained in use

Despite a marked shift away from experimental studies evident in social psychology conducted in a natural environment, there are areas of life where such studies are still carried out. Interestingly, these studies are not conducted to gain new theoretical knowledge or substantiate (or disprove) a theory present in the scientific discourse. Their purpose is to quickly achieve a specific effect: sell more chewing gum, increase the number of calls to a helpline or reduce the number of improvised explosive devices planted along a road connecting two towns somewhere in Afghanistan. In this chapter, we are looking at examples of such studies – first, to demonstrate the methods adopted by their authors (who often remain anonymous) and second, to point out an important fact, namely that when a particular effect is on the line, hardly anyone uses surveys or declarations of attitudes. In such cases, a field experiment is most often applied.

The first area where experiments are used, which we are going to focus on, is the military. "Seriously?" One might ask. The military, the most fossilized, hierarchy-based and reluctant-to-change institution out there, uses experiments? As it turns out, it does – and it does so rather often, particularly in the area of the so-called psychological operations, most commonly referred to as PSYOPS.

According to the *Dictionary of Military and Associated Terms* (2010), psychological operations (abbreviated as PSYOPS) should actually be referred to as MISO (military information support operations) but we will use the term PSYOPS, as it has become widespread. In line with the definition found in the above-mentioned dictionary, PSYOPS are operations designed to communicate selected information to target groups in a planned manner with the intention of affecting their emotions, their motivation, their understanding of the phenomena in their surroundings and, as a result, their behavior. Target groups of such operations are governments, social organizations (both official and unofficial) as well as groups and individuals. In other words, PSYOPS are a non-kinetic (no-force element) form of influencing objects in a zone where military operations are taking place. We are intentionally not using the notion of an enemy here, as PSYOPS affects not just enemy objects – on today's battlefield, a simple enemy/ally division often does not apply, as apart from those two black and white categories, there are all possible shades of gray: from alliance, through neutrality, to complete hostility.

PSYOPS are not a new notion. Psychological operations have been a part of military operations for thousands of years – let us just refer to the use of elephants by Hannibal (which were more of a propaganda tool than actual combat animals) or the dropping of leaflets with false prophecies by Nostradamus during the German attack on France in 1940 (Newcourt-Nowodworski, 1996). However, the establishment of special units responsible for such operations is a relatively new concept.

DOI: 10.4324/9781003092995-14

Table 14.1 Description of PSYOPS Activities

Military operations	*General objectives*	*Examples of PSYOPS activities*
Kinetic activities	Combat and winning the war	Transmitting messages through loudspeakers Distribution of leaflets Broadcasting messages over the radio Face-to-face communication
Non-Kinetic activities	Preventing wars and escalation of conflicts	Training armed forces of a country involved in a conflict Distribution of informational leaflets Production and distribution of TV spots
	Promotion of peace	Production and distribution of informational materials for selected target groups (comic books, newspapers, magazines, posters, etc.)

Source: prepared by the authors.

What are the tasks of PSYOPS? Each unit, depending on the particular army it is a part of, has its unique character but, broadly speaking, the scope of activity of all PSYOPS is similar – as demonstrated in Table 14.1.

In order to demonstrate how operators (or TACOPs, PSYOPS Tactical Operators, as this is the term most often used to refer to PSYOPS soldiers) work, we will describe an exemplary operation (successfully completed, let us add) conducted in Iraq, in the small town of Kufa, located approximately 90 km from Baghdad.

US army officers responsible for keeping the region safe noticed that riots in the town of Kufa always proceeded according to the same and rather repetitive pattern (Duhigg, 2014). A small group of men would appear at one of the major squares in the town; with each hour, the group would grow larger and larger. The more people gathered in the square, the more salesmen, offering mainly water but also snacks, especially kebabs and falafel, which were very popular in that region, would appear around them. At some point, one of the men would throw a stone at security forces (Iraqi or American) and just moments later there would be full-fledged riots taking place in the square, which were difficult to suppress and resulted in heavy losses on both sides of the conflict (Abdullah, 2014).

As it turned out, the commanding officer of the allied forces in that region was an American major who, prior to being assigned to Iraq, was quite thoroughly trained in psychology, particularly in social influence psychology. Having examined the pattern according to which fights and riots would break out in Kufa, the major came up with an idea on how to affect the behavior of the protesters. Namely, he checked to see if it was technically feasible to prevent food vendors from entering the major squares in the town. The Iraqi administrators of Kufa did not understand the purpose it would serve but they admitted that it was possible. Then, the decision was made to implement this idea. After some time it appeared that the solution failed to yield any particular benefit. Exactly as before, a small crowd gathered in one of the major squares in the town and shouted threatening chants; soon, the group grew bigger, into a large mob posing a real threat to security. Local authorities asked the American coalition forces for support, but after a few dozen minutes it became apparent that the support would not be needed this time around. The mob, which had been swirling on the square by Masjid al-Kufa (the town's main mosque), clearly lost its energy and started to look around for street food vendors to replenish their strength with a kebab or falafel. Yet, as we know, there were no vendors to be found in the square. The mob remained at the site for a while, people shouted out a few more chants, and then they simply went home as they got hungry. At approximately 8 p.m., almost no one was left in the square.

This story is an example of just one of many experiments (this solution was tested, with various success rates, in many towns) undertaken by the coalition commanding officers (not just American commanders) in Iraq and Afghanistan. Many of those field (in a dual sense of the word) studies have become elements of trainings prepared for candidates for officers and commanders of units, with both the knowledge gained from the experiments as well as the very method for their execution being elements of the training (Shadrick & Lussier, 2004).

Another example of the practical application of an experiment is the study of the effectiveness of a leaflet conducted by the Polish PSYOPS subunit in Afghanistan in 2007. The leaflet was a part of a larger operation dubbed "Lion Pounce," which targeted the insurgents who acted to the detriment of the local community (and launched their own propaganda campaigns). The leaflet (ID No. IZ07B01ZAdLF7261), resembling a standard format of 6 by 3 inches (15.24 by 7.72 cm), was dropped from helicopters flying over selected villages. Figure 14.1 presents the leaflet in question (in its original form, although the content of the leaflet was written in the language of the local community, which in most cases was Pashto or Dari). A word of explanation needs to be provided as regards the use of the image of a dog – this animal is considered impure and has a special status in the Muslim culture (Foltz, 2014) (to call someone a dog is an extremely grave insult).

The operators conducted intergroup comparisons (between the villages where leaflets were dropped and the control groups, where no such operations were conducted) as well as pretest/posttest comparisons (prior to and after dropping the leaflets). Dependent variables were as follows: the number of IEDs planted along access roads to particular sites, the total number of interventions on the part of the coalition forces caused by the activity of the local terrorist groups, several other variables of specifically military nature and the number of phone calls made to special hot lines established for the purpose of anonymous communication of information on terrorist activities in the given region. The last item was crucial from the perspective of the content of the product. Due to the military

Figure 14.1 The front and back of an exemplary leaflet dropped in Afghanistan under PSYOPS (English translation).

Source: archive of Tomasz Grzyb.

procedures in place, we are not at liberty to present precise data but it should suffice to say that the leaflet turned out to be effective and triggered a whole series of animal-themed leaflets. As a result, images of dogs or rats were used, and the use of an image of a pig was also tested (pigs being considered extremely "impure" in the Muslim culture), although the latter, due to a very marked breach of the cultural taboo, did not make it to mass dissemination. Most importantly, from this chapter's perspective, the procedure described above clearly uses the methodology of a field experiment: there was an experimental and a control group, there were measurements conducted prior to contact with a stimulus designed to cause changes and after its application, and subjects were almost randomly (due to the field conditions complete randomization was not feasible) assigned to the experimental or the control group.

It should be pointed out that the procedure was not an original initiative of the Polish PSYOPS operators – it used a model for conducting studies described in the *PSYOPS Field Manual* (2003). This 250-page text (the full title of the most recent revision, i.e. FM 3-05.301, is *Psychological Operation Process Tactics, Techniques, and Procedures*) describes the basics of activities of PSYOPS operators depending on their involvement variant. Yet what we are most interested in is not the mode of operation but the method applied to measure the effectiveness of such operations and to decide on the approval (or disapproval) of products for dissemination. This information is included in chapter four ("Product development and design") and chapter seven ("Evaluation"). Even though the methods suggested by the manual (pretest examination, random selection of the tested sample in order to test the effectiveness of the stimuli, counting indices and translating them into commonly comprehensible descriptive statistics) would most likely be criticized, in principle, by a scholar who is an expert in statistical analyses, they seem to be a reasonable compromise between methodological purity and how quickly data can be collected and (even more importantly) presented in such conditions, where decisions must be made immediately. They also demonstrate, once again, a characteristic intuitiveness of experimental methods, which, in this case, comes down to the following: "If you do not know whether a leaflet is effective, test it in the simplest way possible – gather those who have seen it, gather those who have not, and see whether there is a difference."

Marketing is another area of our everyday life, which constantly uses field experiments as a day-to-day tool. Obviously, this also applies to analyzing the behavior of humans perceived as consumers, e.g., at catering establishments. An interesting study designed to examine how the behavior of waiters affects tipping was conducted by four psychologists: David Strohmetz, Bruce Rind, Reed Fisher, and Michael Lynn (2002). The researchers decided to make use of an increasingly common custom of bringing a small gift to the table when the customers are getting ready to pay for their meal and leave the restaurant. In most cases, it is a candy, a mint chocolate, or a piece of chewing gum, which is simply brought to the table without a word along with the receipt or handwritten check (the latter being less and less frequent nowadays). As the researchers were perfectly aware of the existence and the strong effect of the reciprocity rule (Cialdini, 2001), they assumed that bringing such a small gift to the table along with the check should result in higher tipping on the part of the customers (in return for the kindness on the part of the waiter). And indeed, the tips were higher in the group in which this technique was used, even though the increase was not what you would call spectacular (3.3%). In the second group the waiter brought not one but two mint chocolates to the customer. Again, as expected, the reciprocity rule had its effect. Where the waiter was twice as nice, the tips increased by as much as 14.1%. The third group was the one that turned out to be the most interesting from the research perspective; here too, the customers received two mint chocolates (similar to the second condition), only the chocolates were given in a peculiar way. First, the waiter approached the table and put the check and a single mint chocolate on the tabletop. He turned around, made half a step, as if he was walking away, and then he stopped for a moment, returned to the table, and smiled as he reached into his pocket to get another mint chocolate while saying: "You've been so nice that I'm going to give you an extra one," then he put another mint chocolate on the table next to the check. As one could expect, the group that received such a treatment repaid the waiter by giving a higher tip but only a select few would be able to accurately estimate the rate of the increase. It was a staggering 23%, almost nine percentage points above the second group, which received, at least theoretically, the same treatment: two mint chocolates.

The results obtained by Strohmetz et al. pointed out several interesting factors that amplify the effect of the reciprocity rule. As proposed by the authors of this study, one will be more willing to repay if the gift they receive is important (not necessarily in a material sense, it can be, e.g., handed over in a peculiar manner to emphasize its importance). Another element that amplifies the reciprocity is the fact that a gift is unexpected (and by the same token, it is not given simply because social norms or the nature of the situation dictates so). The third and the last factor is the personalization of the gift. For our perception of a gift will not be the same when the gift is presented to everyone and when only we (or a very small group of selected individuals) receive it. The studies conducted by Strohmetz et al. have gained a very serious practical application, *inter alia*, thanks to various training courses where they are discussed. Their effect is demonstrated, e.g., by the popularity of personalized calendars, which are given to business partners each new year. Such a calendar (most often in the form of a B5 or A5 format organizer) will usually have the name of its recipient embossed on the front cover. Needless to say, calendars are not prepared for all customers, only for a relatively small group of selected and most valuable business partners. Importantly, they are usually informed about the fact that they belong to such an elite group. This is yet another specific application of the knowledge gained through field experiments to everyday life.

The experiments commissioned by SNCB/NMBS, i.e., Belgian railroad, are another example of studies that were carried out in order to exert real influence on human behavior. The so-called quiet compartments were being introduced on Belgian trains (i.e., assigned zones in trains where everyone is expected to remain quiet so that passengers can rest or work without being disturbed). The problem faced by the Belgian railroad at the initial stage of this project was that a significant number of passengers simply ignored the rules of the quiet compartments. The railroad started testing various types of markings, informational labels, posters, and messages transmitted through loudspeakers (the latter being a rather paradoxical solution). As it turned out, all those methods proved to be ineffective. Therefore, experts in changing human behavior (mainly psychologists) were consulted and they conducted an experiment, namely: in quiet zones of randomly selected cars, a special film with pictures of library-like shelves and books printed on its surface was used to replace the standard paint on the walls of the car. The result was that in those compartments, where the impression of being in a library was created through means of interior decoration, the number of passengers violating the rules in the "quiet zones" dropped significantly. As the study was clearly of a practical type, its authors did not take the trouble of providing an elaborate theoretical justification to explain the effect observed. It can be conservatively assumed that the effect could be reasonably positioned among imprinted scripts of behavior (Carroll & Payne, 2014) – if people have an "imprinted" model for quiet behavior in a library, the presence of signals indicating that they are in a place similar to a library may reinforce their willingness to remain quiet.

Interior design/decoration is also the subject of constant experiments conducted by retail stores and retail chains. Obviously, the majority of results from these types of studies remain confidential and property of the owners of such stores and chains, as well as the consulting agencies working for them (which often hire psychologists as well as talented researchers specializing in field experiments). Sometimes, though, results of similar studies are made public and in some cases they form the basis for scientific texts related predominantly to the area of marketing and sales psychology. That was the case with the studies by Jens Nordfält and his colleagues, who described a series of 12 field experiments conducted in various retail chains designed to investigate the effect that various elements of interior decoration as well as additional stimuli have on customers' behavior (Nordfält, Grewal, Roggeveen, & Hill, 2014). The researchers tested, among other things, the system of positioning products on the shelves (so-called merchandising) and changes in product marking and advertisements affixed to the floor, they verified the effect various scents have on customers' behavior (aroma marketing), etc. All these studies had the following in common: customers were not informed about the studies being conducted, the behavior of the customers (and not declared attitudes) was measured, and the results of the experiments were used in a practical and direct manner. One of the studies (the first one in the series) was to test the effect the store's television system (i.e., the screens usually installed by the cash registers in order to promote various products available in the store) had on the consumers' behavior. The study was conducted in two large supermarkets and two hypermarkets of the Swedish retail chain, ICA. The researchers used the rather simple and yet very solid methodology of the Latin square (Grant, 1948). In the first stage, screens were installed in all locations but they were not turned on. This was considered the baseline: the control measurement. After some time, the screens were turned on in one of the supermarkets and in one of the hypermarkets. Next, after another measurement period, the screens were turned off and turned on in the other two locations. Obviously, the intention was to eliminate the possible influence of store-specific variables or simply to eliminate the changes related to the seasonal nature of some purchases (the study was conducted in December and January, thus such a seasonal effect on shopping before the Christmas as well as new year's sales was very probable).

The dependent variable measured by the researchers was the time spent in the store as well as the amount of money spent by the customers. With the customer tracking and identification system, the data was collected automatically (which, by the way, is an interesting point in the discussion on the voluntary participation of subjects in the experiments).

Due to the obligation to keep the trade secret confidential, the researchers presented their results in an indexed manner, while taking the average values from the control groups as 100. These were grouped in the diagrams. The first one presents the time the subjects spent in the store (Figure 14.2). The second one (Figure 14.3) presents the average amount of money the subjects spent in the store (also an indexed result).

A detailed hypothesis was also tested in the course of this experiment; the researchers wanted to learn the extent to which an active screen modifies customers' behavior defined as approaching (or avoiding) the given stand. In order to do so, two screens were installed on both sides of a banana stand. One of the screens was turned on, while the other was not. The automatic customer tracking system analyzed which side of the stand customers picked bananas up from more frequently. In the analyzed period, the behaviors of 60,000 customers were analyzed, and based on the analysis it was determined that 55% of customers picked up their bananas from the side of the stand with the TV turned on.

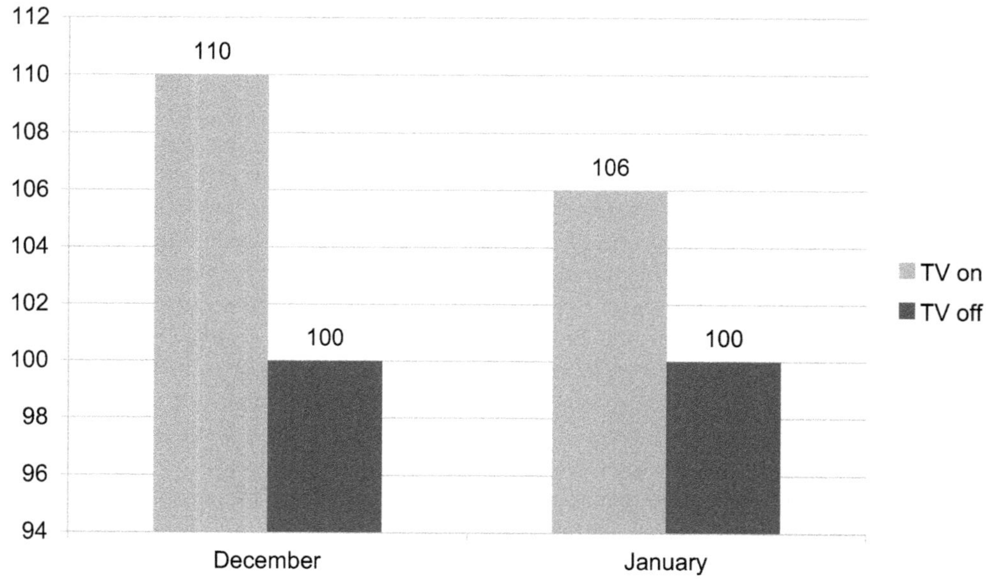

Figure 14.2 Time customers spent in store with TV system turned on or off.

Source: prepared by the authors based on Nordfält et al., 2014.

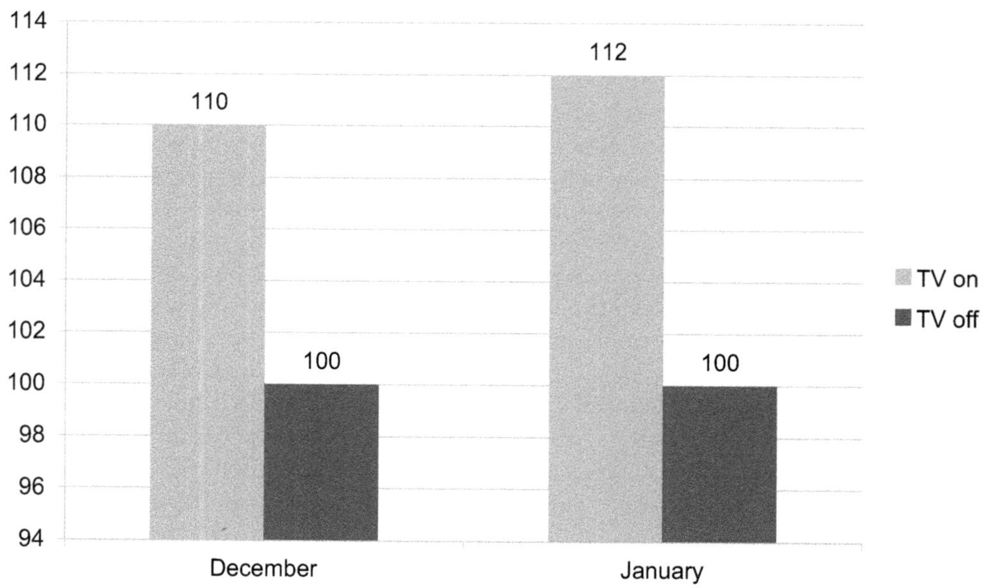

Figure 14.3 Average Amount of Money Customers Spent in the Store (an indexed result) with TV system turned on or off.

Source: prepared by the authors based on Nordfält et al., 2014.

The last of the examples described above is a particularly good illustration for what we would like to discuss in this chapter: there are constantly experiments being conducted of which we are completely unaware. As one can see, their methodology is not particularly sophisticated. One could go as far as to say that their methodological apparatus is, at some points, rather meager, whereas the statistical one is virtually non-existent (in the aforementioned article, the researchers do not go beyond the frequency statistics). Nevertheless, it turns out that the results these experiments yield are absolutely sufficient for practitioners. They are the ones who have to make the decision whether or not to install the TV sets. Let us conduct an experiment: if it turns out that customers stay longer in the store and spend more money, we will keep the TV sets. Otherwise, we will take them down since we will have evidence demonstrating that there is no point in installing them. Once more it turns out, as we already attempted to prove in Chapter 2, that an experiment is a natural way of learning about the surrounding reality.

Let us, for a change, examine a field experiment in the case of which there is no doubt as to its social usefulness. Robert Cialdini and his colleagues decided to verify the effectiveness of referring to various types of social norms in order to deter tourists from destroying wildlife (Cialdini et al., 2006). The entire study was of an experimental nature and conducted in natural conditions in the Arizona's Petrified Forest National Park, USA. The park is located in the Painted Desert, on the border between Apache and Navajo counties in the north-eastern part of Arizona; it is famous for numerous specimens of petrified (or "permineralized," to be precise) trees. The national park was established in 1962 but the first decisions to preserve this site were made by President Theodore Roosevelt. As the park stretches over an area of approximately 200 km^2 and has almost 800,000 tourists visit each year, it is not technically feasible to monitor every square meter of it or all visitors. At the same time, as evidenced by the experience of the park administration, some tourists feel an urge to take with them, as a souvenir, a piece of a petrified tree. It does not take an expert in geology or arithmetic to be able to recognize severe consequences of this problem. Even if only one in every 20 visitors took a piece of petrified wood, soon enough the park might just as well be closed as there would be no exhibits left. Therefore, Cialdini and his colleagues (obviously, acting in consultation with park management) decided to check if there was a way to affect the tendency of visitors to take fragments of petrified trees with them.

The researchers decided to test two things. First, they wanted to see if there would be differences between injunctive norm messages and descriptive norm messages. Second, their objective was to test the focus on the positive and the negative message. As a result, they prepared four types of messages (Table 14.2).

Table 14.2 Types of messages used in National Park Experiment

		Type of norm	
		Injunctive	*Descriptive*
Information	**Positively worded**	1. Please leave the petrified wood in the park	2. The vast majority of past visitors have left the petrified wood in the park, preserving the natural state of the Petrified Forest
	Negatively worded	3. Please don't remove the petrified wood from the park	4. Many past visitors have removed the petrified wood from the park, changing the state of the Petrified Forest

Source: prepared by the authors based on Cialdini et al., 2006.

The captions were accompanied by illustrations:

1. A picture of a tourist admiring fragments of petrified trees and taking pictures of them.
2. A picture of three tourists admiring fragments of petrified trees and taking pictures of them (where the descriptive norm is being used, the number of individuals displaying the given behavior is important and thus the researchers decided to use a picture presenting a small group instead of a single tourist).
3. A picture of a tourist taking a piece of wood in a red circle with a red diagonal line through it.
4. A picture of three tourists, each taking a piece of wood, in a red circle with a red diagonal line through it.

All captions, along with the illustrations, were placed on three-foot-square signs, which were posted in the ground at the starting points of three forest trails (Jasper, Long Logs, and Crystal) where the problem of petrified wood theft occurred. All four types of signs were tested on each of the trails for two-hour sessions.

Of course, the biggest problem was the measurement of the dependent variable, since the researchers wanted it to be actual behavior. For this reason, searching all tourists in order to see how many and what type of items they took with them would be ineffective (additionally, it would introduce a lot of commotion and disrupt the internal accuracy of the study). Therefore, a decision was made to plant, in the exact same locations, specially marked pieces of wood. After each two-hour session, the experimenter's assistant would walk the entire trail in order to count the number of missing wood fragments; he would re-plant new pieces where needed and the session would be re-started (with a new sign erected).

The study covered a group of over 2,655 participants. Table 14.3 presents the percentage of petrified wood pieces that were missing after the session for each variant.

There is a clear interaction between the two independent variables: as much as it did not matter whether the contents referred to the injunctive or the descriptive norm in the case of the positive wording, in the case of the negative wording the injunctive norm was significantly more effective (the descriptive norm was actually counter-productive).

The researchers concluded their results by demonstrating how often mistakes are made when constructing persuasive messages. Even though their experiment clearly proves that pointing to a negative example combined with a descriptive norm is terribly ineffective, such messages are frequently used in many locations (e.g., in national parks). As an example, Cialdini and his colleagues used the following text: "Your national heritage is being destroyed. Each year, 14 tons of petrified wood vanish from the park, piece by

Table 14.3 Percentage of petrified wood pieces taken by tourists per type of norm in message

		Type of norm	
		Injunctive	*Descriptive*
Information	**Positively worded**	5.1	5.0
	Negatively worded	1.5	7.8

Source: prepared by the authors based on Cialdini et al., 2006.

piece." They emphasized that even though the total number of tourists stealing wood fragments is low (estimated at 5%), putting up such a sign makes things even worse, as it refers to the descriptive norm. For if something is common (tourists often do it), they think surely it is not that reprehensible and it is okay for them to do it, too.

To recapitulate this chapter, it is worth noting that there are several qualities shared by all of the field experiments described. All of them were conducted in natural conditions and subjects were not aware of their role in the studies. The dependent variable was always the behavior of the participants: their decision to take or not to take the given action. None of the studies featured debriefing (due to technical reasons, in some cases this would not be possible but still it should be noted that the researchers did not attempt to debrief the subjects, as they believed that the experiment was imperceptible for the participants and thus that debriefing them could possibly do more harm than good). And the final shared element: in the case of each of the studies, the objective was to solve a practical problem or provide an answer to a question not of solely academic nature.

There is one more aspect worth noting there, namely the role of psychologists–researchers as individuals setting (or predestined to set) certain positive standards for functioning within a society. We do not want the reader to be under the impression that our intention, in this chapter, was to search for an excuse ("well others do it, so why can't we?") or to suggest that virtually any study should be allowed without the need to apply for approval from an ethics committee. By no means was it the reason for using the above-mentioned examples of studies. The purpose was for us, the researchers and experimenters, to set certain standards and good practices, so that we could demonstrate that field experiments can be conducted properly while respecting the dignity of the subjects and treating their participation in the experiment seriously, but at the same time conducted in an interesting manner that allows us to analyze the behavior of real people in a real environment. The examples discussed in this chapter may be considered a step in this direction.

15 Good practices

In all previous chapters of this book, we demonstrated that conducting field experiments is a difficult, tiresome, and often unrewarding task that requires a lot of effort and resources, while the effect is uncertain. In this chapter, we will present a few solutions and "hacks" from our own experience, which might make experimental studies a little easier. Perhaps these will serve as ready-made suggestions for those individuals who intend to conduct their studies in the natural environment and register the actual behavior of their subjects. Of course we cannot guarantee that using our solutions will make any field experiment successful, yet our long-term practice, as far as their use is concerned, makes us believe that these are certainly helpful in the everyday work of a researcher–experimenter. The outline of this chapter will be as follows: we pose a few questions similar to those asked daily by individuals conducting field experiments and, obviously, we will do our best to provide a satisfactory answer to each and every one of these questions.

How to collect money legally?

One way of testing people's willingness to give help, applied relatively often in the course of field experiments, particularly those in the area of social influence, is to collect funds for the benefit of a more- or less-known charity. Many authors emphasize the importance of designing one's experiments in this way, chiefly because with the variable operationalized in this manner, it becomes possible to measure a specific altruistic behavior (e.g., Chaudhuri, 2011; Cialdini & Goldstein, 2004; Shang & Croson, 2009). The problem is that in many countries a number of formal requirements must be met before funds can be collected publicly (the most common form used in the case of field experiments). In Poland, where we work and conduct our experiments, one has to do the following in order to be able to do this completely legally:

- set up one's own charity (i.e., draw up the articles of association, appoint a board of directors, file all the required information with the National Court Register, etc.);
- obtain, on behalf of the charity established for the purpose of collecting material or financial donations, a separate permit, issued by the relevant administrative authority for each fundraiser;
- equip collectors with IDs bearing their personal data, photo, data of the fundraiser's organizer, data on the issued permit, and the purpose of the fundraiser;
- prepare, in a prescribed manner, label, secure, and seal money boxes to be used for collecting funds;

DOI: 10.4324/9781003092995-15

- prepare and secure, in a prescribed manner, the donation certificate in the event the fundraiser does not consist of collecting discretionary amounts of money and if the sales figures for the certificate are the dependent variable in the experiment;
- label items sold through an auction or through free sale, each should contain the name of the fundraiser's organizer and the unit price; this requirement pertains to an experimental variant where items are being sold for the purpose of supporting a charity, e.g., lottery tickets (Davis, Razzolini, Reilly, & Wilson, 2006) or various products made for the occasion, cookies, Christmas tree ornaments, etc. (Ebster & Neumayr, 2008; Whithear, 1999).

As one can imagine, it is already the first item on the list above, which, from the perspective of most researchers, is not as much impossible but simply preposterous in the context of the purpose of an experiment. Therefore, it can be safely assumed that if field experiments were to be conducted in this fashion, that is, in compliance with all applicable procedures, no researchers would bother, as they would assume – and rightly so – that it is simply not worth it.

Fortunately, there are other solutions available that are much simpler and still completely legal, as well as – and equally important – socially beneficial. One can simply contact a charity that has been established for some time, has already obtained all the necessary permits and already holds fundraising events (legally and in line with all applicable regulations). Once this cooperation has been established, assistants of the experimenter (acting as volunteers in the experiment) become actual associates of the given charity, go through standard training, receive authentic IDs as well as sealed and approved money boxes; when equipped with the above elements, they conduct the experiment (e.g., by asking for donations in a slightly different manner in the experimental vs. the control group). Obviously, and it must be strongly emphasized, that such cooperation with a charity must be an actual cooperation (it is absolutely unacceptable for experimenters to show up unannounced in order to conduct the experiment without first informing the administration of the given charity about their intention to do so). Based on our experience, we can tell that public benefit organizations often agree to engage in such a cooperation, provided they are treated seriously (i.e., provided they know the plan for the experiment, its purposes, etc.). Needless to say, all donations collected in the course of such an experiment must be transferred to the account of the charity the researchers have been cooperating with.

In the course of our field experiments, we have cooperated with a large number of local (Wrocław Hospice for Children, Destitute Animal Shelter in Wrocław, Homeless Shelter for Men in Wrocław), national (Urszula Jaworska Foundation, Polish Humanitarian Action) as well as international (Amnesty International) charitable organizations. Even though it took some time and getting to know each other, our cooperation with these charities was always very successful and mutually beneficial. The experiments devoted to testing the synergistic effects of using various social influence techniques are just some of the studies we have conducted in cooperation with the Urszula Jaworska Foundation (Dolinski, Grzyb, Olejnik, Prusakowski, & Urban, 2005). Our studies comprised three experiments, with Experiment 1 being conducted jointly with the Foundation (which promotes the registration of bone marrow donors and supports people suffering from leukemia). In the course of the experiment, conducted according to the 2 × 2 scheme, we tested the effectiveness of the "even a penny will help" technique (Cialdini & Schroeder, 1976) as well as the dialogue involvement technique (Dolinski, Nawrat, & Rudak, 2001).

The latter was already discussed in Chapter 5 (a brief reminder: it is more probable for a request to be granted when it is preceded with a casual dialogue), whereas the essence of the "even a penny will help" technique requires explanation. Cialdini and Schroeder (1976) assumed that those who refuse to donate money to charity justify their conduct with themselves by claiming that they are not sufficiently well off in order to be able to help all the needy ones. The "even a penny will help" message (or a similar one, which suggests that the aid may just as well be a token penny) makes this justification invalid (since it would suffice to donate even a very small amount, it does not take a rich person to do it). In this situation, people are more willing to put their hands in their pockets.

One hundred twenty subjects, 50% of which were women, participated in the experiment. The study was conducted in various parts of the town (Opole) and subjects were randomly assigned, in line with the previously conducted randomization, to one of the four groups: the control and three experimental groups. In the control group (where there was no dialogue preceding the request and the "even a penny will help" technique was not used), the subjects were met with the following request:

> Good morning, I am a student at the University of Opole and a volunteer for the Urszula Jaworska Foundation. I am collecting money to benefit people with leukemia. Recently, this serious problem has been brought to public attention. Would you like to join us in this cause?

In the group where the "every penny counts" technique was used (in monologue conditions), the experimenter would end their request with the following phrase: "Even a penny will help."

In dialogue conditions, the experimenter started up a dialogue with the subject with the following:

> Good morning, I am a student at the University of Opole and a volunteer for the Urszula Jaworska Foundation. How serious do you think the problem of leukemia is in our society?

(Here the subject would respond.)

> Do you think is it worth supporting institutions that help deal with this serious problem?

(Here the subject would respond again.)

> I am collecting money to benefit people with leukemia. Recently, this serious problem has been brought to public attention. Would you like to join us in this cause?

In the synergistic conditions, where we attempted to see if the two techniques would affect the decision of the subjects to an even greater extent when used together, the experimenter would add the "Even a penny will help," phrase at the end of the final request.

Four experimenters took part in the study, and their personal effectiveness in terms of making requests was tested with no statistically significant differences identified among them.

The results of the study demonstrated that both the "every penny counts" technique as well as the "involvement in a dialogue" technique were effective in terms of increasing the

Table 15.1 Percentage of persons complying with experimenter's request and mean donation in each experimental condition

	Monologue mode		*Dialogue mode*	
	Even a penny will help	*Standard request*	*Even a penny will help*	*Standard request*
Proportions of persons complying	53.3%	33.3%	83.3%	66.7%
M donation (in Polish zlotys)	1.10	0.49	2.47	1.39

Source: *Journal of Applied Social Psychology*, *35*, p. 1161. Copyright: V.H. Winston & Son, Inc.

Note: In all experimental conditions, N = 30. 1 Polish zloty = approximately US$ 0.25.

chance of donations being made by the participants. Table 15.1 presents the percentage of individuals who granted the request and the average donation amount in each of the groups.

Obviously, the total amount collected (PLN 163.50) was transferred to the Urszula Jaworska Foundation.

Our results confirmed the previously adopted hypotheses. Not only were both techniques effective in terms of increasing compliance on the part of the subjects (all differences were statistically significant), there was also the synergy effect: where the techniques were used simultaneously, both compliance when measured dichotomously (donation or no donation) as well as compliance when measured quantitatively (the average donated amount) were significantly greater.

Nevertheless, it should be pointed out that in order to determine the average donation amount, we had to carefully monitor the number of coins/notes being inserted into the money box (or, in extreme cases, we had to open the box to see how much money had been put in). This was most impractical and led us to another important question:

How to determine the amount donated by each participant?

In a number of studies designed to investigate compliance with various social influence techniques, the dependent variable is operationalized as a donation made by a particular individual (from the given experimental group) for the benefit of a charity. As mentioned earlier, the problem is that each money box, according to applicable regulations, should be sealed and opened only by the organizer of the fundraiser. And even if that were not the case, in would be difficult to constantly open the money box on the street in order to verify the amount of a single donation. Most importantly (aside from problems of a technical nature), we would be putting the goodwill of the collaborating charity at risk. Having a random observer see a volunteer opening a money box with donations might bring about very serious consequences. Thus, it should come as no surprise that, for both legal and practical reasons, opening money boxes in the course of street experiments is not a common practice. Surely the assistants of the experimenter can be instructed to carefully watch how much money is being put into the box but this solution is not perfect either, as subjects often donate a fistful of coins, which makes it impossible to identify the exact amount being donated. What is more, staring at the money being put into the box may affect the donated amount. For this reason, and for quite a long time, we have tried to obtain "counting money boxes," which would automatically record the amount of each individual donation. Initially, we attempted to construct such money boxes in collaboration with companies specializing in the production of slot machines (featuring a system for recognizing and counting coins) but the results of this cooperation were not satisfactory. Suffice it to say that the power draw of such a money box would require a rather large battery, which would make it impractical. Additionally, the mechanism in question would not count banknotes. For these reasons, we decided to abandon this option and started searching for a ready-made solution to our problem. It turned out that the power of the Internet came to our rescue. We found money boxes for children featuring a mechanism which allowed counting inserted coins (as well as recognizing their value based on the circumference of the coin).

The only technical modification that we needed to perform in the design of the money box was moving the reset button, used to reset the calculated amount, to the outside wall of the box (earlier, the button was installed inside the box and thus it would be impossible to reset the "score" without opening it). Currently, what we do is we take a reading from the box to learn the amount donated by an individual once our interaction has come to an end, we record the amount on a log sheet along with additional information (e.g., sex, estimated age, additional comments), and then we reset the counter and move on to another interaction. This solution is not perfect but it is good enough (even more so since once the appropriate holes have been drilled, the box can be sealed using the seal of the charity acting as our partner). What is equally important is that the cost of the device, along with the necessary modifications, is only a dozen euros or so! (Just for the sake of drawing a comparison, the estimated cost quoted by the slot machine companies was around EUR 250 for a single box.) Figure 15.1 presents the money box used in our studies conducted in cooperation with

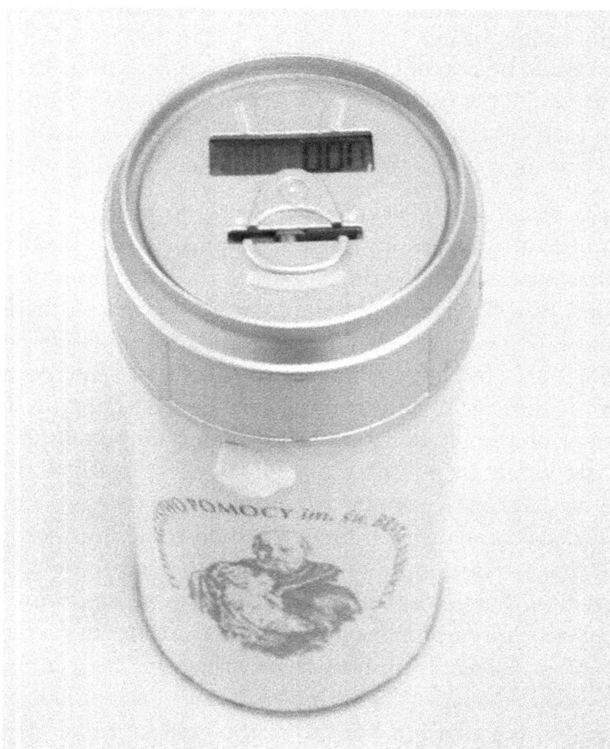

Figure 15.1 A money box with coin-counting mechanism used in field studies.

Source: photo by Michał Jakubowicz.

the St. Brother Albert Homeless Shelter for Men. The figure also shows the digital display indicating the current amount in coins: when conducting an experiment (to make sure the display is not interfering) the whole top of the box can be covered with a piece of cardboard.

How not to get chased away by the police/security services?

Due to their dynamics and duration (in some cases it is necessary to stay in one spot for several hours), studies conducted in natural conditions attract a lot of attention from the local police/security services. Apart from the site security personnel, when the experiment is conducted in or near a building, the police, municipal guard officers, or railroad security officers (if we conduct our experiments near a train station, and we did on several occasions) are also eager to check the experimenters' documents. Based on our experience, we can say that municipal guard officers show up most frequently at the site of the experiment (probably because it is mainly their responsibility to analyze CCTV footage).

How to proceed when it happens? Basically, there are two kinds of approach. The first one being proactive: e.g., we can send a notice to inform the services that street experiments will be conducted on a given day at given locations. The problem with this approach is that in many cases the services interpret such a notice as a request for a permit, which makes the whole thing much more complicated. What is more, said services may refuse to grant such a permit in writing or via e-mail. This would put a researcher in a very uncomfortable position as in most countries there is no defined way to proceed and no procedure for appealing such a decision. Apparently, lawmakers did not expect society to include social psychologists interested in conducting field experiments. On the other hand, considering how rare such experiments have become, it does not exactly come as a surprise.

Therefore, we suggest (this is the option we choose in most cases) that you should not report your intentions to any services. Instead, make sure the experimenters (and particularly the troubleshooter, discussed below in more detail) have several certificates and documents stamped with as many official seals as possible. Therefore, each experimenter should have a "Certificate regarding the execution of the studies," which states that X, born on … in …, etc., is conducting studies under the project (title, number, series). It is also advisable to include in the information that, if necessary, his/her identity can be confirmed via telephone at the given telephone number, and that a person with a professor's degree is the supervisor for the experiment. If such a document is issued on letterhead and is stamped with numerous color seals, it will be sufficient for most police/municipal guard officers as confirmation attesting to the fact that the study has been legally sanctioned. In case it is not, the experimenters should also be provided with an official "Request for assistance" addressed "To Whom It May Concern." The request should basically restate all the details included in the certificates and, additionally, contain the following sentence: "Due to the complex nature of the studies being conducted and since it is necessary for the studies to be carried out in a natural environment, all parties whom it may concern are kindly requested to assist the experimenters in any manner possible." Obviously, the request should also be signed by a person with a professor's degree and stamped with seals. Fans of *The Three Musketeers* by Alexandre Dumas might find the content of the above-mentioned request to suspiciously resemble the famous letter by Cardinal Richelieu ("The bearer of this letter has acted under my orders and for the good of the state") but it has one undeniable advantage: it works. We have used this method dozens of times, experimenters' assistants had their documents checked on numerous occasions by representatives of various services and presenting the aforementioned documents always resolved the situation – particularly if done by a troubleshooter, whom we are going to introduce next.

How to keep the experiment site in order?
The online version of Merriam-Webster's Dictionary offers three definitions of the term ("Troubleshooter | Definition of Troubleshooter by Merriam-Webster"):

1 a skilled worker employed to locate trouble and make repairs in machinery and technical equipment.
2 an expert in resolving diplomatic or political disputes: a mediator of disputes that are at an impasse.
3 a person skilled at solving or anticipating problems or difficulties.

In our case, clearly, when we use the term troubleshooter, we refer to the second and third definitions, even though in some instances there might emerge technical issues that a troubleshooter can resolve. This is an additional member of the research team, most likely an experienced experimenter who is not directly involved in conducting the study as an assistant of the experimenter or a confederate but who supervises the course of the experiment. Responsibilities of a troubleshooter include the following:

- keeping an eye on the entire experimental situation and taking notes on whether the assistants of the experimenter act as instructed;
- watching over the randomization process, in some cases, e.g., when equipped with a walkie-talkie, a troubleshooter can identify (based on a previously developed framework) individuals to be tested; this is important, as in the past it happened that assistants did not approach some of the individuals who should have been chosen according to the rules of randomization (e.g., scary-looking individuals or those with a simply unpleasant appearance); assigning the task of choosing the subjects to the troubleshooter eliminates this problem;
- as mentioned earlier, dealing with police/security services; a troubleshooter is a perfect partner for them;
- making sure a high ethical standard of the study is maintained (this crucial task also involves observing those individuals who have finished their interaction with the experimenter's assistant, as the troubleshooter makes sure these people do not display any alarming symptoms); in the event there are any signs indicating that something is not quite right, it is the role of the troubleshooter to approach such individuals and explain the situation to them (this is particularly significant in the case of experimental procedures with no subject debriefing);
- if debriefing is included in the procedure of the given study, it can be handled by a separate designated person or by the troubleshooter (if the latter is the case, the experimenters should pause the experiment for the duration of the debriefing).

Based on our experience, we can state that appointing a troubleshooter has nothing but positive aspects. First, the experimenters are supervised but also feel safer, as they know that, should the situation become problematic, there will be someone to help them out. Second, with a troubleshooter involved in the course of the experiment, things simply run much smoother; all difficult situations can be clarified by a person who is not directly involved in the experimental procedure. Third, the presence of a troubleshooter ensures a higher degree of certainty as regards standard behavior on the part of the assistants of the experimenter (they are unaware of some of their actions affecting the result of the experiment and these may only be spotted by an outside observer).

Where do "strong variables" come from in field experiments?

Even though, in principle, this book does not cover, at least not in detail, the statistical tools used for the purpose of analyzing the results of field experiments, one should know a rather basic principle related to the classification of arithmetic operations performed on particular variables. According to the Stevens' typology (Gardner, 1975; Stevens, 1975) there are four types of variables: nominal, ordinal, interval, and ratio variables (although in psychology, the latter two are usually combined to form a single category of quantitative variables, which is done for practical reasons even though it is not entirely correct from the methodological perspective). The nominal variable is a fairly natural dependent variable in field studies. After all, when examining one's behavior, we most typically interpret it in a binary manner: the subject did or did not help, signed or did not sign a petition, responded to an instruction or ignored it. And, of course, this interpretation method is by all means valid, and one might even venture to claim that it's natural. We addressed this problem in detail in the initial sections of this book. The problem is that in some cases this dichotomous distinction is insufficient for at least two reasons.

First, as we know, "higher" scales are more sensitive, which means they are more suitable for noticing differences in one's behavior. In the event we want to see how a given social influence technique affects a change in the behavior of a particular individual, it is better to formulate two questions instead of one. Apart from the question of whether or not the behavior of the subjects changed as a result of the social influence technique applied, it is worth asking: "To what extent did it change?" When we ask, for example, for a donation for the benefit of a charity, we should not only be interested in whether or not the given subject made a donation but also in the difference between his/her donation and the one made by, e.g., the person from the control group. If a fundraiser is held for a noble cause, it might be the case that virtually everyone gives some money regardless of their assignment to the experimental or the control group. In such a case, exclusively recording the fact that a donation was or was not made is simply ineffective, as it does not allow us to identify the differences between the groups. Obviously, one can imagine a reversed situation, where all or almost all subjects from one group donate EUR 1 each and 20% of the subjects from the other group donate EUR 5 each. Naturally, this is only a theoretical possibility but it manages to demonstrate how important it is to analyze not only the dichotomous variable (donation/no donation) but also the quantitative one (how much was donated).

Another reason to operationalize dependent variables in field studies in such a manner as to make them (also) quantitative variables is because editors of numerous journals and many reviewers have grown accustomed to this measurement method. Although it should be said that based on the experience we had with reviews over the years, it is very rare for reviewers to openly declare a binary measurement of behavior as inappropriate. It is rather suggested to us that "perhaps another, e.g., quantitative, method should be used." Obviously, if such suggestions are made when the article is already being reviewed, changes can only be made in a replication of the study and thus it is advisable to consider a quantitative measurement of the dependent variable in the initial stages of designing the experimental scheme.

How to do it? How to operationalize a typically dichotomous variable to make it also quantitative? There is no single rule here and it all depends on the situational context, the site where the experiment is being conducted and the people involved in the process.

Below we present a few options that we have already implemented in our studies and we also address disadvantages of those solutions, which, attractive as they may be, did not work out for us. We have divided our suggestions into two groups: group A, when somebody is asked to help a particular person (most often a confederate seemingly in need of assistance), or group B, when support for an organization is sought. We are intentionally omitting all issues related to money donated by subjects. This is because with a money box featuring a built-in coin-counting mechanism or with subjects transferring money to a bank account, the problem is solved: we can measure both the dichotomous variable (donation/no donation) and the donated amount. Yet, the situation is not always as comfortable as this for experimenters. Help given to another individual can take various forms. Tables 15.2 and 15.3 present examples of the operationalization of dependent variables related to giving help in case A (helping a particular individual) and case B (supporting an organization).

Of course, the variables descried above are only examples of operationalization. Each particular experimental scheme follows its own rules and thus requires the tasks for the subjects to be designed in a slightly different manner. Nevertheless, we believe that these ideas may be useful; even if they do not provide ready-made solutions, they should at least be a source of ideas for scholars conducting street experiments.

How to document the course of a study?

Research designed to analyze the content of posts published on social media demonstrates that each year the number of words an average Facebook post is comprised of declines (Zajac & Cyprowski, 2016). Additionally, a change has been observed as far as the types of posts are concerned. Table 15.4 illustrates this process in detail by listing the percentage of posts from each category.

Table 15.2 Examples of various operationalization of dependent variables in field experiments that allow measurement at the interval level (dependent variable equals help given to a particular individual, e.g., the confederate)

Case A – the dependent variable is help given to a particular person

General description of the variable	*Detailed examples*
Time spent on giving help	Time spent by the subject to help pick up scattered items (sheets of paper, pencils, toys, groceries*).
	Time spent by the subject on the favor the experimenter asks (watching a bicycle, holding a ladder).
Physical involvement in giving help	The distance (in meters) walked by the subject with the experimenter to show him/her the way to a given location.
	The number of packages carried by the subject and the experimenter to the car.
	The number of items, which the experimenter had dropped, picked up by the subject (sheets of paper or pencils).
Declaration of help	The number of specific tasks (assembling pens, solving math problems, affixing postage stamps, manually addressing envelopes) the subject declares he/she will perform for the experimenter.

Source: prepared by the authors.

* In one of the studies, a female assistant of the experimenter dropped (seemingly by accident) oranges. We do not recommend this option and suggest using items that are more durable (less perishable).

Table 15.3 Examples of various operationalization of dependent variables in field experiments that allow measurement at the interval level (dependent variable equals help given to an organization)

Case B – the dependent variable is help given to an organization

General description of the variable	*Detailed examples*
Time spent on giving help	Declared (or, if possible, actual) time spent on helping the organization as a volunteer.
	Time spent on distribution of leaflets together with the experimenter.
Involvement in giving help	The number of signatures on a petition, e.g., addressed to town/city authorities regarding a ban on circus shows, collected by the subject (or the number of signatures the subject declared he/she would collect).
	The number of leaflets (on a charity) the subject takes to distribute among his/her friends.
	The number of friends brought by the subject (or the number of friends the subject declared he/she would bring) to a briefing held by the organization.

Source: prepared by the authors.

Table 15.4 Percentage of text, links, photographs and videos in Facebook posts in the 2012–2015 period

Content type	*Year*			
	2012	*2013*	*2014*	*2015*
Text	28	24	18	13
Link	35	34	36	41
Photo	34	38	39	39
Video	3	4	7	7

Source: prepared by the authors based on Zajac & Cyprowski, 2016.

This impression of the return to image-based culture (Jenks, 1995; Mirzoeff, 2010) may also be experienced by those observing trends in presenting content at scientific conferences. For many years now, a person who does not use a slide projector for their presentation causes quite a sensation among the audience. Actually, each session starts with a ritual loading of PowerPoint files onto the chairperson's laptop, and a growing number of speakers, apart from presenting results of their studies, use photographs and videos to illustrate the course of their study. On one occasion, after we presented our results, a member of the audience (a world-famous psychologist) asked us to share our results and insisted we include a video file illustrating the course of the experiment in the data provided.

All these processes should encourage psychologists conducting field experiments to fully document their studies. There are at least three reasons to do so:

- it enables interfering variables that might affect the results of the experiment to be recorded and to analyze the effect they may have had on said results;
- individuals who participated in the study as subjects may file lawsuits;
- it enables the work of the experimenters to be supervised and to analyze the accuracy of their work.

It appears that the first and third reasons are rather obvious and as such do not require further explanation, particularly in the light of the considerations included in the chapters devoted to analyzing interfering variables and the work of experimenters who receive imprecise instructions. The one that deserves additional attention is reason number two.

Nowadays (particularly in some countries), legal proceedings instigated against various institutions and organizations by individuals who claim that they have suffered more or less tangible losses are very common. As a result, a manual for a hair dryer will warn users not to put the appliance into a bathtub full of water when it is plugged in; a manual for children's building blocks will tell you not to swallow the blocks; and a manual for a refrigerator will tell you not to position the fridge with the door against a wall. On the other hand, it was many years ago that we witnessed a marked increase in the amount of third-party liability insurance purchased by physicians and teachers (some of this insurance has become mandatory). It appears that a lawsuit brought against an experimenter conducting studies in a non-laboratory environment is also a real possibility. It should be noted that the phrase "studies involving people," especially "unaware people," would clearly suggest that the researcher is guilty (even more so when we consider the attention from the media, which such a case would undoubtedly attract) even if the procedure was simply to ask an individual for 1 euro to buy coffee for a homeless person sitting nearby. In such a case, a video documenting the course of the interaction may become vital evidence attesting to the due diligence on the part of the experimenter and his/her concern for the well-being of the subjects.

Speaking of legal aspects, one should also remember the regulations on recording people without their consent. We will not address this topic in detail, as regulations regarding this problem may vary from one country to another. Nevertheless, we have no doubts that even if the misdemeanor law is not completely clear on this, the right to protect one's image should be protected for purely ethical reasons, and as researchers who actually use the subjects, their time, and their voluntary involvement for our benefit, we should feel particularly obligated to do whatever is necessary to protect it. Therefore, it should be clearly emphasized that any materials recorded in the course of an experiment may only be used exclusively for academic and documentary purposes and must not, in any case, be published. If we want to have an "illustration" of the course of the experiment, e.g., in order to include it in a presentation on the results of our studies, we should use material recorded separately featuring an informed actor or a student hired to play the role of a subject. This way we will have interesting material that could even become a tool for promoting science (at various scientific and popular science events) and we will make sure the image and dignity of those whom our fate depends on, i.e., the actual subjects, is protected.

To conclude the discussion on practical solutions to the problems related to conducting street experiments, we should address one more aspect. Designing and conducting field experiments is always a fascinating adventure that involves creativity and thinking outside of the box. The potential solutions for certain typical and recurring problems proposed in this chapter are merely suggestions: only some problems can be solved in the manner described herein. They should not be considered a model or a standard for one's conduct; they are only ideas we have used and tested. As far as finding solutions to problems that may arise in future experiments, the authors of these experiments will have to rely on their own ingenuity.

16 Final remarks

On November 8, 2016, presidential elections were held in the United States of America and Donald Trump was elected as the new president of the country. It was only a few days after the elections when speculations started to emerge suggesting that Trump had won thanks to a specific algorithm that enabled a prediction of personality traits of users of such social media platforms as Facebook or Twitter based on their behavior online and sent them personalized information tailored in terms of argumentation and communication tools. According to the information published by the press, Cambridge Analytica used the knowledge from earlier studies, demonstrating the relation between online behavior and traits of one's personality to send to social media users information agitating for Trump, which was composed in such a manner as to use precisely selected, and thus convincing, arguments (Bachrach, Kosinski, Graepel, Kohli, & Stillwell, 2012; Kosinski, Stillwell, & Graepel, 2013; Quercia, Lambiotte, Stillwell, Kosinski, & Crowcroft, 2012). And even though the actual effect the efforts made by Cambridge Analytica had on the result of the presidential elections in the United States is still being (and probably will be) debated (Bershidsky, 2016), the whole story tells us something very important. Namely, that while enjoying all the benefits of the digital revolution, a contemporary man discloses large volumes of sensitive data to individuals who can use it: marketing experts (specializing in selling both goods and ideas). Such experts, while respecting no rules of ethical approach to studies, conduct experiments to see which form of presenting an offer for a new mortgage loan, an electric kettle, or a presidential candidate is most effective. Are they breaking the law? Interestingly enough, they are not. When setting up a Facebook account, you basically say: "I agree that everything I have is now yours."

The same problem is illustrated even more evidently by another incident, which demonstrates the precision with which customer profiling works (customers are identified by, e.g., the numbers on their loyalty cards, theoretically meant to give access to attractive discounts but in reality issued predominantly to enable hundreds of variables describing a particular holder). One day, an angry customer rushed into a Target (a popular retail chain in America) store; right from the door he was shouting intimidating remarks addressed to the entire retail chain in general, and the management of that specific location in particular. The reason for all that commotion was that his teenage daughter started receiving advertisements for and samples of products for young mothers – a baby formula, cosmetics, etc. The father was angry as his daughter was still in high school and he believed that such promotional activities might encourage her to become pregnant (which, apparently, he did not wish to happen). The personnel of the store apologized to the man and explained that such mistakes could happen: it was simply an algorithm that

DOI: 10.4324/9781003092995-16

suggested products the given customer should find useful based on their purchase history; obviously, the algorithm was not perfect or 100% error-free (Duhigg, 2014).

This just as well could have been the end of it, if it had not been for one tiny detail: a few days after his previous visit to the store, the man returned. This time to apologize to the personnel of the store for his earlier behavior. As it turned out, his daughter was actually pregnant but did not tell her parents about it. The computer system used by the Target retail chain turned out to be a more insightful observer of actual behavior of the teenage girl (who had purchased, e.g., multivitamins or a stretch mark cream in the second trimester) than her own father.

Why are we using these examples as a starting point for concluding our reflections on field experiments? Chiefly because of one of the most important problems, or rather ethical charges, formulated against their authors, namely no respect for the autonomy and freedom of the subjects. True, in the majority of field studies (which we pointed out many times earlier in this book), participants are not informed about the fact that a study is being conducted. In some cases (although, let us make it absolutely clear, not always), the participants remain unaware even once the experiment has ended. Therefore, an outside observer might draw the following conclusion: there is no difference between you. You researchers are exactly the same as marketing experts trying to hustle white goods only because somebody has Googled the phrase, "my washing machine won't spin dry."

Or are we? Let us reflect on the ultimate objectives for both sides: there is no doubt as to the motives behind the measures undertaken by marketing experts, they simply want to boost sales. It is quite a different story with field studies conducted by social psychologists; their purpose is to expand our knowledge of how human beings function in their natural environment. They want to see whether psychological theories work as expected in the real world and, ultimately, they want to amend these theories and modify them in the event that the data obtained through field experiments justify doing so. But does the different motivation mean they can ignore ethical aspects? We could not be further from proposing such a thesis! Actually, they care a lot about the ethical aspects (to be completely honest, they sort of have to, as each experimental scheme must be approved by the relevant Ethics Committee prior to implementation). Obviously, it is not a strictly yes or no affair, i.e., it is not that the Ethics Committee exclusively accepts those projects that entail absolutely no negative consequences for the subjects. It is quite often that the Committee expects researchers to display a certain degree of sensitivity to the well-being of individuals participating in their experiments and to propose procedures that will minimize the negative consequences (and mitigate the expected ones).

The aspects related to conducting field experiments and addressed in this book pertain to numerous areas, such as the very positioning of a field experiment in the entire chain of studies, the rather complex methodology (as compared to other types of experiments), and the chance for publication of articles based on field experiments. Additionally, a lot of attention was devoted to ethical aspects as well as various dilemmas researchers have to face in this respect. And yet, despite all this, we should not perceive field experiments as too difficult, too complex, or too ethically doubtful to be actually feasible. Quite the opposite, it is the hardship related to preparing and conducting such experiments that should encourage us to perform them. The ancients used to say: *per aspera ad astra* – "through hardships to the stars."

In any case, we do not look at field experiments only from the perspective of hardships and problems related to their preparation and execution. As we agree with the opinion of Klaus Fiedler (2018), who claims that while trying to encourage the psychological milieu to engage in studies conducted within a particular methodological framework one should focus on the positives, we wanted to demonstrate in this book the extent to which field experiments contribute to the increase in knowledge about psychology and that sometimes, at least equally importantly, they lead psychologists to question knowledge acquired previously resulting from, e.g., survey-based studies.

Even if only a certain share of the readers believe this book was worth reading, we, as the authors, will consider our job to be well done. Even if only a few researchers come to the conclusion that sometimes they should step out of their laboratories and add a field experiment to their studies, we will be satisfied. And even if only some academics are persuaded to devote more attention to field experiments than before at their classes on the methodology of psychological research, we will be happy. After all, that is why we wrote this book in the first place.

References

Abdullah, T. (2014). *A short history of Iraq*. London: Routledge.

Adair, J.G. (1984). The Hawthorne effect: A reconsideration of the methodological artifact. *Journal of Applied Psychology, 69*, 334–345.

Ajzen, I. (1987). Attitudes, traits, and actions: Dispositional prediction of behavior in personality and social psychology. *Advances in Experimental Social Psychology, 20*, 1–63.

Ajzen, I., & Fishbein, M. (1975). *Belief, attitude, intention and behavior: An introduction to theory and research*. Reading, MA: Addison-Wesley.

Ajzen, I., & Fishbein, M. (1977). Attitude–behavior relations: A theoretical analysis and review of empirical research. *Psychological Bulletin, 84*, 888–918.

American Psychologist (2009). vol. *64* issue 1 [whole special issue "Obedience – then and now"].

American Psychological Association. (2017). *Ethical principles of psychologists and code of conduct* (2002, amended effective June 1, 2010, and January 1, 2017). www.apa.org/ethics/code/.

Anderegg, W.R., Prall, J.W., Harold, J., & Schneider, S.H. (2010). Expert credibility in climate change. *Proceedings of the National Academy of Sciences, 107*, 12107–12109.

Anderson, C.J., Bahník, Š., Barnett-Cowan, M., Bosco, F.A., Chandler, J., Chartier, C.R., Cheung, F., Christopherson, C.D., Cordes, A., Cremata, E.J., Penna, N.D., Estel, V., Fedro, A., Fitneva, S.A., Frank, M.C., Grange, J.A., Harsthorne, J.K., Hasselman, F., Henninger, F., van der Hulst, M., Jonas, K.J., Lai, C.K., Levitan, C.A., Miller, J.K., Moore, K.S., Meixner, J.M., Munafo, M.R., Neijenhuijs, K.I., Nilsonne, G., Nosek, B, A., Plessow, F., Prenoveau, J.M., Ricker, A.A., Schmidt, K., Spies, J.R., Stieger, S., Strohminger, N., Sullivan, G.B., van Aert, R.C.M., van Assen, M.A.L.M., Vanpaemel, W., Vianello, M., Voracek, M., & Zuni, K.

(2016). Response to comment on "estimating the reproducibility of psychological science." *Science, 351*, 1037–1037.

Aron, A., Dutton, D.G., Aron, E.N., & Iverson, A. (1989). Experiences of falling in love. *Journal of Social and Personal Relationships, 6*, 243–257.

Aronson, E. (2010). *Not by chance alone: My life as a social psychologist*. New York, NY: Basic Books.

Aronson, E., & Aronson, J. (2018). *The social animal*. New York, NY: Worth Publishers.

Aronson, E., & Carlsmith, J.M. (1968). Experimentation in social psychology. In: G. Lindzey & E. Aronson (Eds.) *The Handbook of Social Psychology*, vol. 2 (pp. 1–79). Reading, MA: Addison-Wesley.

Aronson, E., Wilson, T.D., & Akert, R.M. (1994). *Social psychology: The heart and the mind*. New York, NY: Harper Collins.

Asch, S.E. (1951). Effects of group pressure upon the modification and distortion of judgments. In: H.S. Guetzkow (Ed.), *Groups, leadership, and men* (pp. 222–236). Pittsburgh, PA: Carnegie Press.

Babad, E.Y., Inbar, J., & Rosenthal, R. (1982). Pygmalion, Galatea, and the Golem: Investigations of biased and unbiased teachers. *Journal of Educational Psychology, 74*, 459–474.

Bachrach, Y., Kosinski, M., Graepel, T., Kohli, P., & Stillwell, D. (2012). Personality and patterns of Facebook usage. In: *Proceedings of the 4th Annual ACM Web Science Conference* (pp. 24–32). Evanston, IL: ACM.

Bain, R. (1928). An attitude on attitude research. *American Journal of Sociology, 33*, 940–957.

Bain, R. (1930). Theory and measurement of attitudes and opinions. *Psychological Bulletin, 27*, 357–379.

Barber, T.X., Forgione, A., Chaves, J.F., Calverley, D.S., McPeake, J.D., & Bowen, B. (1969). Five attempts to replicate the experimenter bias effect. *Journal of Consulting and Clinical Psychology, 33*, 1–6.

Barnett, S.A. (2007). *The rat: A study in behavior.* New York and London: Routledge.

Barrett, D.W. (2016). *Doing research: An introduction to research methods.* London: Sage

Baumeister, R. F., Vohs, K. D., & Funder, D. C. (2007). Psychology as the science of self reports and finger movements: Whatever happened to actual behavior? *Perspectives on Psychological Science, 2*, 396–403.

Baumrind, D. (1964). Some thoughts on ethics of research: After reading Milgram's "Behavioral Study of Obedience." *American Psychologist, 19*, 421–423.

Bavel, J.J.V., Mende-Siedlecki, P., Brady, W.J., & Reinero, D.A. (2016). Contextual sensitivity in scientific reproducibility. *Proceedings of the National Academy of Sciences, 113*, 6454–6459.

Beckers, R., Deneubourg, J.-L., Goss, S., & Pasteels, J.M. (1990). Collective decision making through food recruitment. *Insectes Sociaux, 37*, 258–267.

Bègue, L., Beauvois, J.L., Courbet, D., Oberlé, D., Lepage, J., Duke A.A. (2015). Personality predicts obedience in a Milgram paradigm. *Journal of Personality, 83*, 299–306.

Belmont Report (1979). The National Commission for the protection of human subjects of biomedical and behavioral research. Washington, DC: U.S. Government Printing Office.

Bem, D.J. (1972). Self-perception theory. *Advances in Experimental Social Psychology, 6*, 1–62.

Bem, D.J., & Lord, C.G. (1979). Template matching: A proposal for probing the ecological validity of experimental settings in social psychology. *Journal of Personality and Social Psychology, 37*, 833–846.

Berns, G.S., Chappelow, J., Zink, C.F., Pagnoni, G., Martin-Skurski, M.E., & Richards, J. (2005). Neurobiological correlates of social conformity and independence during mental rotation. *Biological Psychiatry, 58*, 245–253.

Bersheid, E., & Walster, E. (1974). A little bit about love. In: T.L. Huston (Eds.) *Foundations of interpersonal attraction* (pp. 355–381). New York: Academic Press.

Bershidsky, L. (2016, 8.12). No, big data didn't win the U.S. Election. *Bloomberg Opinion, 8 December 2016.* Retrieved 22nd December 2020 from: www.bloomberg.com/view/articles/2016-12-08/no-big-data-didn-t-win-the-u-s-election

Bickman, L., & Zarantonello, M. (1978). The effects of deception and level of obedience on subjects' ratings of the Milgram study. *Personality and Social Psychology Bulletin, 4*, 81–85.

Bilewicz, M., Winiewski, M., Kofta, M., & Wójcik, A. (2013). Harmful ideas, the structure and consequences of anti-Semitic beliefs in Poland. *Political Psychology, 34*, 821–839.

Birnbaum, M.H. (2000). *Psychological experiments on the Internet.* Amsterdam: Elsevier.

Blasi, A. (1980). Bridging moral cognition and moral action: A critical review of the literature. *Psychological Bulletin, 88*, 1–45.

Bock, D.C., & Warren, N.C. (1972). Religious belief as a factor in obedience to destructive commands. *Review of Religious Research, 13*, 185-191.

Bogardus, E.S. (1925). Measuring social distance. *Journal of Applied Sociology, 9*, 299–308.

Bohannon, J. (2013). Who's afraid of peer review? *Science, 342*, 60–65,

Bond, R., Smith, P.B. (1996). Culture and conformity: A meta-analysis of studies using Asch's (1952b, 1956) line judgment task. *Psychological Bulletin, 119*, 111–137.

Borchardt, K. O. (2003). Kolebka nawigatorów. Gdynia: Morska Oficyna Wydawnicza.

Bradbury, J.W., & Vehrencamp, S.L. (1998). *Principles of animal communication.* Retrieved 22nd December, 2020 from: http://sites.sinauer.com/animalcommunication2e/litcite/PoAC%202e%20Literature%20Cited%20(All%20Chapters).pdf.

Brannigan, A. (2004). *The rise and fall of social psychology: The use and misuse of the experimental method.* New Brunswick, NJ: Transaction Publishers.

Brown, N., & Heathers, J. (2017). The GRIM test: A simple technique detects numerous anomalies in the reporting of results in psychology. *Personality and Social Psychology Bulletin, 8*, 363–369.

Bryden, M.P. (1988). *An overview of the dichotic listening procedure and its relation to cerebral organization.* Retrieved 22nd December, 2020 from: http://psycnet.apa.org/psycinfo/1988-98844-001.

Byrka, K., Grzyb, T., & Dolinski, D. (2015). Attitudes, behavior, democracy, and dialogue. In: K. Jezierska & L. Koczanowicz (Eds.) *Democracy in dialogue, dialogue in democracy: The politic of dialogue in theory and practice* (pp. 139–157). Farnham, UK: Ashgate Publishers.

Brzezinski, J.M. (2016). Towards a comprehensive model of scientific research and professional practice in psychology. *Current Issues in Personality Psychology, 4*, 1–10.

Brzezinski, J. M. (2017). Data integration levels: Between scientific research and professional practice in clinical psychology. *Current Issues in Personality Psychology, 5*, 163–171.

Bucknall, T.K. (2000). Critical care nurses' decision-making activities in the natural clinical setting. *Journal of Clinical Nursing, 9*, 25–36.

Burger, J.M., & Guadagno, R.E. (2003). Self-concept clarity and the foot-in-the-door procedure. *Basic and Applied Social Psychology, 25*, 79–86.

Burgoon, J.K., Guerrero, L.K., & Floyd, K. (2016). *Nonverbal communication*. New York, NY: Routledge.

Butler, D. (2013). Investigating journals: The dark side of publishing. *Nature, 495*, 433–435.

Camerer, C. (2003). *Behavioral game theory: Experiments in strategic interaction*. Princeton, NJ: Princeton University Press.

Campbell, D.T., & Stanley, J.C. (1963). *Experimental and quasi-experimental designs for research*. Boston, MA: Houghton Mifflin.

Carroll, J.S., & Payne, J.W. (2014). *Cognition and social behavior*. New York, NY: Psychology Press.

Carr, N. (2015). Is Google making us stupid? What the Internet is doing to our brains, "The Composition of Everyday Life, Concise," *The Atlantic*. Retrieved 22nd December, 2020 from: www.theatlantic.com/magazine/archive/2008/07/is-google-making-us-stupid/306868/.

Chandler, J.J., & Paolacci, G. (2017). Life for a dime: When most prescreening responses are honest but most study participants are impostors. *Social Psychological and Personality Science, 8*, 500–508.

Chaudhuri, A. (2011). Sustaining cooperation in laboratory public goods experiments: A selective survey of the literature. *Experimental Economics, 14*, 47–83.

Chou, E.Y., Halevy, N., Galinsky, A.D., & Murnighan, J.K. (2017). The Goldilocks contract: The synergistic benefits of combining structure and autonomy for persistence, creativity, and cooperation. *Journal of Personality and Social Psychology, 113*, 393–412.

Cialdini, R.B. (1980). Full-cycle social psychology. *Applied Social Psychology Annual, 1*, 21-47.

Cialdini, R. B. (2009). We have to break up. *Perspectives on Psychological Science, 4*, 5–6.

Cialdini, R.B. (2001). Influence. Science and practice (4th ed.). Needham Heights, MA: Allyn & Bacon.

Cialdini, R.B., Demaine, L.J., Sagarin, B.J., Barrett, D.W., Rhoads, K., & Winter, P.L. (2006). Managing social norms for persuasive impact. *Social Influence, 1*, 3–15.

Cialdini, R.B., & Goldstein, N.J. (2004). Social influence: Compliance and conformity. *Annual Review of Psychology, 55*, 591–621.

Cialdini, R.B., Kallgren, C.A., & Reno, R.R. (1991). A focus theory of normative conduct. *Advances in Experimental Social Psychology, 24*, 201–234.

Cialdini, R.B., & Schroeder, D.A. (1976). Increasing compliance by legitimizing paltry contributions: When even a penny helps. *Journal of Personality and Social Psychology, 34*, 599–604.

Cialdini, R.B., Trost, M.R., & Newsom, J.T. (1995). Preference for consistency: The development of valid measure and the discovery of surprising behavioral implications. *Journal of Personality and Social Psychology, 69*, 318–328.

Condon, P. (2016). *Getting starting with the open science framework*. Retrieved 22nd December 2020 from: http://scholars.unh.edu/cgi/viewcontent.cgi?article=1010&context=oaw.

Cohen, J. (1990). Things I have learned (so far). *American Psychologist, 45*, 1304–1312.

Cohen, J. (1994). The earth is round (p<.05). *American Psychologist, 49*, 997–1003.

Colquitt, J.A. (2008). From the editors publishing laboratory research in AMJ: A question of when, not if. *Academy of Management Journal, 51*, 616–620.

Cook, C., Goodman, N.D., & Schulz, L.E. (2011). Where science starts: Spontaneous experiments in preschoolers' exploratory play. *Cognition, 120*, 341–349.

Cook, J., Oreskes, N., Doran, P.T., Anderegg, W.R., Verheggen, B, Maibach, E.W., et al. (2016). Consensus on consensus: A synthesis of consensus estimates on human-caused global warming. *Environmental Research Letters, 11*, 048002.

Cook, T.D., & Campbell, D.T. (1979). *Quasi experimentation: Design and analysis issues for field settings.* Boston, MA: Houghton Mifflin.

Corfield, V.K. (1969). The role of arousal and cognitive complexity in susceptibility to social influence. *Journal of Personality, 37*, 554–566.

Cronbach, L.J. (1957). The two disciplines of scientific psychology. *American Psychologist, 12*, 671–684.

Darley, J.M., & Batson, C.D. (1973). "From Jerusalem to Jericho": A study of situational and dispositional variables in helping behavior. *Journal of Personality and Social Psychology, 27*, 100–108.

Darley, J.M., & Latané, B. (1968). Bystander intervention in emergencies: Diffusion of responsibility. *Journal of Personality and Social Psychology, 8*, 377–383.

Darnon, C., & Klein, O. (2019). Expression of concern regarding six articles by Dr. Nicolas Guéguen. *International Review of Social Psychology, 32*, 1–3.

Davis, D.D., Razzolini, L., Reilly, R.J., & Wilson, B.J. (2006). Raising revenues for charity: Auctions versus lotteries. In: R.M. Isaac, & D.D. Davis (Eds.) *Experiments investigating fundraising and charitable contributors* (pp. 47–91). Bingley, UK: Emerald Group Publishing Limited.

Davis, P. (2013). *Open access "Sting" reveals deception, missed opportunities.* Retrieved 22nd December, 2020 from: https://scholarlykitchen.sspnet.org/2013/10/04/open-access-sting-reveals-deception-missed-opportunities/.

Deutsche Bank. (2014). *Raport Finansowy Polaków 2014. Plany na 2015 rok.* Retrieved 22nd December, 2020 from: www.deutschebank.pl/raport-portret-finansowy-polakow-2014.pdf.

Dictionary of Military and Associated Terms (2010). Retrieved 22nd December, 2020 from: http://Doctrine/pubs/dictionary.pdf. jcs.mil?Portals/36/Documents/.

Dillard, J.P. (1990). A goal-driven model of interpersonal influence. In: J.P. Dillard (Ed.), *Seeking compliance: The production of interpersonal influence messages (*pp. 41–56). Scottsdale, AZ: Gorsuch Scarisbrick.

Dolinska, B., & Dolinski, D. (2014). Fear-then-relief, legitimizing a paltry contribution, and charity. *European Review of Applied Psychology, 64*, 29-34.

Dolinska, B., Jarzabek, J., & Dolinski, D. (2020). I like you even less at Christmas dinner: Prejudice level as a function of an approaching national or religious holiday. *Basic and Applied Social Psychology, 42*, 88-97.

Dolinski, D. (1996). The mystery of the Polish soul. B.W. Johnson's effect à rebours. *European Journal of Social Psychology, 26*, 1001–1005.

Dolinski, D. (2001). Emotional seesaw, compliance, and mindlessness. *European Psychologist, 6*, 194–203.

Dolinski, D. (2010). Touch, compliance, and homophobia. *Journal of Nonverbal Behavior, 34*,179–192.

Dolinski, D. (2016). *Techniques of social influence: The psychology of gaining compliance.* New York and London: Routledge.

Dolinski, D. (2018a) Is psychology still a science of behavior? *Social Psychological Bulletin, 13*(2), 1–14.

Dolinski, D. (2018b). Social psychology should be a science of feelings, thoughts and behaviour. *Social Psychological Bulletin, 13*(2), 1–13.

Dolinski, D., & Grzyb, T. (2016). One serious shock versus gradated series of shocks: Does "Multiple Feet-in-the-Door" explain obedience in Milgram studies? *Basic and Applied Social Psychology, 38*, 276–283. 1–8.

Dolinski, D., & Grzyb, T. (2020). *The social psychology of obedience towards authority: An empirical tribute to Stanley Milgram.* New York and London: Routledge.

Dolinski, D., Grzyb, T., Olejnik, J., Prusakowski, S., & Urban, K. (2005). Let's dialogue about penny. *Journal of Applied Social Psychology, 35*, 1150–1170.

Dolinski, D., Nawrat, M., & Rudak, I. (2001). Dialogue involvement as a social influence technique. *Personality and Social Psychology Bulletin, 27*, 1395–1406.

Dolinski, D., & Nawrat, R. (1998). "Fear-then-relief" procedure for producing compliance: Beware when the danger is over. *Journal of Experimental Social Psychology, 34*, 27–50.

Dolinski, D., & Odachowska, E. (2018). Beware when danger on the road has passed. The state of relief impairs a driver's ability to avoid accidents. *Accident Analysis and Prevention, 115*, 73–78.

Duhigg, Ch. (2014). *The power of habit: Why we do what we do in life and business.* New York, NY: Random House.

Dunbar, R. (2004). *The Human Story: A new history of mankind's evolution*. London: Faber & Faber.

Dunn, D. S. (2012). *The practical researcher: A student guide to conducting psychological research*. Hoboken, NJ: Wiley.

Dutton, G.D., & Aron, A.P. (1974). Some evidence for heightened sexual attraction under conditions of high anxiety. *Journal of Personality and Social Psychology*, *30*, 510–517.

Ebster, C., & Neumayr, B. (2008). Applying the door-in-the-face compliance technique to retailing. *The International Review of Retail, Distribution and Consumer Research*, *18*, 121–128.

Empson, R. A., & Miskelly, C. M. (1999). The risks, costs and benefits of using brodifacoum to eradicate rats from Kapiti Island, New Zealand. *New Zealand Journal of Ecology*, 23, 241–254.

Endler, N.S., & Speer, R.L. (1998). Personality psychology: Research trends for 1993–1995. *Journal of Personality*, *66*, 621–669.

Ethical Principles of Psychologists and Code of Conduct (2016). Washington, DC: American Psychological Association.

Faber, J., & Fonseca, L. M. (2014). How sample size influences research outcomes. *Dental Press Journal of Orthodontics*, *19*, 27–29.

Farber, M.L. (1952). The college student as laboratory animal. *American Psychologist*, 7, 102.

Faris, E. (1928). Attitudes and behavior. *American Journal of Sociology*, *34*, 271–281.

Fazio, R.H., Chen, J.-M., McDonel, E.C., & Sherman, S.J. (1982). Attitude accessibility, attitude-behavior consistency, and the strength of the object-evaluation association. *Journal of Experimental Social Psychology*, *18*, 339–357.

Fiedler, K. (2018). How to make psychology a genuine science of behavior: Comments on Dolinski's thoughtful paper. *Social Psychological Bulletin*, *13*(2), 1–7.

Fiedler, K., & Kareev, Y. (2006). Does decision quality (always) increase with the size of information samples? Some vicissitudes in applying the law of large numbers. *Journal of Experimental Psychology: Learning, Memory, and Cognition*, *32*, 883–903.

Fiedler, K., & Kareev, Y. (2011). Clarifying the advantage of small samples: As it relates to statistical wisdom and Cahan's (2010) normative intuitions. *Journal of Experimental Psychology: Learning, Memory, and Cognition*, *37*, 1039-1043.

Fisher, C.T. (1968). Ethical issues in the use of human subjects. *American Psychologist*, *23*, 532.

Fisher, J. (1992). Testing the effect of road traffic signs' informational value on driver behavior. *Human Factors: The Journal of the Human Factors and Ergonomics Society*, *34*, 231–237.

Fischer, P., Krueger, J. I., Greitemeyer, T., Vogrincic, C., Kastenmüller, A., Frey, D., Heene, M., Wicher, M., & Kainbacher, M. (2011). The bystander-effect: a meta-analytic review on bystander intervention in dangerous and non-dangerous emergencies. *Psychological Bulletin*, *137*, 517.

Fiske, S.T., Gilbert, D.T., & Lindzey, G. (2010). *Handbook of social psychology (vol. 2)*. New York, NY: John Wiley & Sons.

Fleming, A. et al. (1946). *Penicillin. Its practical application*. Retrieved 22nd December, 2020 from: www.cabdirect.org/cabdirect/abstract/19472201476.

Flower, T. P., Gribble, M., & Ridley, A. R. (2014). Deception by flexible alarm mimicry in an African bird. *Science*, *344*, 513-516.

Foltz, R. (2014). *Animals in Islamic traditions and Muslim cultures*. Oxford, UK: Oneworld Publications.

Freedman, J.L., Fraser, S.C. (1966). Compliance without pressure: The foot-in-the-door technique. *Journal of Personality and Social Psychology*, *4*, 195–202.

Friend, R., Rafferty, Y., Bramel, D. (1990). A puzzling misinterpretation of the Asch "conformity" study. *European Journal of Social Psychology*, *20*, 29–44.

Frith, J. (2013). Turning life into a game: Foursquare, gamification, and personal mobility. *Mobile Media in Communication*, *1*, 248–262.

Gardner, P.L. (1975). Scales and statistics. *Review of Educational Research*, *45*, 43–57.

Gilbert, D.T., King, G., Pettigrew, S., Wilson, T.D. (2016). *Comment on "Estimating the reproducibility of psychological science."* Retrieved 22nd December 2020 from: http://projects.iq.harvard.edu/files/psychology-replications/files/gkpw_post_publication_response.pdf.

Gilbert, S.J. (1981). Another look at the Milgram obedience studies: The role of the gradated series of shocks. *Personality and Social Psychology Bulletin*, 7, 690–695.

Goffman, E. (1963). *Behavior in public place*. New York, Glencoe: The Free Press.

Goldman, M., Kiyohara, O., & Pfannensteil, D.A. (2001). Interpersonal touch, social labeling, and the foot-in-the-door effect. *Journal of Social Psychology, 152*, 143–147.

Goldstein, N.J., & Cialdini, R.B. (2007). The spyglass self: A model of vicarious self-perception. *Journal of Personality and Social Psychology, 92*(3), 402–417. https://doi.org/10.1037/0022-3514.92.3.402

Golec de Zavala, A., Federico, Ch. M., Sedikides, C., Guerra, R., Lantos, D., Mrozinski, B., Cypryanska, M., & Baran, T. (2020). Low self-esteem predicts out-group derogation via collective narcissism, but this relation is obscured by in-group satisfaction. *Journal of Personality and Social Psychology, 119*, 741–764.

Gomez, B.T., Hansford, T.G., & Krause, G.A. (2007). The Republicans should pray for rain: Weather, turnout, and voting in US presidential elections. *Journal of Politics, 69*, 649–663.

Goodman, J.K., Cryder, C.E., & Cheema, A. (2013). Data collection in a flat world: The strengths and weaknesses of Mechanical Turk samples. *Journal of Behavioral Decision Making, 26*, 213–224.

Gosling, S.D., Vazire, S., Srivastava, S., & John, O.P. (2004). Should we trust web-based studies? A comparative analysis of six preconceptions about internet questionnaires. *American Psychologist, 59*, 93–104.

Grant, D.A. (1948). The Latin square principle in the design and analysis of psychological experiments. *Psychological Bulletin, 45*, 427–438.

Greenberg, M.S. (1967). Role playing: An alternative to deception? *Journal of Personality and Social Psychology, 7*, 152–157.

Greenwood, J.D. (1983). Role-playing as an experimental strategy in social psychology. *European Journal of Social Psychology, 13*, 235–254.

Griffith, R. (1987). *The politics of fear: Joseph R. McCarthy and the Senate*. Amherst, MA: University of Massachusetts Press.

Griskevicius, V., Tybur, J.M., Sundie, J.M., Cialdini, R.B., Miller, G..F., & Kenrick, D.T. (2007). Blatant benevolence and conspicuous consumption: When romantic motives elicit strategic costly signals. *Journal of Personality and Social Psychology, 93*, 85–102.

Grzyb, T. (2003). *Skutecznosc huśtawki emocjonalnej jako techniki stosowanej w warunkach prośby telefonicznej*. Unpublished Master Thesis, Opole University.

Grzyb, T. (2005). *Badania Solomona Ascha nad konformizmem realizowane za pomocą eksperymentu terenowego*. Wrocław: Unpublished Research Report.

Grzyb, T. (2016). Why can't we just ask? The influence of research methods on results. The case of "bystander effect". *Polish Psychological Bulletin, 47*, 276–283.

Grzyb, T., & Dolinski, D. (2017). Beliefs about obedience levels in studies conducted within the Milgram paradigm: Better than average effect and comparisons of typical behaviors by of different countries. *Frontiers in Psychology, 8*, 1632.

Grzyb, T., & Dolinski, D. (2021). Multiple feet-in-the-door and obedience. *Basic and Applied Social Psychology, 43*, 81–89.

Grzyb, T., Dolinski, D., & Kulesza, W. (2021). Dialogue and labeling. Are these helpful in finding volunteers? *The Journal of Social Psychology, 161*, 63–71.

Grzyb, T., & Steposz, M. (2016). *The number of studies per article and the year of publication: Analysis of the flagship journals of social psychology*. Unpublished research report.

Guadagno, R.E., Asher, T., Demaine, L.J., & Cialdini, R.B. (2001). When saying yes leads to saying no: Preference for consistency and the reverse foot-in-the-door effect. *Personality and Social Psychology Bulletin, 7*, 859–867.

Guadagno, R.E., & Cialdini, R.B. (2010). Preference for consistency and social influence: A review of current research findings. *Social Influence, 5*, 152–163.

Guéguen, N. (2012). "Say it … Near the flower shop": Further evidence of the effect of flowers on mating. *The Journal of Social Psychology, 152*, 529–532.

Guéguen, N., & Jacob, C. (2006). The effect of tactile stimulation on the purchasing behavior of consumers: An experimental study in natural setting. *International Journal of Management, 23*, 24–33.

Guéguen, N., & Fischer-Lokou, J. (2002). An evaluation of touch on a large request: A field setting. *Psychological Reports, 90*, 267–269.

Guéguen, N., & Lamy, L. (2013). Weather and helping: Additional evidence of the effect of the sunshine Samaritan. *The Journal of Social Psychology, 153*, 123–126.

Guéguen, N., & Pascual, A. (2000). Evocation of freedom and compliance: The "But you are free of…" technique. *Current Research in Social Psychology, 5*, 264–270.

Güth, W., Schmittberger, R., & Schwarze, B. (1982). An experimental analysis of ultimatum bargaining. *Journal of Economic Behavior & Organization, 3*, 367–388.

Haney, C., Banks, C., & Zimbardo, P. (1973). A study of prisoners and guards in a simulated prison. *Naval Research Review, 30*, 4–17.

Haslam, S.A., Reicher, S.D., & Birney, M.E. (2014). Nothing by mere authority: Evidence that in an experimental analogue of the Milgram paradigm participants are motivated not by orders but by appeals to science. *Journal of Social Issues, 70*, 473–488.

Haslam, S.A., Reicher, S.D., & Millard, K. (2015). Shock treatment: Using immersive digital realism to restage and re-examine Milgram's "Obedience to Authority" research. *PloS One, 10*(3), e109015.

Heinzen, T., & Goodfriend, W. (2017). *Social psychology*. London: Sage

Henrich, J.P., Boyd, R., Bowles, S., Camerer, C., Fehr, E, & Gintis, H. (2004). *Foundations of human sociality: Economic experiments and ethnographic evidence from fifteen small-scale societies*. Oxford: Oxford University Press.

Hock, R.R. (2015). *Forty studies that changed psychology*. New York, NY: Pearson Higher Education.

Holland, J., Silva, A.S., & Mace, R. (2012). Lost letter measure of variation in altruistic behaviour in 20 neighbourhoods. *PloS one*, 7(8), e43294.

Hofling, C.K., Brotzman, E., Dalrymple, S., Graves, N., Pierce, C.M. (1966). An experimental study in nurse-physician relationships. *The Journal of Nervous and Mental Disease, 143*, 171–180.

Hornik, J. (1987). The effect of touch and gaze upon compliance and interest of interviewees. *Journal of Social Psychology, 127*, 681–683.

Hornik, J., & Ellis, S. (1988). Strategies to secure compliance for a mail interview. *Public Opinion Quarterly, 52*, 539–551.

Howard, D.J. (1990). The influence of verbal responses to common greetings on compliance behavior: The foot-in-the-mouth effect. *Journal of Applied Social Psychology, 20*, 1185–1196.

Hsee, C.K., & Ruan, B. (2016). The Pandora effect: The power and peril of curiosity. *Psychological Science, 27*, 659–666.

Ioannidis, J.P. (2016). Anticipating consequences of sharing raw data and code and of awarding badges for sharing. *Journal of Clinical Epidemiology, 70*, 258–260.

Ipeirotis, P.G. (2010). *Demographics of mechanical turk*. Retrieved 22nd December 2020 from: http://papers.ssrn.com/sol3/papers.cfm?abstract_id=1585030.

Iphofen, R. (2011). *Ethical decision making in social research: A practical guide*. Basingstoke, UK: Palgrave Macmillan.

Isen, A.M., & Levin, P.F. (1972). Effect of feeling good on helping: Cookies and kindness. *Journal of Personality and Social Psychology, 21*, 384–388.

Isen, A.M., Shalker, T., Clark, M., & Karp. P. (1978). Affect, accessibility of material in memory, and behavior: A cognitive loop? *Journal of Personality and Social Psychology, 36*, 1–12.

Isen, A.M., & Simmonds, F. (1978). The effect of feeling good on a helping task that is incompatible with good mood. *Social Psychology, 41*, 346–349.

Jackson, M. (1997). *Michael Jackson's beer companion: The world's great beer styles, gastronomy, and traditions.* London: Running Press Book Publishers.

Jacobson, R.P., Mortensen, Ch.R., & Cialdini, R.B. (2011). Bodies obliged and unbound: Differentiated response tendencies for injuctive and descriptive norms. *Journal of Personality and Social Psychology, 100*, 433–448.

Jalalian, M. (2015). The story of fake impact factor companies and how we detected them. *Electronic Physician*, 7, 1069–1072.

Jenks, Ch. (1995). *Visual culture*. Hove, UK: Psychology Press.

Johnson, W.B. (1937). Euphoric and depressed mood in normal subjects. *Character and Personality, 6*, 79–98.

Jones, D.N., & Paulhus, D.L. (2017). Duplicity among the dark triad: Three faces of deceit. *Journal of Personality and Social Psychology, 113*, 329–342.

Kaczmarek, M.C., & Steffens, M.C. (2017). Mindlessly polite: A conceptual replication of the emotional seesaw effect on compliance and information processing. *Frontiers in Psychology, 8*, 329.

Kaczmarek, M.C., & Steffens, M.C. (2019). "Mind full or mindful" – can mere cognitive busyness lead to compliance similar to an emotional seesaw? *Social Influence, 14*, 117–132.

Kahneman, D. (2016). 36 heuristics and biases. In: R.J. Sternberg (Ed.), *Scientists making a difference: One hundred eminent behavioral and brain scientists talk about their most important contributions* (pp. 171– 193). New York: Cambridge University Press.

Kahneman, D., Knetsch, J.L., & Thaler, R.H. (1986). Fairness and the assumptions of economics. *Journal of Business, 59*, S285–S300.

Kahneman, D., & Tversky, A. (1972). Subjective probability: A judgment of representativeness. *Cognitive Psychology, 3*, 430–454.

Kantowitz, B.H., Roediger III, H.L., & Elmes, D.G. (2014). *Experimental psychology*. Scarborough, UK: Nelson Education.

Kaplan, H.R. (1987). Lottery winners: The myth and reality. *Journal of Gambling Behavior, 3*, 168–178.

Kasser, T., & Ryan, R.M. (1993). A dark side of the American dream: Correlates of financial success as a central life aspiration. *Journal of Personality and Social Psychology, 65*, 410–422.

Katz, D., & Braly, K. (1933). Racial stereotypes of one hundred college students. *Journal of Abnormal and Social Psychology, 28*, 280–290.

Kaufmann, H. (1967). The price of obedience and the price of knowledge. *American Psychologist, 22*, 321–322.

Kayser, D.N., Greitemeyer, T., Fischer, P., & Frey, D. (2010). Why mood affects help giving, but not moral courage: Comparing two types of prosocial behaviour. *European Journal of Social Psychology, 40*, 1136–1157.

Kemp, E., & Creyer, E.H. (2007). Increasing persuasion, reducing resistance: Maximizing the efficacy of persuasive appeals for aesthetic product consumption. *Advances in Consumer Research, 34*, 337–339.

Kelln, B.R., & Ellard, J.H. (1999). An equity theory analysis of the impact of forgiveness and retribution on transgressor compliance. *Personality and Social Psychology Bulletin, 25*, 864–872.

Kelman, H.C. (1967). Human use of human subjects: The problem of deception in social psychological experiments. *Psychological Bulletin, 67*, 1–11.

Kenrick, D.T., & Cialdini, R.B. (1977). Romantic attraction: Missatribution versus reinforcement explanations. *Journal of Personality and Social Psychology, 35*, 381–391.

Kenrick, D.T., Neuberg, S.L., & Cialdini, R.B. (2020). *Social psychology: Goals in interaction*. Essex, UK: Pearson.

Kilham, W., & Mann, L. (1974). Level of destructive obedience as a function of transmitter and executant roles in the Milgram obedience paradigm. *Journal of Personality and Social Psychology, 29*, 696–702.

Kimura, D. (1961). Cerebral dominance and the perception of verbal stimuli. *Canadian Journal of Psychology/Revue Canadienne de Psychologie, 15*, 166–171.

Klebaniuk, J. (2012). Profesor Stapel na dopingu. O upiekszaniu psychologii spolecznej. *Psychologia Spoleczna, 3*, 213–217.

Kleinke, Ch. L. (1977). Compliance to request made by gazing and touching experiments in a field settings. *Journal of Experimental Social Psychology, 13*, 218–223.

Kleinke, Ch.L. (1986). Gaze and eye contact: A research review. *Psychological Bulletin, 100*, 78–100.

Knapp, M.L., Hall, J.A., & Horgan, T.G. (2013). *Nonverbal communication in human interaction*. Boston, MA: Wadsworth Cengage Learning.

Knowles, E.S., Linn, J.A. (2004a). Approach-avoidance model of persuasion: Alpha and Omega strategies for change. In. Knowles, E.S., Linn, J.A. (Eds.). *Resistance and persuasion* (pp. 117–148). Mahwah, NJ: Lawrence Erlbaum Associates.

Knowles, E.S., Linn, J.A. (Eds.) (2004b). *Resistance and persuasion*. Mahwah, NJ: Lawrence Erlbaum Associates Publishers.

Kohn, A. (1998). *What to look for in a classroom … and other essays*. San Francisco, CA: Jossey-Bass.

Kolata, G. (2007). *Rethinking thin: The new science of weight loss – and the myths and realities of dieting*. New York, NY: Farrar, Straus & Giroux.

Kołakowska, Z. (2005). *Metodologiczne problemy zjawiska niedostępności w badaniach sondażowych*. Unpublished Master Theses. Warsaw University.

Kosinski, M., Stillwell, D., & Graepel, T. (2013). Private traits and attributes are predictable from digital records of human behavior. *Proceedings of the National Academy of Sciences*, *110*, 5802–5805.

Krackow, A., & Blass, T. (1995). When nurses obey or defy inappropriate physician orders: Attributional differences. *Journal of Social Behavior and Personality*, *10*, 585–594.

Krantz, J. H., & Dalal, R. (2000). *Validity of Web-based psychological research*. San Diego, CA: Academic Press

Kraut, R., Olson, J., Banaji, M., Bruckman, A., Cohen, J., & Couper, M. (2004). Psychological research online: report of Board of Scientific Affairs' Advisory Group on the Conduct of Research on the Internet. *American Psychologist*, *59*, 105–117.

Lake, D.A., & Rothchild, D.S. (1998). *The international spread of ethnic conflict: Fear, diffusion, and escalation*. Princeton, NJ: Princeton University Press.

Lamy, L., Fischer-Lokou, J., & Guéguen, N. (2015). Places for help: Micro-level variation in helping behavior toward a stranger. *Psychological Reports*, *116*, 242–248.

Langer, E. J. (1989). Minding matters: The consequences of mindlessness-mindfulness. *Advances in Experimental Social Psychology*, *22*, 137–173.

Langer, E.J., Blank, A., & Chanowitz, B. (1978). The mindlessness of ostensibly thoughtful action. The role of "placebic" information in interpersonal interaction. *Journal of Personality and Social Psychology*, *36*, 635–642.

Langer, E.J., & Moldoveanu, M. (2000). The construct of mindfulness. *Journal of Social Issues*, *56*, 1–9.

LaPiere, R.T. (1934). Attitudes vs. actions. *Social Forces*, *13*, 230–237.

Latané, B., & Darley, J.M. (1968). Group inhibition of bystander intervention in emergencies. *Journal of Personality and Social Psychology*, *10*, 215–221.

Latané, B., & Darley, J.M. (1969). Bystander "apathy." *American Scientist*, *57*, 244–268.

Latané, B., & Darley, J.M. (1970). *The unresponsive bystander: Why doesn't he help?* New York, NY: Appleton Century Crofts.

Lederer, S., & Davis, A.B. (1995). Subjected to science: Human experimentation in America before the Second World War. *History: Reviews of New Books*, *24*, 13.

Leoniak, K.L., & Cwalina, W. (2019). The role of normative prompts and norm support cues in promoting light-switching behavior: A field study. *Journal of Environmental Psychology*, *64*, 1–11.

Levine, R.V., Norenzayan, A., & Philbrick, K. (2001). Cross-cultural differences in helping strangers. *Journal of Cross-Cultural Psychology*, *32*, 543–560.

Levitt, S.D., & Dubner, S.J. (2009). *Superfreakonomics: Global cooling, patriotic prostitutes and why suicide bombers should buy insurance*. New York: William Morrow HarperCollins.

Levitt, S.D., & List, J.A. (2007). What do laboratory experiments measuring social preferences reveal about the real world?. *The Journal of Economic Perspectives*, *21*, 153–174.

Lewis-Beck, M.S., & Stegmaier, M. (2014). Weather, forecasts, elections: After Richardson. *Political Science and Politics*, *47*, 322–325.

Ley, P. (1981). Professional non-compliance: A neglected problem. *British Journal of Clinical Psychology*, *20*, 151–154.

Liska, A.E. (1984). A critical examination of the causal structure of the Fishbein/Ajzen attitude-behavior model. *Social Psychology Quarterly*, *47*, 61–74.

Lynn, M., Le, J.-M., & Sherwyn, D.S. (1998). Reach out and touch your customers. *The Cornell Hotel and Restaurant Administration Quarterly*, *39*, 60–65.

Lynam, D., Moffitt, T., & Stouthamer-Loeber, M. (1993). Explaining the relation between IQ and delinquency: Class, race, test motivation, school failure, or self-control? *Journal of Abnormal Psychology*, *102*, 187–196.

Maksim, A., & Spiewak, S. (2017). Zwiazek pomiędzy wiekiem, preferencja spojnosci i skutecznoscia techniki wpływu społecznego "stopa w drzwiach." *Psychologia Spoleczna*, *12*, 21–29.

Marzoli, D., & Tommasi, L. (2009). Side biases in humans (Homo sapiens): Three ecological studies on hemispheric asymmetries. *Naturwissenschaften, 96*, 1099–1106.

Mason, W., & Suri, S. (2012). Conducting behavioral research on Amazon's Mechanical Turk. *Behavior Research Methods, 44*, 1–23.

Mayo, E. (1949). *The social problems of an industrial civilisation*. Cambridge, MA: Harvard University Press.

Mayo, E., Lombard, G.F.F. (1944). *Teamwork and labor turnover in the aircraft industry of Southern California*. Cambridge, MA: Harvard University Press.

McConahay, J.B. (1986). Modern racism, ambivalence, and the modern racism scale. In: J.F. Dovidio, & S.L. Gaertner (Eds.) *Prejudice, discrimination, and racism* (pp. 91–125). San Diego, CA: Academic Press.

McIntosh, D.N. (1996). Facial feedback hypotheses: Evidence, implications, and directions. *Motivation and Emotion, 20*, 121–147.

Meineri, S., Guéguen, N. (2011). "I hope I'm not disturbing you, am I?" Another operationalization of the foot-in-the-mouth paradigm. *Journal of Applied Social Psychology, 41*, 965–975.

Merton, R.K. (1948). The self-fulfilling prophecy. *The Antioch Review, 8*, 193–210.

Meeus, W.H., & Raaijmakers, Q.A. (1995). Obedience in modern society: The Utrecht studies. *Journal of Social Issues, 51*, 155–175.

Milgram, S. (1963). Behavioral study of obedience. *Journal of Abnormal and Social Psychology, 67*, 371–378.

Milgram, S. (1965). Some conditions of obedience and disobedience to authority. *Human Relations, 18*, 57–75.

Milgram, S. (1974). *Obedience to authority: An experimental view*. New York: Harper & Row.

Milgram, S., Mann, L., Harter, S. (1965). The lost-letter technique: A tool of social research. *Public Opinion Quarterly, 29*, 437–438.

Mirzoeff, N. (2010). Visual culture. *The Year's Work in Critical and Cultural Theory, 18*, 327–337.

Misra, B. (2016). Ten "personal" reasons why I am skeptical about Open Access (OA): Thoughts of an individual researcher. *The Winnower*, 7:e145789.92186.

Mixon, D. (1972). Instead of deception. *Journal for the Theory of Social Behaviour, 2*, 145–178.

Mook, D.G. (1983). In defense of external invalidity. *American Psychologist, 34*, 379–387.

Mortensen, Ch., R., & Cialdini, R.B. (2010). Full cycle social psychology for theory and application. *Social and Personality Psychology Compass, 4*, 53–63.

Nagel, T. (1979). *Mortal questions*. Cambridge, UK: Cambridge University Press.

Nawrat, R., & Dolinski, D. (2007). "Seesaw of emotions" and compliance. Beyond the fear-then-relief rule. *The Journal of Social Psychology, 147*, 556–571.

Neal, J.W., Durbin, C.E., Gornik, A.E., & Lo, S.L. (2017). Codevelopment of preschoolers' temperament traits and social play networks over an entire school year. *Journal of Personality and Social Psychology, 113*, 627–640.

Newcourt-Nowodworski, S. (1996). *Black propaganda in the Second World War*. Stroud, UK: The History Press.

Nilsen, W.J., & Pavel, M. (2013). Moving behavioral theories into the 21st century: Technological advancements for improving quality of life. *IEEE Pulse, 4*, 25–28.

Nisbett, R.E., & Cohen, D. (1996). *Culture of honor: The psychology of violence in the south*. Boulder, CO: Westview Press.

Nordfält, J., Grewal, D., Roggeveen, A.L., & Hill, K.M. (2014). Insights from in-store marketing experiments. In: D. Grewal, A.L. Roggeveen, & J. Nordfält (Eds.) *Shopper marketing and the role of in-store marketing* (pp. 127–146). Bingley, UK: Emerald Group Publishing Limited.

Nosek, B. A., Banaji, M., & Greenwald, A. G. (2002). Harvesting implicit group attitudes and beliefs from a demonstration web site. *Group Dynamics: Theory, Research, and Practice, 6*, 101–115.

Open Science Collaboration (2015). Estimating the reproducibility of psychological science. *Science, 349*(6251), aac4716.

Orne, M.T. (1962). On the social psychology of the psychological experiment: With particular reference to demand characteristics and their implications. *American Psychologist, 17*, 776–783.

Orne, M.T., & Holland, C.H. (1968). On the ecological validity of laboratory deceptions. *International Journal of Psychiatry, 6*, 282–293.

Patterson, M.L. (2008). Back to social behavior: Mining the mundane. *Basic and Applied Social Psychology, 30*, 93–101.

Pawlowski, B., & Koziel, S. (2002). The impact of traits offered in personal advertisements on response rates. *Evolution and Human Behavior*, 23, 139–149.

Peng, K., Nisbett, R.E., & Wong, N.Y.C. (1997). Validity problems comparing values across cultures and possible solutions. *Psychological Methods, 2*, 329–344.

Perrin, S., Spencer, C. (1980). The Asch effect: A child of its time. *Bulletin of the British Psychological Society, 32*, 405–406.

Perry, G. (2013). *Behind the shock machine: The untold story of the notorious Milgram psychology experiments*. New York, NY: The New Press.

Persson, M., Sundell, A., & Öhrvall, R. (2014). Does Election Day weather affect voter turnout? Evidence from Swedish elections. *Electoral Studies, 33*, 335–342.

Peterson, R.A., & Merunka, D.R. (2014). Convenience samples of college students and research reproducibility. *Journal of Business Research, 67*, 1035–1041.

Pettigrew, T.F., & Meertens, R.W. (1995). Subtle and blatant prejudice in Western Europe. *European Journal of Social Psychology, 25*, 57–75.

Piliavin, I.M., Piliavin, J.A., & Rodin, J. (1975). Costs, diffusion, and the stigmatized victim. *Journal of Personality and Social Psychology, 32*, 429–438.

Piliavin, I.M., Rodin, J., & Piliavin, J.A. (1969). Good samaritanism: An underground phenomenon? *Journal of Personality and Social Psychology, 13*, 289–299.

PSYOPS Field Manual (2003). Washington, DC: Headquarters Department of the Army.

Quercia, D., Lambiotte, R., Stillwell, D., Kosinski, M., & Crowcroft, J. (2012). The personality of popular Facebook users. In: *Proceedings of the ACM 2012 conference on computer supported cooperative work* (pp. 955–964). Retrieved 22nd December 2020 from: http://dl.acm.org/citation.cfm?id=2145346.

Rank, S.G., & Jacobson, C.K. (1977). Hospital nurses' compliance with medication overdose orders: A failure to replicate. *Journal of Health and Social Behavior, 18*, 188–193.

Raudenbush, S.W. (1984). Magnitude of teacher expectancy effects on pupil IQ as a function of the credibility of expectancy induction: A synthesis of findings from 18 experiments. *Journal of Educational Psychology, 76*, 85–97.

Reips, U-D. (2000). The Web experiment method: Advantages, disadvantages, and solutions. In: M.H. Birnbaum (Ed.) *The psychology experiments on the Internet* (pp. 89–117). San Diego, CA: Psychology Press.

Reips, U.-D., Birnbaum, M.H. (2011). *27 Behavioral research and data collection via the Internet*. In: K-P. L. Vu & R. Proctor (Eds.) Handbook of human factors in web design (pp. 563–585). Hove, UK: Routledge.

Reis, H.T., & Gosling, S.D. (2010). Social psychological methods outside the laboratory. In: S.T. Fiske, D.T. Gilbert, & G. Lindzey (Eds.) *Handbook of social psychology, vol. 1*, 5th ed., (pp. 82-114). New York, NY: Wiley.

Richard, F.D., Bond, C.F., & Stokes-Zoota, J.J. (2003). One hundred years of social psychology quantitatively described. *Review of General Psychology*, 7, 331–363.

Ritchie, D.A., & Shopes, L. (2003). Oral history excluded from IRB review. *OHA Newsletter, 37*, 1.

Roethlisberger, F.J.,& Dickson, W.J. (2003). *Management and the worker (vol. 5)*. Hove, UK: Psychology Press.

Rosenberg, M.J. (1965). When dissonance fails: On eliminating evaluation apprehension from attitude measurement. *Journal of Personality and Social Psychology, 1*, 28–42.

Rosenthal, R. (1966). *Experimenter effects in behavioral research*. New York, NY: Appleton Century Crofts.

Rosenthal, R. (1994). Science and ethics in conducting, analyzing, and reporting psychological research. *Psychological Science, 5*, 127–134.

Rosenthal, R. (2002). Experimenter and clinician effects in scientific inquiry and clinical practice. *Prevention & Treatment, 5*, Article 38.

Rosenthal, R., & Jacobson, L. (1968). *Pygmalion in the classroom*. New York, NY: Holt, Rinehart & Winston.

Rosnow, R.L., & Rosenthal, R. (1989). Statistical procedure and the justifications of knowledge in psychological science. *American Psychologist, 44*, 1276–1284.

Ross, A. S. (2019). *Experimental and nonexperimental designs in social psychology*. New York & London: Routledge

Rozin, P. (1976). The selection of food by rats, humans and other animals. In: J. Rosenblatt, R. A. Hinde, C. Beer, & E. Shaw (Eds.) *Advances in the Study of Behavior, Vol. 6*. (pp. 21–76). New York, NY: Academic Press.

Savani, K., & Job, V. (2017). Reverse ego-depletion: Acts of self-control can improve subsequent performance in Indian cultural contexts. *Journal of Personality and Social Psychology, 113*, 589–607.

Scandura, T.A., & Williams, E.A. (2000). Research methodology in management: Current practices, trends, and implications for future research. *Academy of Management Journal, 43*, 1248–1264.

Schachter, S. (1964). The interaction of cognitive and physiological determinants of emotional state. *Advances in Experimental Social Psychology, 1*, 48–81.

Schachter, S., & Singer, J.E. (1962). Cognitive, social and psychological components of the emotional state. *Psychological Review, 69*, 379–399.

Schroeder, J., Fishbach, A., Schein, Ch., & Gray, K. (2017). Functional intimacy: Needing – but not wanting – the touch of a stranger. *Journal of Personality and Social Psychology, 113*, 910–924.

Schultz, P.W., Nolan, J.M., Cialdini, R.B., Goldstein, N.J., & Griskevicius, V. (2007). The constructive, destructive, and reconstructive power of social norms. *Psychological Science, 18*, 429–434.

Schwarzwald, J., Bizman, A., & Raz, M. (1983). The foot-in-the-door paradigm: Effects of second request size on donation probability and donor generosity. *Personality and Social Psychology Bulletin, 9*, 443–450.

Scott, C.A. (1977). Modifying socially-conscious behavior: The foot-in-the-door technique. *Journal of Consumer Research, 4*, 156–164.

Sears, D.O. (1986). College sophomores in the laboratory: Influences of a narrow data base on social psychology's view of human nature. *Journal of Personality and Social Psychology, 51*, 515–530.

Shadish, W.R., Cook, T.D., & Campbell, D.T. (2002). *Experimental and quasi-experimental designs for generalized causal inference*. Boston, MA: Houghton, Mifflin & Company.

Shadrick, S.B., & Lussier, J.W. (2004). *Assessment of the Think Like a Commander training program*. Research Report 1824. Arlington, VA: U.S. Army Research Institute for the Behavioral and Social Sciences.

Shalvi, S., Baas, M., Handgraaf, M.J., & De Dreu, C.K. (2010). Write when hot – Submit when not: Seasonal bias in peer review or acceptance? *Learned Publishing, 23*, 117–123.

Shanab, M.E., & Yahya, K.A. (1978). A cross-cultural study of obedience. *Bulletin of the Psychonomic Society, 11*, 267–269.

Shang, J., & Croson, R. (2009). A field experiment in charitable contribution: The impact of social information on the voluntary provision of public goods. *The Economic Journal, 119*, 1422–1439.

Shariff, A.F., & Norenzayan, A. (2007). God is watching you priming: God concepts increases prosocial behavior in an anonymous economic game. *Psychological Science, 18*, 803–809.

Sherif, M., Harvey, O.J., White, B.J., Hood, W.R., & Sherif, C.W. (1961). *Intergroup conflict and cooperation: The Robbers Cave experiment*. Norman, OK: University of Oklahoma Book Exchange.

Shotland, R.L., Berger, W.G., & Forsythe, R. (1970). A validation of the lost-letter technique. *The Public Opinion Quarterly, 34*, 278–281.

Siegman, A.W., & Feldstein, S. (2014). *Nonverbal behavior and communication*. Hove, UK: Psychology Press.

Sims, J.M. (2010). A brief review of the Belmont report. *Dimensions of Critical Care Nursing, 29*, 173–174.

Skitka, L. J., & Sargis, E. G. (2006). The Internet as psychological laboratory. *Annual Review of Psychology, 57*, 529–555.

Slater, M., Antley, A., Davison, A., Swapp, D., Guger, C., Barker, C., Pistrang, N., & Sanchez-Vives, M.V. (2006). A virtual reprise of the Stanley Milgram obedience experiments. *PloS one, 1*(1), e39.

Snow, R.E. (1995). Pygmalion and intelligence? *Current Directions in Psychological Science, 4*, 169–171.

Sotirovic, M. (2016). Heuristic information-processing. *The International Encyclopedia of Political Communication.* Retrieved 22nd December, 2020 from: http://onlinelibrary.wiley.com/doi/10.1002/9781118541555.wbiepc033/full.

Spears, T., & Spears, O.C.M. (2017). World's main list of "predatory" science publishers vanishes with no warning. Retrieved 22nd December, 2020 from: http://ottawacitizen.com/news/local-news/worlds-main-list-of-science-predators-vanishes-with-no-warning.

Standage, T. (2005). *A history of the world in 6 glasses.* New York, NY: Washer & Company.

Steele-Johnson, D., Beauregard, R.S., Hoover, P.B., Schmidt, A.M. (2000). Goal orientation and task demand effects on motivation, affect, and performance. *Journal of Applied Psychology, 85,* 724–738.

Stern, S.E., Faber, J.E. (1997). The lost e-mail method: Milgram's lost-letter technique in the age of the Internet. *Behavior Research Methods, Instruments, & Computers, 29,* 260–263.

Stevens, S.S. (1975). *Psychophysics.* Piscataway, NJ: Transaction Publishers.

Straumshein, C. (2017). Librarian's list of "predatory" journals reportedly removed due to "threats and politics." Retrieved 22nd December, 2020 from: www.insidehighered.com/news/2017/01/18/librarians-list-predatory-journals-reportedly-removed-due-threats-and-politics.

Strack, F., Martin, L.L.,& Stepper, S. (1988). Inhibiting and facilitating conditions of the human smile: A nonobtrusive test of the facial feedback hypothesis. *Journal of Personality and Social Psychology, 54,* 768–777.

Strack, F., & Neumann, R. (2000). Furrowing the brow may undermine perceived fame: The role of facial feedback in judgments of celebrity. *Personality and Social Psychology Bulletin, 26,* 762–768.

Strohmetz, D.B., Rind, B., Fisher, R., & Lynn, M. (2002). Sweetening the till: The use of candy to increase restaurant tipping 1. *Journal of Applied Social Psychology, 32,* 300–309.

Szczepanowski, R., Folwarczny, M., Krol, M., Dolinski, D., & Budzisz, J. (2019). Electrophysiological correlates of emotional see-saw effect on a go/no-go task. *Current Psychology, 38,* 533–541.

Szczucka, K. (2012). Attraction at first fright? What Dutton and Aron really demonstrated almost 40 years ago. *Polish Psychological Bulletin, 43,* 191–198.

Szpitalak, M., & Polczyk, R. (2010). Warning against warnings: Alerted subjects may perform worse: misinformation, involvement and warning as determinants of witness testimony. *Polish Psychological Bulletin, 41,* 105–112.

Trafimow, D. (2014). Editorial. *Basic and Applied Social Psychology, 36,* 1–2.

Trafimow, D., & Marks, M. (2015). Editorial. *Basic and Applied Social Psychology, 37,* 1–2.

Tschudin, A., Call, J., Dunbar, R.I., Harris, G., & van der Elst, C. (2001). Comprehension of signs by dolphins (Tursiops truncatus). *Journal of Comparative Psychology, 115,* 100–105.

Vallace, J., & Sadalla, E. (1966). Behavioral consequences of transgression: I. The effects of social recognition. *Journal of Experimental Research in Personality, 1,* 187–194.

Vanhove, A.J., & Harms, P.D. (2015). Reconciling the two disciplines of organisational science: A comparison of findings from lab and field research. *Applied Psychology, 64,* 637–673.

Wagenmakers, E.-J., Beek, T., Dijkhoff, L. et al. (2016). Registered Replication Report Strack, Martin, & Stepper (1988). *Perspectives on Psychological Science, 11,* 917–928.

Walster, E. (1966). Assignment of responsibility for an accident. *Journal of Personality and Social Psychology, 3,* 73–79.

Walster, E., Aronson, E., & Abrahams, D. (1966). On increasing the persuasiveness of a low prestige communicator. *Journal of Experimental Social Psychology, 2,* 325–342.

Wasserstein, R.L., Schrim, A.L., & Lazar, N.A. (2019). Moving to a world beyond "p < 0.05". *The American Statistician, 73,* sup.1, 1–19.

Weber, S.J., & Cook, T.D. (1972). Subject effects in laboratory research: An examination of subject roles, demand characteristics, and valid inference. *Psychological Bulletin, 77,* 273–295.

Webster, D.M., & Kruglanski, A.W. (1994). Individual differences in need for cognitive closure. *Journal of Personality and Social Psychology, 67,* 1049–1062.

Wells, W.D. (1993). Discovery-oriented consumer research. *Journal of Consumer Research, 19,* 489–504.

West, S. G., Cham, H., & Liu, Y. (2014). Causal inference and generalization in field settings: Experimental and quasi-experimental designs. In H. T. Reis & C. M. Judd (Eds.) *Handbook of research methods in social and personality psychology* (p. 49–80). Cambridge, UK: Cambridge University Press.

White, P., & Selwyn, N. (2013). Moving on-line? An analysis of patterns of adult Internet use in the UK, 2002–2010. *Information, Communication & Society, 16*, 1–27.

Whitehead, T.N. (1938). *The industrial worker.* Retrieved 22 December, 2020 from: http://psycnet.apa.org/psycinfo/1938-04315-000.

Whithear, R. (1999). Charity shop volunteers: A case for „tender loving care". *International Journal of Nonprofit and Voluntary Sector Marketing, 4*, 107–120.

Wicker, A.W. (1969). A failure to validate the lost-letter technique. *The Public Opinion Quarterly, 33*, 260–262.

Wicker, A.W. (1971). An examination of the „other variables" explanation of attitude-behavior inconsistency. *Journal of Personality and Social Psychology, 19*, 18–30.

Wintre, M.G., North, C., & Sugar, L.A. (2001). Psychologists' response to criticisms about research based on undergraduate participants: A developmental perspective. *Canadian Psychology, 42*, 216–225.

Wojciszke, B. (2011). Systematycznie Modyfikowane Autoreplikacje: logika programu bada empirycznych w psychologii. In: J. Brzeziński (Ed.), *Metodologia badan psychologicznych. Wybor tekstow* (pp. 44–68). Warszawa: Wydawnictwo Naukowe PWN.

Yong, E. (2014). *The Bird That Cries Wolf Changes Its Lies. National Geographic.* Retrieved 22 December, 2020 from: http://phenomena.nationalgeographic.com/2014/05/01/the-bird-that-cries-wolf-changes-its-lies/.

Zajac, J., & Cyprowski, F. (2016). *Czego dowiedzieliśmy się o Polakach, badajac social media.* Retrieved 22nd December, 2020 from: www.sotrender.com/blog/pl/2016/03/badania-gustow-w-social-media/.

Zeigler-Hill, V., Southard, A.C., Archer, L.M., & Donohoe, P.L. (2013). Neuroticism and negative affect influence the reluctance to engage in destructive obedience in the Milgram paradigm. *Journal of Social Psychology, 153*, 161–174.

Zhou, H., & Fishbach, A. (2016). The pitfall of experimenting on the web: How unattended selective attrition leads to surprising (yet false) research conclusions. *Journal of Personality and Social Psychology, 111*, 493–504.

Zimbardo, P.G. (2007). *Lucifer effect.* New York, NY: Wiley.

Index

Taylor & Francis Group
an **informa** business

Taylor & Francis eBooks

www.taylorfrancis.com

A single destination for eBooks from Taylor & Francis with increased functionality and an improved user experience to meet the needs of our customers.

90,000+ eBooks of award-winning academic content in Humanities, Social Science, Science, Technology, Engineering, and Medical written by a global network of editors and authors.

TAYLOR & FRANCIS EBOOKS OFFERS:

- A streamlined experience for our library customers
- A single point of discovery for all of our eBook content
- Improved search and discovery of content at both book and chapter level

REQUEST A FREE TRIAL

support@taylorfrancis.com

Routledge
Taylor & Francis Group

CRC Press
Taylor & Francis Group

For Product Safety Concerns and Information please contact our EU
representative GPSR@taylorandfrancis.com
Taylor & Francis Verlag GmbH, Kaufingerstraße 24, 80331 München, Germany

www.ingramcontent.com/pod-product-compliance
Ingram Content Group UK Ltd.
Pitfield, Milton Keynes, MK11 3LW, UK
UKHW050759180926
475701UK00008B/1135
* 9 7 8 0 3 6 7 5 5 5 5 6 6 *